Muhajababes

*meet the new middle east –
cool, sexy and devout*

Allegra Stratton

CONSTABLE • LONDON

For Mum, Dad and Rob

Constable & Robinson Ltd
3 The Lanchesters
162 Fulham Palace Road
London W6 9ER
www.constablerobinson.com

This edition published by Constable,
an imprint of Constable & Robinson Ltd, 2006

A copy of the British Library Cataloguing in
Publication data is available from the British Library

ISBN-13: 978-1-84529-427-4
ISBN-10: 1-84529-427-0

Printed and bound in the EU

1 3 5 7 9 10 8 6 4 2

Muhajababes

Contents

Introduction

In early 2003 one of my friends found a house in Spitalfields, east London, and I left home to live in it. We were a bunch of five first-jobbers and the house Tash had found was a cheap, tall, thin Huguenot thing that we quickly developed grand plans for: it could be a one-stop welfare state, a salon, a club, there could be a printing press in the basement, waifs and strays could bed down in the attic and so on. On one weekend in February I showed it to my sister. She was waif and stray specimen A. Mum and dad's marriage was in meltdown and the one-room-wide, one-room-deep, five-storeys-high building would, with our family about to leave London, probably now become her base as well. It was an Important Day.

The front of the house on the first floor was covered in Tardis-blue shop panels that, it being the end of winter, we left on the house to keep it warm. These panels meant that from the outside you couldn't see whether anyone was inside, and inside there was little natural light except that coming in above the front door. The Saturday that I showed my sister round, her possible new home looked like the inner sanctum of anarchists. Half-finished anti-war banners and placards lay at sixes and sevens, paint pots and felt-tip pens decorated the unvarnished pine floorboards, reels of gaffer tape festooned the room and off-cuts of balsa-wood and dowelling stuck up at odd brachial angles. What was obviously a trial run of Tash's younger brother's placard was propped on a chair in the corner of the room pointing out that 'Bombing for Democracy is Like Fucking for Chastity'. There were also a few plain white umbrellas – two still rolled, one open and propped jauntily on the kitchen table with NO WAR stencilled in black. That afternoon two million people would march through the centre of London against the Iraq war. My housemates were among them.

When they got back, ruddy cheeked, righteous and proud, I picked a fight with Tash, starting with what a mess they'd left the front room in – which was the nuclear option given the house ethos we'd crafted together a couple of weeks earlier. Didn't she know it was my sister's first visit? To her possible new home. She doesn't have another home, and so on. A lot of sentimental nonsense that I sort of felt, but sort of didn't. What I was really angry about was that she was against the war. My housemate and I were on opposite sides of a major argument.

Tash's point was less grand than mine: the West had meddled with the Middle East already, what evidence was there that we'd do it any better this time around? She had other points but, basically, barely three months out of a history degree she was as suspicious of big, ideological, political projects as a modern education system can make someone. Me? I was a less recent graduate who had been working on a newspaper for a year before moving on to the BBC. I was more susceptible to the opiate of sweeping narratives like bringing freedom to Iraqis and democracy to the Middle East.

As the year went on it became obvious that Tash had won the argument. This was inconvenient. She was my friend and housemate. Obviously we managed to share a fridge and resolve issues of council tax, just. We weren't so earnest we couldn't. But as we passed on the narrow house stairs, it was always hanging in the air that I was the warmonger. Being on the losing side of the argument, the onus was on me to do the soul-searching.

I started to go to Arabic lessons and read serious journals the size and width of mini *Glamour* but where articles have footnotes and you get small change from a tenner. One particular issue caught me. With former Baathists – Saddam's men – barred from positions of power, 400,000 ex-soldiers unemployed after the disbanding of the Iraqi army and the US preferring to hire workers from Bangladesh and India instead of Iraqis, unemployment was high.

I could see this happening from the comfort of BBC Westminster where I worked. Here, everyone has a telly on their desk. More TVs are mounted on walls, lurk over your shoulder, hang above doors and there might even be one playing away, mute, in the corner of a meeting. If you wanted you could watch what seemed like an almost continuous narrative of these young, unemployed Iraqis kicking pebbles around on the corner of a street in Baghdad.

There was, my expensive foreign-affairs magazines told me, a word for these men: *hayateen*. It means 'men who lean against walls'. They merited their own term because of their increasing numbers. The Middle East's infant-mortality rates had fallen to such an extent that two thirds of Arabs are 25 or younger. This makes 250 million – a quarter of a billion –

young Arabs. The experts called it a 'youth bulge'. Academic studies showed a firm link between conflict and a youthful demographic. The United Nations said that 16 of the world's 25 youngest countries have experienced major civil conflicts since 1995.

If I continued to feel rubbish about my colossal error of judgement about the war, looking at these men 'propping up walls' made me feel I might not have been such an idiot. Those of us in favour of the war weren't to know the Americans would disband the army. The evidence suggested the US was aware of the Middle East's pear-shaped population. At least half the 9/11 hijackers had been under 25 and six months before the Twin Towers were felled, the CIA had reported on 'the doomed future of youngsters living in the Middle East'. In Bosnia, the US had learnt that you have to put the idle, angry, young men to work. But the Bush administration didn't seem to agree.

By now I was in quite deep. My sister, by the way, had liked the scenes of anarchy and had moved into the house while I'd moved out. The foreign-affairs mags had given way to webchats, which in turn had given way to interviews on phones with sociologists in Cairo and New York. The last time Western countries had a big youth bulge was in the late 1960s, as the products of the post-war baby boom came of age. The result was student rebellion and the Summer of Love.

My TV showed shots of dejection and boredom on a dust track in some neglected suburb of Baghdad or the 110 per cent effort of the Palestinian kid lobbing a stone at an Israeli tank. But maybe they were not the whole story. The World Bank suggested this oversized generation were leaning on school desks rather than against walls: their stats showed the Middle East and North Africa, including Iran, had experienced the 'fastest expansion in educational attainment in the world between 1980 and 2000'. The new generation of Arabs, male and female, is 'the most educated in the region's history'.

I was now plugged into a feverish academic subculture. In baby-boomer temples like Harvard and Stanford, professors I spoke to were peddling a worldview of social change for the Middle East. They saw in the Middle East's large cohort of clever clogs enough parallels with the causes of 1968, the English Civil War and the French Revolution that they penned papers and wrote lectures. What creates unrest, they told me, in return for the money I was haemorrhaging on long-distance phone calls, was not just an increase in the numbers of young people but also in the numbers of educated young people with no increase in jobs. The World Bank estimates that over the next ten years the Middle East will need to create 37 million new jobs for first-time job-seekers. Prior to the English Civil War of 1640 there had been an almost 400 per cent increase in enrolments at Oxbridge but no such increase in jobs. Similarly, before the French Revolution, the number of law students at the best universities rose by nearly 80 per cent while the population itself increased by only 20 per cent.

In January 2005, two years after Tash and I had had our big cat fight, Iraq's elections approached. Except nearly half the population of Iraq would not be voting that 30 January, because the median age (there's equal numbers above and below) in Iraq is 19 (it is 38 in Europe). With the voting age at 21, the kids would be omitted.

It now struck me that if the professors were right, there might be pockets of people – my age and just having left home as well – also adapting to paying their own taxes and taxies, organizing Arab Haight-Ashburys or penning poems in a Levantine Greenwich Village. Were Arabs very similar or very different from Tash and me? Were there knots of graduates, living in the centres of their cities, talking and clashing about politics, tidiness and food bills? Thinking of running a printing press from their basement and a salon from their attic? It sounds very middle class, but that was the point. What did the middle-class Arab kids look like? What did they have to say? After the French Revolution the word *'socialisme'* entered the dictionary. Were there Arab words about to be invented? Or would I just find 'men who lean against walls', as the TV on my desk at work would suggest?

I decided my money would be better spent going to the Middle East than on magazines and phone calls to Ivy League professors. I'd go there and see whether their young population – in all its puppy-fat enormity – was taking form as the profs would like it to. I wasn't going to get into Iraq but I could go to countries near it.

Muhajababes is a record of what I found, of the young people I met and the conversations we had. This was as I planned it to be – I wanted it to be a book full of conversations. What didn't go as planned was the itinerary. After Lebanon and Jordan, I got to the border with Jerusalem and wasn't allowed in. Supposedly, there was a black mark next to my name. So instead I visited Cairo before flying across the Gulf to Dubai and Kuwait and then nipping back to

Damascus. So remember this order: Beirut, Amman, Cairo, Dubai, Kuwait and Damascus.

My methodology was to talk to everyone I met who seemed my age. I started with my industry – working for the BBC it was pretty easy to line up a visit to a TV station in Beirut. Other than that, I had only a few contacts before I left London. Instead, I got around – cheekily purloining mobiles and emails of anybody interesting mentioned in conversation and knocking on doors. Because of this methodology, most of my interviewees were relative strangers, though some – as a function of how the region really was a region – sent me on to other countries and places with contacts of theirs to pursue. While sometimes I felt ill-equipped, it forced me to find the synapses of whatever nascent youth culture the region had. Some of you will probably tick me off for spending as much time as I do with people who you think are dossers. If I'd gone with any more interviews set up I'd probably have been even more guilty of that.

Age? I didn't always ask how old people were – it seemed to be a mind-set. With its ceiling at 30. OK, in one exception I interview a 35-year-old at length but he is the exception. Language? We spoke a mixture of languages. I have pidgin Arabic that is occasionally and always unexpectedly quite good but by no means reliable enough to sustain a conversation. So I talked with them in a mixture of translated Arabic, my own faltering Arabic, English, American and even French. It was a mix that seemed to work. This book's interviews not having been in fluent Arabic might have been a problem if I had felt I wasn't getting an interesting picture, but I didn't think this was true.

I wrote down every single thing most of them said to me and they will remember me as the English journalist who 'was always writing very fast' and had, for a culture that is quite strict about neat handwriting, what they saw to be 'bad handwriting'. In circumstances where I couldn't write things down – when I just didn't have my notebook out or it would have been inappropriate to get it out mid-conversation (a sure sign to the person speaking that they were suddenly saying something unexpectedly interesting and they might like to reconsider whether it is for public consumption or not) – I would make emergency trips to the loo and write down an as-near-as-damn-it version. It seemed better to get what these people said to an audience back here than to omit their *bons mots*. These nearly missed conversations aside, most of the time I had my notepad firmly in hand. I made notes lying in bed, in nightclubs, in taxis, private cars, standing in the street and sitting on the curb.

Most of the names of the people I spoke to have been changed. This is because they *wanted* me to change their names. In some instances – if they were taking drugs, were politically over-active or were being bitchy – it is because they would only speak to me on conditions of anonymity. But those people who didn't stipulate anonymity were perhaps a bit cavalier and I took the executive decision to change all names. So I'm sorry, Elton, I've changed your name. ('Elton' is the gay Kuwaiti exhibitionist who was insistent that Islamist segregation *encouraged* homosexual relations and who pleaded with me to use his real name. It was all about being proud of who you were.) I haven't changed Hind's name as her situation hasn't been anonymous for a long time. I have changed the names of less famous bands but not of more famous ones, nor the famous figures.

I went looking for a way round and then out of an argument. I came back having found a new political and religious force: the muhajababes. I think the professors of baby-booming might get a kind of revolution: an Egyptian Haight-Ashbury, Carnaby Street in Beirut or *Spare Rib* in Kuwait… But religion will feature too. An Arab Pete Townsend writing the song 'My Generation' in 2005 would probably use the word 'veneration' instead.

1

Requiem for Zen
Beirut

It was a large white Ottoman mansion with an irregular roofline of turrets, out of which stuck satellite dishes. Inside, the stairwell had the languid air of an ancient climbing tree. People were balancing their bums on banisters and leaning against walls, lockers, railings and each other on all of its levels. One of them on the second floor gestured for me to come up. The first girl I passed mumbled something like 'I'm nervous'; a boy slightly ahead of me told his friend they were late for their 'meeting', and just before I reached the second floor a girl at the back of a group of three making their way down the stairs was looking into her mobile and reporting, to no one in particular, that she had a 'missed call'. Down a corridor, stout as a chess piece on a chequered floor, Jad, the executive producer of Zen TV, stood hovering in a doorway.

'I'm sure I just heard a Beiruti say they were nervous,' I said, catching up with him and following him into his room, 'in English.'

'Yup, there's no Arabic for being nervous. I'm afraid it's just you Brits.'

Inside the room there were two people, two desks, two computers, two chairs, two electric heaters humming, a cabinet bursting with videotapes, a few pens, one TV and maybe five billboard-size posters on the walls: *The Tailor of Panama*; *Hannibal*; *The Insider* and other box-office thrillers that were in cinemas a while ago. One hundred years before the films' release this room might have been a eunuch's ante-chamber. Compared to the dimensions of the stairs and hall, it was smaller, but the proportions were still stretched. This room of anachronisms – 1990s film posters, 1970s heaters, 1950s furniture inside an Ottoman shell – was the control room of the Arab world's only youth television channel, Zen TV.

Zen – pronounced 'Zayne', and meaning 'good' – scheduled talk shows, game shows and dubbed movies to fill the down time of a larger than ever pan-Arab audience under the age of 25. Its website was a masterpiece of giddy graphic design, and since its launch a couple of years ago it had sent a respectable number of controversial shockwaves round the region's newspapers. Its parent company was Future TV and it was to Future TV's buildings that I'd now come. 'Safa, here is our English visitor,' Jad said to a woman sitting at her desk with a rug on her knees. The rug, the grand period window behind her and the rudimentary pencil and paper she used made her resemble a Bletchley Park secretary. Jad raised his voice to address me over the noise of the chair he was dragging into position in front of the TV.

'I've just moved house so will be popping in and out all day. But you don't really need me. You have a lot of TV to watch,' and then to Safa, wincing with the effort of trying to count items on a spreadsheet, regardless of our arrival, 'Make sure she doesn't switch.' With this, Jad turned up the TV's sound, picked up his keys and left. It was a short introduction

11

but I supposed it made sense for me to watch some of Zen TV before talking about it or meeting the people who made it.

First I introduced myself to Safa, who I was now sitting next to. I asked what she did and interrupted her second attempt at counting boxes on large gridded sheets. In between the Arabic numbers 17 and 18 she said, *'sabatashar* , I buy programmes, *tamantashar*. Jad wants you to watch this channel. So watch it.'

The channel Jad had left me watching seemed to be Arab MTV – Arab video-clips on loop. Video-clips are what Arabs call music videos and much like any music video, they always have a mini-narrative. There has been a huge video-clip industry in the Middle East since the 1990s but it was only much more recently with the proliferation of satellite channels that video-clips multiplied. After watching a couple of them, I wondered after how many songs it would be polite to get up and leave. Or at least go and take up smoking with the people I'd passed on the stairs. I could even hear some of them cackling about something: one now said very loudly, 'Anjaad'?, meaning 'really?', usually said with the stress on the last As and accompanied by eyes popping out of the head. Clearly, something very interesting had just been revealed. This place rattled with documentary projects conceived, programme meetings convened and staff gossip confirmed, but I was stuck watching prize winningly bad TV next to a woman and her spreadsheet.

The night before in a Beirut bar the owner had been kinder to me. It was one of my first nights in the city, and I probably cut quite a gauche and lonely figure. It felt ridiculous to tell people I was researching a book on 'youth culture'. Was I going to interview every one of the some 200 million Arabs under 25; was I looking for some kind of zany *Why Don't You?* bunch, expressing their creativity with coloured paper, glue and scissors; was I going to swallow the press-released cant of the region's well-intentioned army of NGOs that work with youth groups; should I march straight up to the boys skateboarding in central Beirut and ask them the name of their favourite band? How was I going to deal with it when they said Green Day? I'm sure they liked Western bands, but I'd hear the shrieks of my university anthropology supervisor asking me if I really believed Green Day would be the sound-track to anyone's revolution, let alone an Arab's. I must have reeked of this apprehension – the bar manager tranquillized me with free mojitos and a seat behind the DJ's decks.

In actual fact my spirits hadn't been *too* low that night as I'd been due to visit Zen TV the next day. I thought of Zen as a convenience store of youth culture. If something *happening* were happening, surely the station's TV producers would have spotted it and be broadcasting it. The DJ I was now introduced to only bolstered this expectation: when I asked him whether he'd heard of Zen his reaction was chemical. Though the track was past the halfway point he took off his earphones to indulge in a short but purple rhapsody about the genius of the TV station and its staff.

'It is of international standard. The first time decent televi-sion has come to the Middle East. I applied to be a sound engineer but it didn't surprise me that with Arabs from all over the world applying, I missed out. I'm not sad, because it is good that all these people came back home,' and then he talked about everyone being a winner and voiced other platitudes of the loser. He'd been so hushed and breathless about Zen that it had been difficult to hear him over the low beats of his record – a DJ Shadow track.

In front of the TV the next day, it didn't seem right that a channel a DJ Shadow fan would deify was the rubbish I was watching: men in spray-on tight shirts, women in even less singing '*habibi*' ['my love'], most often at a camera but sometimes at each other. Writhing on sands, walking on beaches, dancing at weddings and splashing in courtyard fountains. Each had end credits implying the people responsible were proud of their product.

I scanned Safa's desk for some relief and found it. To one side of her a tower of VHSs was topped with one labelled *What Not To Wear*.

'Trinny and Susannah! Are you going to air that?' Safa panicked. She was not comfortable that somebody else's guest was now unaccompanied and sitting so near to her, but she soon found what I was looking at and relaxed.

'Oh, thaaat? No. That pile of VHSs is my *Out*box.'

She rested the pencil on the paper grid – next week's TV schedule – and put her hand to her heart. 'Personally? I loved it. I would have loved to have seen old Arab women getting a makeover. It would have been the best television. But this would have been the problem too. Too much flesh. I thought and thought about whether there was a way we could get round it. But there wasn't. The programme concept needs flesh. And there was no way we'd get away with that kind of thing. Any more.'

Of course. That they wouldn't get away with too much flesh was a well-worn-shapeless-ill-fitting-baggy-burqa stereotype of the Arab world. But the video-clip now showing starred an artiste wearing only bed sheets. Why could she, if Trinny and Susannah couldn't?

'Is it because she is a Christian?', I asked, wondering if Christians had laxer rules on flesh.

As soon as I'd said it, I knew she'd shoot me down. Lebanon has 18 sects, and they exploded into a civil war in 1975. It officially ended in 1991, but things are so sensitive there hasn't been a census since 1932. People don't want to know how many of which sects there are in the country. And the pretence is that you aren't able, nor would you want to, 'tell a person's sect by their looks', as Safa now put it, before picking up her pencil and re-entering her grids. Later I realized just how stupid a question it had been. Even if the singer had been Christian, as Elissa, one of the most famous Arab singers is, most of her audience wasn't. The number of Muslims watching a near-naked Elissa is always massive, and only 10 per cent of Arabs are Christian.

Evidence of the general reach of these singers was that one of them, Haifa Wehbe – Ms Lebanon in 1995 and a Christian – has been voted the 'ultimate sex symbol' by all Arab youth who could be bothered to respond to a poll; a Cairo newspaper's young readers voted Egyptian singer Ruby the most popular personality in their country; and Nancy Ajram had been voted by the Arabic version of *Newsweek* as one of the region's most influential Arabs.

As Safa took *What Not To Wear* and put it in a drawer, a man popped his head round the door and asked for Jad. His eyes locked on the TV and he walked towards it, crouching and squinting like he'd seen a spider in the hair of the singer now on TV.

'He's one of ours, isn't he?' he asked of no one in particular.

Safa introduced Musa, executive producer of another of Future TV's programmes, *Superstar*. She told him that the singer was indeed one of his finalists. Musa was short and wearing a navy duffle-coat. Though he must have been in his forties he had the sartorial sav of Gap does Paddington Bear: a very Western look – grungy and preppy – probably developed at Harvard.

'You're looking for Zen TV, aren't you?' he asked, turning to me and straightening up. 'Youth programming was another thing we tried and failed to steal from you Brits. Like *The Weakest Link*, which was a complete flop in Arabia. You Brits are decent-nasty … you think, If I'm going to be nasty, I need to be nice-nasty – tell it to someone's face. Not Arabs – it is secret scheming through and through. We *did* find a woman who was as nasty as Anne Robinson, but no one stood up to her. Which is the other problem. Arab subservience killed another TV concept.'

With a flourish he flung his short arms towards the TV. 'But we did OK for *him*,' and he now looked at his pop star like he was a painting he'd just finished. '*Superstar* was off-this-planet successful. The ratings for the last episode of the first series of *Superstar* were sky high – I think we hit about 90 per cent of the market share in Lebanon. Even about 50 per cent of the audience in Saudi Arabia.'

This region-wide success was unusual for the Middle East. The sheer number of channels, he said, normally meant a 20 per cent share was the max. 'But that night in Lebanon the streets were as empty as after curfew during the war.'

Gaddafi came on board, meeting all the finalists. Yassir Arafat was also very pleased but Palestinian Islamist groups Hamas and Islamic Jihad were less tickled, thinking the timing of the first *Superstar* series – the second Palestinian uprising against Israeli occupation, or intifada, began in September 2000 – wasn't a good time to divert the attention of young people away from the Israeli–Palestinian issue. But, he said, Palestinian doubters and sheikhs from the Gulf were the only critics.

'Apart from that it was, how you say?, "a runaway success". We've had stage fright since. So what have we commissioned? Another series of *Superstar*.'

Though he hadn't taken off his duffle-coat he was now comfortable in Jad's chair and evidently philosophical about *Superstar*'s success.

'In my opinion, the only thing that unites the Arab world is the Arab language, and the Koran. Other than that there is nothing. That's why *Superstar* is television in its purest Arab form.'

'It's true,' added Safa, still not looking up from her schedules but much more relaxed with someone else there to baby-sit me. The Middle East's regional differences were magnified by *Superstar*, Musa explained. I thought he meant dialects. Differences in dialects mean that the Arabic a Kuwaiti or Iraqi speaks is different from that of a Beiruti and different again from a Cairene. He did mean that. As well as politics.

'*Superstar* worked because it magnified those differences. Television in this region doesn't work when it is trying to *unite* the Arab world. *Superstar* isn't interested in this. It wants them to vote against each other as much as possible. The Lebanese won't vote for the Libyans. The Jordanians won't support the Palestinians.' And so on. He didn't seem to have seen the Eurovision Song Contest. For that matter, he didn't seem to have seen al-Jazeera. Wasn't Jazeera supposed to have brought the Middle East closer together? I asked. Musa's face dropped, he said something about the Brits being 'so nice' and left.

Safa pushed her chair away from her desk to place a little more distance between us and addressed me.

'There are 150 satellite channels in the Arab world but the only one people like you talk about is Jazeera. Kids I know, though not my kids, stay in all day watching Jazeera. They know more about Rumsfeld than I do. They become insomniacs … they stay awake all night wanting news of what's happening in Iraq and in Palestine. But why do they care what's happening in Palestine? Just because they're bored.'

She explained that Musa liked to think, though he'd never say it, that *Superstar* is better than Jazeera. While al-Jazeera does get between 40 million and 50 million regular viewers, 15 million voted on the outcome of *Superstar*, 'more Arabs than have ever cast ballots in a free election'.

❖

By the time Jad came back, Safa had gone home. I'd been watching TV for about four hours. He returned chuckling at the news that Prince Harry was in trouble for dressing up as a Nazi, and I refocused on a semi-naked woman being served breakfast in bed by a bunny rabbit.

'It's porn, isn't it?' he said, pointing at the TV as he finally settled down at his desk beneath Cate Blanchett's metre-wide face in the *Elizabeth* film poster. He began to concentrate. 'OK. From the beginning. It was my idea. Basically. I was the executive producer. You know we're owned by Mr Lebanon?'

I did know this and that Rafiq Hariri had been prime minister of Lebanon twice, only stepping down for the second time a few months earlier in October 2004. He'd done so in fury at some illicit constitutional tinkering. The presidency was meant to be restricted to one six-year term but, supposedly under pressure from Syria, in autumn 2004 parliament voted for the presidential term to be extended three years. This would allow pro-Syrian president – Emile Lahoud – to continue.

Hariri had worked with Syrian support for years – Lebanon's larger Syrian neighbours had, with Lebanese permission, got the country out of scrapes and scuffles since sending 40,000 troops in 1976. They were dispatched to support Christians worried they were being overrun by Palestinians. After the civil war 14,000 troops (and spooks) stayed on in *petite* Lebanon and the relative peace they secured was known in Washington, DC, as Pax Syriana. Public opinion was now turning – the dominant suspicion was that Syria saw Lebanon as theirs. Since the journey between Beirut and Damascus is only three hours, some estimate that there are half a million Syrians living in Syria and commuting to Beirut daily. In Beirut they make money, untaxed, that they send home to Syria where, with life being cheaper, it goes further. But it was the constitutional fiddling, coupled with a day-to-day blocking of Hariri's reforms by Lahoud and nearly 20 pro-Syrian ministers that pushed Hariri. The day after he resigned the pro-Syrian Omar Karami was made prime minister in his stead.

But this was Hariri's *second* resignation. There had also been all the drama of a *first* resignation in 1998. Hariri had been around such a long time that his thick black calligraphic eyebrows occupied a place in Lebanese life similar to Denis Healey's in the UK. From a lowly Sunni farming background he had headed to Saudi Arabia in his twenties. He arrived in time for the oil boom of the 1970s and became the personal contractor to the then Prince Fahd who went on to become king of Saudi Arabia. The Saudi royals made him a Saudi citizen and Hariri made a fortune – so rich he made it on to *Forbes'* list of the world's 100 richest men. From the desert he kept an eye on little Levantine Lebanon, donating \$12 million to victims of the Israeli invasion in 1982, and it was, in part, his elbow grease and money that helped bring about the 1989 Taif Accords that began to end the civil war. In 1992 he returned to Lebanon as prime minister. After a civil war dominated by competing militia, the entry into politics of someone not clearly aligned to any one faction, and more into JCBs, skips and hard hats, was *supposed* to bring a breath of fresh air into Lebanon.

A decade or so later he was popularly seen as having blown the life out of Beirut's heart. Though there were showers of personal generosity – 30,000 students were put through college because of him – his profile had suffered from being in power. It was his construction company Solidere that got the city's rebuilding contracts and turned the carbonized carcass of Beirut's centre into today's plaza. I could see the aesthetic grievance: the sandblasted yellow stone looks like the inside of a Cadbury's Crunchie.

'It's a doll's house in denial that place, it's been so airbrushed that some people can't bear to even walk through it,' Jad said. 'But that's Hariri. He came back from the Gulf believing that the way to solve Lebanon's financial problems was through privatization. Dunkin' Donuts, Nike and TGI Friday's.' Hariri was Jad's boss but as he listed these companies I sensed his small curlicue moustache curl a little tighter and the flimsy desk in front of him levitate, perhaps pushed up by knees tensed beneath. It wasn't a massive punt that he'd be pissed off with Hariri, whose free-market strategy and borrow-and-build schemes had left a massive public debt of about $30 billion.

After a few hours of video-clips I was keen to get on with it, past Zen TV's creation story.

'This is very interesting, Jad, but I'd like to go and see the Zen TV studios. Are any programmes being made today? Would it be possible to see any being broadcast? Or meet a few producers? You know my job back in London is TV production. That's why I'm really –'

Jad held up his finger, asking for patience. As Hariri rebuilt, he continued, he also refurbished.

'In 1993 he bought and then founded his TV station in this mansion, a building formerly home to Lebanon's first post-independence president, Bechara al-Khoury. Egypt and Lebanon's media industries are like America's and England's. Hariri knew how important his TV station was. He gave it an important building.'

Jad was now rustling around in one of his desk drawers. As if pulling up a turnip from beneath a weight of soil, he looked up from below his desk tugging and talking at the same time.

'They wanted to put $20 million into youth programming – to be completely cynical I suppose they thought they could make money out of programming for this huge youth demographic.'

He sprang back up having loosened and pulled out whatever he was niggling at.

'The rhetoric was about this new generation of Arabs being more positive than their parents – tired after living through more civil war than their kids. They'd commissioned some Dubai research centre to conduct an in-depth study of the likes and dislikes of young people in the region. And there we go.' The first Arabic channel dedicated to viewers aged between 13 and 35. Jad's turnip was a VHS and he now walked over to Safa's desk and put it in the machine.

I watched Jad spooling through videos of Zen TV presenters chatting like canary birds: the set's primary-coloured furniture and the presenters' primary-coloured clothes actually looked a little melancholic in their fast-forwarded helium chirpiness. In the corner of the screen was the Zen TV logo. A cartoon-rendered piece of DNA.

'The presenters of Zen's shows were the generation returning home,' Jad said.

No accurate numbers for the size of this generation exist. Some say there are 15 million people around the world of Lebanese descent, mostly Christian (maybe even 80 per cent) and Druze (another Lebanese sect that had morphed out of the Shia Ismaili sect to be no longer Muslim). Others say significantly less. But there are thought to be around seven million people of Lebanese descent in Brazil alone. The joke about Lebanon is that, at a population of four million, there are more Lebanese outside it than inside it. Under Syrian influence, Beirut passed legislation stopping second-generation Lebanese from automatically getting citizenship. Since the diaspora is predominantly Christian, if it did get the right to vote it would completely change the electoral landscape. But these people had cemented their lives abroad. Jad was more likely talking about the one million people who fled Lebanon during the civil war.

'Half Lebanese and the other half British, American, French. They were returning home and we were going to televise it … In fact, the prospect of working for Zen TV could even be said to have *brought* them home,' he said, liking the sound of this last line and giving it an upswing at the end. In the absence of any reconciliation commission, TV *was* the post-war healing.

'We aired concerts in ruins, live on television, and we also *destroyed*, live on air, some of the city's ruined buildings that were too ruined to renovate.' And they did well. One study – commissioned by the channel so perhaps it should come with a health warning – put Zen TV's viewer base at over 2.5 million: a quarter of them in the Kingdom of Saudi Arabia, a fifth in Jordan, next Egypt, UAE (United Arab Emirates) and Lebanon.

The first programme we watched was Jad's favourite. Called *Dardachat* or *Chitchat*, it went out daily between 6:30 pm and 8:30 pm, and its set was designed like MTV's *Real World*: all lounging loft living and jerky abstract camera shots. Men and women sitting on plump red sofas, possibly remaindered from the West they were such a tired TV cliché. Some had their feet up on coffee tables, others were wearing strapless tops that revealed fresh tan lines from that morning's sunbathing somewhere on the Beirut Corniche. In one episode *Dardachat*'s geeky character talked about things he'd found on the net that day, before the camera sped over to the kitchen area of the apartment to discover that another 'flat-mate'/TV presenter had rustled up a student meal.

The next time Jad stopped the tape was during a discussion about how bras and underwear had become over-wear. Halfway through, one of the presenters put on a big curly pink wig, to illustrate what point I wasn't sure, but this was clearly one of Jad's favourite moments and he took over. 'To go on air then with a man wearing shorts was incredibly brave. Boys with earrings and dyed hair. Girls putting their feet up on the table and putting on wigs, for fun. This stuff you are watching, this stuff is all taboo. In one programme they even went out on to the streets with a camera and asked people what sound you make when having an orgasm.' That question would also go down pretty badly in Walthamstow or Oxford.

24

'Arab leaders complained,' Jad went on – indeed, the imam of the Grand Mosque in Mecca called reality television shows like *Dardachat* 'weapons of mass destruction that kill values and virtue'. Jad continued, 'Because Saudi Arabia is responsible for four-fifths of Arab advertising spending, advertisers started staying away. Even people who owned cable pirate – that's people who watched cable channels illegally – started to ask for it to be taken off their subscription. Imagine the irony? Imagine the ignominy? What *they* were doing is illegal but still they wanted to ban us.'

Hariri, the hands-off owner whom Jad had barely seen in seven years, then got more hands-on. In 2004, Hariri closed down Zen TV. I was a year too late. Now I understood why Jad's grammatic groove was the past tense. This VHS was the station's black box. Someone should put a notice on the website, I suggested, probably quite tersely. My object had disappeared in front of my very eyes.

But Jad was in no mood for Zen TV housekeeping. He was wondering whether his critics might have had a point.

'The channel's viewers. They were not like this. Drugs, sexuality, relationships, suicides … these are not yet problems for the vast majority of Arabs … at least not in the same way that they were for Zen TV's employees.'

Khalid, a producer in his mid-twenties, arrived in the middle of Jad's Zen requiem: 'new ideas inciting people to demand change … Saudi women seeing on their television women, not just in America but in the countries next to them – Kuwait and Dubai – driving around unaccompanied by men. That was meant to make them think, Why not us?'

Looking at his watch, Khalid pulled up a chair with us and spoke quickly. The matter was simple, he said. Had I seen lots of people from Saudi Arabia in and around Beirut? Pristine-white dishdashas (ankle-length robes)? He called them Khaleejis, meaning 'people from the Gulf', and said they had loads of money. With freedom in Saudi Arabia, or what he actually called KSA (the Kingdom of Saudi Arabia), so constrained, they travel. Since 9/11 and the attacks on NYC they've been unable to visit America and instead they've come to Lebanon. Their presence, he said looking at his watch one more time, was skewing Beirut politics. 'You've seen that big mosque being rebuilt in central Beirut? That's being funded by KSA.'

In his opinion they were, in effect, re-religionifying the area. 'They never liked Zen TV anyway. The channel was being beamed into, among other places, KSA. I have female cousins in the compounds and whenever I was putting a programme out I would make myself think how would they feel about it. And in retrospect I was feeling pretty guilty quite a lot of the time. I've got to go –.'

'Go with him,' Jad said with something approaching urgency. 'See what's left of Zen TV.'

I followed the clanging sound Khalid made up the central stair-well, now empty of Future TV staff, into the eaves of the mansion. Off to the right, where all the action seemed to be, was the staff smoking room, but I found Khalid in a small cubby-hole to the left – his gallery, from which the TV programme would be directed. His programme had already kicked off. On two monitors a man was visible, sitting on a barstool surrounded by a fake newsroom (it was actually a graphic and had been superimposed).

'The trouble was,' Khalid said, 'that the Saudi kids in the compounds get up to stuff – it's just they do so in secret. Zen TV couldn't help them by tackling issues affecting them because that would have meant blowing their cover.'

We were standing in the gallery watching his presenter read out text messages that ran along the bottom of the screen. Khalid's director was a woman sitting in front of the control panel doing not very much, but I suppose she was there and walkie-talkied up in case there was a problem.

'Like, for instance, I really wanted to make a programme about the increasing number of Saudis who buy cars, drive really fast and kill themselves. There is a road in Saudi Arabia where you'll probably die if you walk along it just before prayer times, as kids race from more liberal Bahrain back into KSA to do their prayers. The other thing is alcohol dependency. The Saudis don't have alcohol – OK, they sort of have alcohol: they brew grapes down in the cellar for a few months and they get medical alcohol. And they sort of have drugs: UHU glue sticks. But I knew I couldn't make programmes about any of this.

'There was a Zen TV presenter who had been trained in the West as a psychologist. Her role was to receive, read out and discuss viewers' personal problems as they were emailed in: depression, identity crises, relationship aches. The sheikhs weren't keen on this. Then they liked her even less when she got cancer and went on TV with no hair after the effects of chemo.' So, one morning, the Saudi sheikhs made a phone call to Hariri. 'Jad says he has made you watch video-clips all day. That's what has replaced us. Zen TV was taken off the air because there was more talking around and about sex than pictures of sex.' It was the big bucks Hariri and his advisers prophesied it to be – it's just there's no 'discussion'. 'It is all video-clips on loop. Trash has invaded the region … the most successful channels now are music channels like the one you watched. Right now Arabs would rather watch either Haifa [Wehbe] or Jazeera's news from Iraq … nothing in between.'

Along the bottom of the screen in front of which we were standing ran a ticker-tape of text messages – notes of love and friendship in Arabic but written in English with numbers replacing those Arab sounds for which there is no English equivalent. It was the presenter's job to read out the gist of these anyway abbreviated messages. Every 15 minutes this routine was interrupted by a short game. On the other side of the screen from the presenter appeared a Rubik's cube of a famous person's face, scrambled. Viewers who guessed the identity – J-Lo, Gwen Stefani, Madonna or Cher the day I watched – could text in. There was no bra-strap on show, no discussion of orgasms. The camera shot held steady and someone must have put the big red sofa in the props cupboard.

2

Generation Returned

Beirut

Leaving the Zen TV building, right would have taken me past Beirut's Holiday Inn so I went left. Jad had depressed me with a line about the building being a metaphor for everything that was crap about the Lebanese: designed to withstand an earthquake, it opened only shortly before civil war broke out in 1975 and in week one of its life it became used, because of its height, as a militia sniper position. Too large to demolish, its empty skeleton still stands above Beirut with the hundreds of would-be hotel rooms open to the atmosphere.

Ahead of me was an open gate with lots of people gathered around. The general direction of the crowd's slow movement was up some stairs and into the house. Whatever event there was, it didn't seem that private, so I joined the back of a group of five women entering. It wasn't particularly adventurous – being barely four buildings from where I'd been all day – but there was obviously something happening. If I'd relied on Zen TV to be a laboratory of youth culture, then it had just been bombed and precious samples destroyed. I'd have to do some work instead.

Though the hall was crammed with people, under a hundred shoes the same black and white tessellated floors of Future TV were visible. I pushed through the crowd to the door of a central room, where a man wearing a flat-cap cocked to two o'clock handed me a leaflet with boxes to tick. Seated on a white plastic garden chair at the back of the room I was offered a drink. As I drank tentatively, wondering if someone might take it off me because I wasn't a proper guest, a girl clambered on to something to make herself visible and called people's attention. There was a din as chairs were scraped into rough lines, and a screen was pulled down the end wall. As the lights dimmed, a balding man crept into the room and sat on a chair near the door, drawing a few cheers from people who had caught his entrance.

I'd found myself in an end-of-year show by advertising students and the form I'd been handed was for me to fill in the pieces I liked. The room was crowded with raven-haired French Arabs. Some of those I'd pushed past in the corridor had been conversing in French. Most were speaking in Arabic and French. Those conversing in something unrecognizable were probably speaking their made-up mixture of the two languages. And Jean-Luc Godard would have been pleased. The girls wore polka-dot print blouses, vermilion lipstick; their hair was unbrushed. The boys wore stripes and no lipstick but perhaps some eyeliner and hair just as tousled. Was this what my professors of baby-booming had envisaged when they'd talked breathlessly about the forthcoming Arab world's own *soixante-huit* revolution? A carbon-copy model? This tableau was Zen TV's generation returned. Now I understood why they'd broadcast those ridiculous vox-pops on orgasms. It was vintage *Amélie* whimsy – taken straight out of the scene from the film where Amélie takes a moment to muse on how many people in Paris at that precise moment are having an orgasm.

Francophilia reigned supreme. Some arse, just off the plane from exile in Paris, bringing Gaullist sentimentalism to Zen TV, had enraged the religious authorities.

France has a special relationship with Lebanon. Following the collapse of the Ottoman Empire after the First World War, the League of Nations mandated the five provinces that make up present-day Lebanon to the direct control of France. Lebanon gained peaceful independence in 1943, French troops withdrew in 1946 and when civil war broke out, France returned the hospitality by accepting Lebanese exiles. Chirac and Hariri were firm friends with Hariri being the political figure most often received by the French President. With the civil war having been over for more than a decade families had now returned. More French than the French: one of the next adverts was a pastiche of the French dialogue-free 1956 classic, *The Red Balloon*, in which a small child scampers around Paris chasing his escaped balloon. Not for them the grit of the Paris *banlieue*. No one's adverts owed anything to *La Haine*.

Fifteen minutes into the screening, the projector broke down and when the lights and voices were raised, the man next to me looked at my sheet, introduced himself as Michel and said in French, 'I am very relieved you liked my advert enough to tick my box.'

'Me too,' I answered in English. 'That could have been quite awkward.'

'Ah, so, you're English?' I nodded. 'You're English and yet you liked my advert?' It hadn't been so very bad. 'The reason I am amazed is that the best adverts come from England. Guinness sea horses, Dyson making vacuum cleaners sexy, so on.' Arabs, he said, had particular problems, and while they fixed their projector he launched a paranoid defence of his classmates' adverts.

'An Arab audience is not as sophisticated – I can not be sure of the language capacity of my audience so have to keep jokes and puns to a minimum.' His advert – for cigarettes told from the perspective of the inside of the packet – had already been given full marks by his professor, he said. Because there were no words. 'Words are something of a sin on adverts, according to my professor.'

Michel had lived in Paris from 1988 to 2000 – from eight to 20 – returning when Hariri became PM the second time. 'I didn't go to university in France – mum and dad couldn't afford it. But there's a certain amount of *stuff* you pick up by growing up in the West. I tested myself by seeing if I understood all the adverts.'

'So is it frustrating to not be able to make adverts like those in France you tested your cultural knowledge on?'

'Of course, but that is the price of coming home.' Now, like the kids who had worked at Zen TV next door, he too had returned from the urbane and knowing culture of the West with new tricks and knowledge to be told: no words. Words only alienate. No clever tricks.

'For a lot of us our next step will be a stint in KSA,' Michel said when the show was over. 'That's where the money is.' Zen TV's Khalid might have been thinking of Michel when he gave me the potted history of the station's demise.

I asked him whether the older man who had been cheered as he arrived was his professor. He shook his head. It was someone called Xiad. The house was Xiad House.

I'd heard of Xiad and Xiad House. In fact, I planned to try and find him in a couple of days. The luck of gatecrashing this party made up for the bad luck of Zen TV. As I sat there, waiting for them to fix the projector, I saw the older man I now knew as Xiad slip out as quickly as he'd arrived. The only place he could have gone was up the dark staircase near the entrance. I followed him. On the next landing was an open door where he stood as I felt my way up in the dark.

'You were downstairs but you're not an advertising student?'

'Er, yup. I'm a journalist.'

'Mmm. Yes. Sort of advertising.'

He sent me through into his main room while he made coffee. A large cubic room, its high ceilings, square proportions and triple-arched windows meant it was like sitting in a large birdcage. I perched on the red velvet cushion on the antique bed sofa next to the open windows, and heard the show downstairs turn into a party. Many sets of lanky doors opened off all the walls except one, on which hung a large canvas – a black sky above a grey landscape with a square of sky blue cut into it.

'That's Beirut,' he said entering the room and pointing with his elbow at the canvas because he was carrying Nescafé mugs with both hands.

Xiad House was famous in Beirut for its open-door policy. Xiad had lived in the house all his life. In his early twenties when his father had wanted to sell it, Xiad, a young artist, took it over. Now, events like the advertising graduate show were held there every other night. The house functioned as an enclosure for young artists and musicians to graze in. One of the rooms downstairs was the office for Helem, Beirut's famous gay-rights movement – Arabic for 'dream', Helem is the first and only gay advocacy group in the Middle East. If, loosely speaking, it was fair to assume that Xiad was a lefty, then why was he sitting in front of me now drinking Nescafé when the Lebanese make perfectly good coffee?

Lefties drinking American coffee and young expat Arabs pursuing careers in advertising suggested the Battle of Seattle, Genoa riots and Naomi Klein's *No Logo* hadn't reached Beirut. Despite the activities against Israel, America, Syria and the government, they were quite into their brands. Adverts and big brands were revered in Beirut. At that moment one superstore, Aishti – Beirut's version of H&M – had bought almost *all* of the billboard space in the city and its adverts appeared as frequently as street signs. Its advertising budget for 2005 was $3 million. But at least it was a Lebanese company. The lights went out, cries came up from the downstairs party and Xiad made a sibilant sound somewhere in the black.

'We are reminded of how crap this government is at least once a day when the power fails.'

Xiad's rates were cheaper than my hotel and he let me stay. Later that night I moved in. The room he gave me was the back part of his drawing room – the two parts separated by triple glass doors – large enough for a family of six. Though only glass doors separated my room from the main living space, large canvases of fully clothed footballers and naked men and women hung on the doors provided privacy. Only light spilled over the top. Windows on the other side of the bedroom looked on to Xiad's garden, where more canvases were propped against the back wall. At bedtime there was light coming from a shed and I saw a hand go up and draw the curtain – he'd got us crammed in everywhere. Despite the Nescafé and advertising, it was very spirit of '68.

Though it was raining the next day when I arrived at Beirut sport stadium there was already a huge crowd clogging up the entrance. Of the maybe 500 present there were 50 women. The average man wore tight jeans, tight shirts, shoes with slight heels, gelled hair and there were a fair few checking teeth and nostril hair in hand and car-wing mirrors. They were an unlikely lot to need controlling by the Lebanese army, but as I tried to get to the front two men collapsed at my feet in a ball of fists and kicks and a dozen Lebanese soldiers piled on top of them. Inside, one half of the basketball court was cordoned off. In this pen, hundreds of hopefuls were practising their singing and the arena hummed. By contrast, the other side of the stadium was empty save for the desk of Future TV's production staff. It was 10 am and *Superstar* auditions were just beginning for the day. Officious miked-up producers assembled two single lines in the centre of the court.

Musa was busy – he was judging all day – so he palmed me off on to someone with expensive skin: Mahmood, the presenter of *Superstar*. A sometime Egyptian catalogue model with one of the best-known faces in the Arab world, he'd turned his back on modelling for London – only to return a few years later having been head-hunted back again.

35

He'd now been presenting *Superstar* for three years – since he was 22.

'Last year we got around 4.8 million viewers, this year we want 6 million.' He sounded like a stockbroker: 'Last time round we auditioned 40,000, whittling it down to 83 from 15 Arab countries.' Auditionees approached him and I thought it impressive that he seemed to know quite a few of them. 'Some people have gone to every audition in every country they can get into. Every year,' he explained. Someone now shouted a suggestion to Mahmood from the audition pen. 'Are you going to Iraq? If so, why don't you call it Super-shaheed?' *Shaheed* means 'martyr' in Arabic.

Mahmood's work today involved being fired off into the crowd to keep it happy. At one stage he and a camera crew clambered to reach a small man standing in the gods. He was belting out a song that seemed to come from his toenails and his entire extended family – arranged round him in a family portrait – were singing.

I had left Mahmood's side and clambered high up on the other empty side of the stadium to get a better view. I sat down with a young woman who was waiting for her brother. From this side of the stadium we could see Mahmood holding the microphone up to an auditionee. When this man finished the crowd erupted, as did Samar, the person I was sitting next to. A slight woman wearing a brown headscarf, she slapped her knees in delight.

'A real mountain voice. You don't hear that much any more. It's all video-clips … and everybody knows that comes from a machine in a recording studio. But that man drinks hard mountain water that gives him a hard heart and a hard voice – not Lipton Ice.' (Lipton, alongside Nescafé, were the programme sponsors.) 'I bet he doesn't get through to the next round.' She certainly seemed to know her voices. So why wasn't she entering? She sneered in the same way I might have done if I were asked why I wasn't entering UK *Pop Idol*. But her shyness didn't explain why there were so few other women auditioning.

'This competition is not about singing,' she said, 'but about being watched. It's not proper for women to be so, er, how you say, "showy".'

The auditions had now been under way for 20 minutes and the first successful auditionee now emerged. She was very short, wore tight hipster jeans and had hair down to her bum. Cameras stuck to her like iron filings as she did a slow victory walk around the court.

'What about her then? She's wearing quite revealing clothes.'

'Maybe she's Christian.'

'But they called out her name. Fatima. Are Christians called Fatima?' Samar shifted her bum on the bucket seat and looked pointedly over my shoulder where there were members of the army. As I turned to look I could see Musa's press officer pointing me out to Mahmood. He was obviously being berated for letting me out of eye- and ear-shot and climbing up the stands towards us, addressed us when he got close enough:

'At last a woman has got through. When I took this job they told me that I was going to meet loads of young women. But actually the only people that seem to audition are thousands of unemployed young men, who can't sing.'

The Arab world's women were largely too modest for Mahmood. So how did the music channels recruit?

Mahmood took me downstairs and we passed Musa who wanted to show us the entry form for one candidate.

'An Iraqi. All his paperwork is intact, so he is here legally. But it says here he left last year. Imagine. Rushing out of Iraq, getting into Beirut legally and within a year thinking something like this might be a good way to make money.' I suppose Musa imagined it was further testament to people wanting to sing rather than fight. And appear on Future TV instead of al-Jazeera. Mahmood got me into the back of one of the audition rooms before another hopeful arrived. Half of the room was draped in blue material with the yellow *Superstar* logo printed in Arabic – except it read *Suberstar* because there is no Arabic letter for 'p'. In front of the row of judges there was marked a spot on the ground, above which a microphone dangled. The other side of the room was crammed with producers, directors and crew. On this untelevised half of the room the changing rooms' lockers remained uncovered and the soundman next to me was drawing a penis in heavy black biro.

Over the next hour they saw 15 hopefuls, three of whom were women and five of whom got through to the next round. They were told they could sing only in Arabic and couldn't sing foreign songs. The judges let through a less attractive couple of boys with 'mountain voices' but otherwise this was video-clip kindergarten, the engine of an industry that churned out the overly sexy music stars, as Musa had implied, by spotting previous year's Superstars on the music channels. The first thing that each contestant had to say, after their name, was where they were from. Most of those who auditioned while I was watching were Lebanese, a few had come not too far from Damascus and quite a distance from Cairo, but the man in front of us was a Palestinian, from the Beirut refugee camp Bourg al-Barajneh. His singing was excruciating and the sole female judge stopped him as abruptly as taking the needle off a record. The penis-drawing soundman was now translating for me:

'She doesn't like it. She says it's too much. But the other judge likes him so they are fighting.' Even without translation it was clear the female judge was really angry as opposed to the cod angry of Simon Cowell.

'She has now told him that his singing is too emotional.' Too Palestinian, the soundman said. This, apparently, was nothing unusual. In the first series there had been a Palestinian finalist who sang Fayrouz's 'Jerusalem' – written in 1971 to mourn the fall of Arab Jerusalem to Israel in 1967. This same judge had believed the finalist's rendition used emotional blackmail to get more people to vote for him. At the time the Palestinian finalist released a statement trying to have it both ways. On the one hand he said, 'She [the judge] has to understand that [Palestinians] are my people, and this is what I feel,' and on the other hand he argued that she was wrong. Most of his votes were coming from Abu Dhabi, he said, and for that constituency an overtly political performance might actually lose him votes. He got through but didn't win. One supporter in Jerusalem said he'd lost out because the rest of the Arab world doesn't support the Palestinian cause. The Palestinian before the judge now didn't get through.

By now I was bruised by an accumulation of losses. I'd thought the Palestinian issue was something I could count on as unifying young, and old, Arabs. Now I wasn't sure. And if I'd left Future TV in mourning for an ironic golden age of Arab discussion programmes and documentary-making, after this day spent watching Superstar after Superstar hanker after fame, I knew it was buried.

3

Wasta

Beirut

Upstairs in the basketball court, there were still probably one hundred waiting to audition, but there was less singing. People were tired. One man was away from the coop, leaning against the railings watching them all. I was talked out but he had a notepad that he kept fishing out of his pocket and I was nosey. He told me he had successfully auditioned yesterday and now he was back to check out the opposition.

'I can't think about anything else. Before the audition I got so nervous I was nauseous.' Jad was wrong that it was just the English who got nervous. 'I lost 5/6lb in two days, and I fainted at work.'

He didn't look a faint-heart. Ahmed was a 20-year-old hotelier, who along with his hotelier family came from Tripoli, a Sunni town and Lebanon's second largest. *Superstar*, he said, was the best thing to hit the Arab world. From my afternoon watching video-clips and then a near full day at the *Superstar* auditions I felt I had a pretty good insight into what was required, and his nicely spoken voice and neotenous symmetrical looks might have been it. It was the Boyzone effect on music that grizzly rock critics rail against back home, but to the power of 10.

Why was he so enthusiastic?

'Stop being so cynical,' he said. I'd perhaps sounded chippier than I meant to but he seemed to be happier now he was distracted from the competition. Leaning away from the railings, he explained:

'In *Suberstar* there is no *wasta*. There are no, how you say it?, "connections". There is everywhere else – in becoming a politician, in getting a job, in getting a visa. Like, take me and Mahmood, for instance,' he said, referring to the weary TV presenter now sitting on the Future TV production table. 'I have very bad *wasta* … but Mahmood's *wasta* is excellent.'

We looked at Mahmood talking with his female co-presenter. 'His mother was an actor. Not many people know this. But I've heard it is true. Anyway, he is the exception. Apart from Mahmood I don't think there is any *wasta* in *Suberstar*.' Now he had stood up straight again. 'They can't let people through on the strength of *wasta* alone because the viewers of the TV programme would be the ultimate judges of whether people were good singers or not.'

Then, once through to the final, he said, public voting was a double insurance against *wasta*. Reports from the time of *Superstar*'s launch recorded a producer saying, 'At the end of the day, the audience decides everything.'

Ahmed put it a different way: 'The ear hears all voices… it's democracy,' he summed up. 'When the first series was coming to an end and we suspected a little bit of cheating, my friends and me demonstrated outside the television station … TV stations care about their viewers more than the government does about the people.'

The scandal to which he was referring involved the last three contestants: female singers from Syria and Jordan and a man named Melhem Zein from Lebanon. When Zein was eliminated, the Beirut audience lost it. Both women fainted amid a tumult of flying chairs and had to be rushed to hospital. A crowd gathered in front of the studio and began a well-known Arabic chant that is usually reserved for far more serious strife. But time and again people made the comparison with democracy, half in jest, half seriously. Despite a Jordanian winning, she did so by only 52 per cent to 48 per cent in a region 'where presidents always win by 99 per cent'. 'That's why *Superstar* is the beginning of change for us,' Ahmed said.

The duffle-coated Musa, talking at Future TV on my first day, certainly hadn't called it democracy. Safa had hinted that Musa *might* have grand sentiments about his TV shows' effect on democracy, but I hadn't heard this from Musa's mouth so I couldn't be sure. What I *had* heard – the stuff about Lebanese pitted against Libyans and so on – was the opposite of Ahmed's high-falutin ideas of democracy. The Iraq elections were on the horizon in the next week and the Palestinians had just turned out to vote, despite being under occupation, for the president of the organization internationally recognized as representing them: the PA, or Palestinian Authority. The results were reassuringly inexact – 62 per cent of the votes cast went to the winner. But Musa was having none of this easy reading of the *Zeitgeist*. For him his programme's success was regional politics magnified: the Lebanese being happiest when the Egyptian candidate gets knocked out, and happier still when the Syrian, Palestinian, Emirati then the Algerian entrants topple. For Musa, it worked because it played to the region's internal divisions.

The reality of the voting process was also far from democracy. In Libya, where voting was difficult because of a lack of phone lines, Libyans who wanted to vote piled into internet cafés where the café owners were rumoured to refuse to let them use machines unless they voted for the Libyan entrant. There were rumours too that the entire Jordanian army had been ordered to vote for Jordan's contestant. During the first series, Lebanon's leaders were criticized as failing the nation by *not* mobilizing support for Zein. Maybe, at this stage, in the sweaty, smelly stadium basements, *wasta* was more irrelevant than usual. Maybe all this voting was great news and heralded a new age of Arab democracy. But democracy it wasn't. At around 6 pm I left Ahmed to his note-making about all those that emerged from the bowels of the stadium victorious.

The door of Xiad House was open and Xiad stood outside with a well-dressed woman as if they were checking tickets for entry to a play – a distinct possibility. There had been concert piano playing into the early hours of the morning the night before. Instead the woman had her car keys out ready and they were evidently waiting for someone – probably the man who was in the sitting room, absorbed in a phone call, when I walked through to my room. Dressed all in black with a light silver thread for a pinstripe running through the jacket, his hair was a messy black-biro scribble but his back was to the room so I couldn't see his face.

I'd made it to my bedroom door when the man I came to know as Walid called me back: 'You will be joining us …'

'I'm making a film about the revolution that must happen in Beirut.' We were crammed into Xiad's sister Marie's Renault 5 driving across to East Beirut. I was in the back seat with Walid and listening to his detailed plans for a revolution in Beirut. They were so uncannily perfect maybe he was the place man of the professors of baby booming. The car was so small that if you talked, you talked to everyone in it.

'You're so immature. It's a stupid, stupid, dangerous idea. Go back to Paris,' Marie berated Walid from the driver's seat.

Xiad stared out of the window, hissing obscenities. Walid ignored them. It wasn't clear how Walid knew Xiad and Marie and why, given they were talking to each other in such venomous tones, they were all going for a drink with each other. Walid asked me a lot of questions in quick succession, each unrelated to the one before, and felt his hair when listening to me. A clutch of random questions in, he stopped me mid-answer. He hadn't been understanding much. Perhaps I would try to speak in an American accent. We were stuck in a traffic jam on the flyover above Beirut, only about halfway to the East so silence wasn't an option, nor would clearer annunciation help – it would just make my voice more clipped. So I opted for a bout of American accent so bad and unconvincing that he got distracted by my jacket. The only one I had with me, it was a faux-Edwardian thing from Top Shop in brown and cream tweed, with large fur lapels and a belt tie. He now asked if we could swap jackets. On girls this looked as intended. On him, it sat more like a shrug around his shoulder blades. But it didn't look wrong. In turn,

I had to put on his blazer. I looked inartistically androgynous and worried about the smell of the only jacket that I'd worn every day so far.

One thin street in Gemmayze – an area of Ottoman buildings with little balconies above street level – is lined with bars and restaurants, each one a little, narrow and deep glorified wine cellar. Along the street, faded and tattered, like posters for a gig, were plastered sea-blue UN Resolution 1559 posters – sponsored by the USA and France and calling for Syria to end its presence in Lebanon. This UN Resolution was adopted in 2004 and signalled America and France's first rapprochement since falling out over the Iraq war the year before. France acted because its ex-colony Lebanon was like family, America acted because it saw in Lebanon a more liberal democracy than Syria.

Here the bars' clientele are the same 200 or so people in rotation. Entering one bar this evening Xiad and Walid forked off into the downstairs room while I went with Marie upstairs, where she began asking me my advice on a film she thought needed making to publicize her work, 'promoting the use of electronic signatures to reduce credit-card fraud'. Walid caught up with us on the stairs and heard a chunk of Marie's pitch before accelerating past and on to the landing to inspect himself in his new jacket in one of the mirrors there.

'Fuck credit-card fraud ... let it happen,' he said, projecting his voice through the strains of an Umm Kulthoum track and over the small and densely packed second-floor balcony. (Umm Kulthoum was the queen mother of Arabian singing who could make one song last a couple of hours; her funeral, 30 years earlier, had been attended by 4 million people.)

'Steal from the rich to give to the poor. Lebanon needs life made easier for Robin Hood. Not harder.' I was impressed that he name-checked an English hero but Marie pursed her lips: his silly, glib talk of revolution and bad grasp of Beirut's recent history were, she said, spoiling his good looks. 'Walid, you are not revolutionary and Beirut does not need a revolution. Since the civil war we have nearly achieved prosperity, and now you want us to go backwards. You are so handsome but so stupid,' she said. Walid was a lucky mixture of the best bits of some of the world's foxier men. What Mr Potato Head would look like if he had David Bowie's frame, Bob Dylan's head, shoulders and slouch, and Jimi Hendrix's mania. Even as we were speaking someone in the bar's corner was drawing a sketch of him. Xiad joined in: 'It will be very easy to incite revolution, Walid. Our government is rare for not having a monopoly on power'– there is no centralized police force and Hizbollah is allowed to carry arms. 'The difficulty in Lebanon,' Xiad continued, 'is keeping the peace not making the war.' Having only heard the bare bones of Walid's plan for an uprising it did seem to be against a cliché of an autocratic Arab government, which, in many ways, Lebanon's government was not. The central government is frail, there's no oil money to lubricate international affairs and no adequately trained riot police to face down Walid-style revolutions. And, most importantly, the Lebanese government had Hizbollah to contend with. It was in recognition of this fact that UN Resolution 1559 also called for Hizbollah to disarm. As the group was thought to be partly controlled by Syria, disarming Hizbollah would be another way of disarming Syria.

Hizbollah was formed roughly halfway through Lebanon's civil war, in 1982. Shortly after Lebanon had gained independence in 1943, the 1948 Arab–Israeli war pushed about 100,000 Palestinian refugees into Lebanon. Lebanon's Christians fretted about this influx of Sunni Muslims and the effect they would have on the finely balanced political compromise of Lebanon's post-colonial period. Neighbouring secular Syria, also worried about this possible imbalance, moved into Lebanon. The presence of Syria led to a short break in the fighting, which resumed in south Lebanon – an area controlled first by the Palestine Liberation Organization (PLO), and then occupied by Israel in 1978 and 1982. (Israel pulled back to a 'security zone' in 1985 from which it withdrew in May 2000.) In 1982, just three years after its own revolution, Iran poured 1,500 Iranian Revolutionary Guards into south Lebanon and set up Hizbollah. Reflecting this, Hizbollah's first manifesto in 1985 aimed to establish an Islamic state like Iran's theocracy. Today it has quietly dropped this talk and instead focuses on its popular resistance against Israel, typified by President Lahoud's comment that 'for us Lebanese, and, I can tell you, the majority of Lebanese, Hizbollah is a national resistance movement. If it wasn't for them we couldn't have liberated our land.'

Walid was cutting a cigar and had his spider legs wrapped one over the other. He shook his mop, undefeated.

'I have a story for you, Xiad. Today I was so bored I went to the cinema to watch a film that I'd already seen in Paris. It was a Tarantino film and I couldn't believe they'd edited it. They'd censored a Tarantino film. That's pretty low, huh? While the rest of the world was kicking down class, deference and sexual inhibitions – the playing out during the 1980s of the West's 1960s liberal revolutions – the Lebanese were busy having a war for the wrong reasons. I believe that if the civil war had played itself out – rather than stopping when bourgeois people like you and Marie got tired – Lebanese people today would be able to watch Tarantino films as Tarantino intended them. We don't produce anything ourselves that we can be proud of, and stuff from outside we censor. We live in a Beirut of absolute stifling boredom. When someone is "splenetic" it means they're kind of irritable and hostile. That's us – because of the complete inability to do anything in Lebanon if you're not of the right sect, if you don't have the right *wasta*. Our culture is in crisis. If people can get out, they will.'

Despite the gradual return of that million displaced abroad by the civil war, those who could get to the West were doing so. Some 300,000 had emigrated since 1995 because, Walid argued, there were no prospects for them in Beirut.

'But if they can't get out of this country then I say that people need to go back to their houses and get out their guns.'

For this reason his film, he told me, would be shot as if the camera crew were a militia squad, ambushing each interviewee. He would also hire a helicopter to transport his crew. The sound of the helicopter would remind viewers of the civil war. He got up again, still wearing my jacket, now suiting him so well I wondered if I'd get it back. At the bar he greeted a girl whom I recognized as one of Future TV Khalid's producers.

Walid had told me earlier that he was diagnosed as being *hyperactif*. If the people round this table were anything to go by, most just thought him a dickhead. But I liked him. In the

49

week or so that I spent with him he always turned down Nescafé and his bugbears most mirrored those of the poorer people I met. Like superstar Ahmed he hated *wasta* but though the two were united in their bilious critique of Arabian old school ties, they disagreed about the solution.

'*Superstar*? Churning out the same shit Arab music and for what? So you can be on one of those shit music channels.'

A few days later I watched Walid's first film, *Spleen*. Walid had arrived unannounced at Xiad House and we found the video player in a side room where another Xiad Houser, Fatima, was working on the artwork for a poster of a forthcoming exhibition. She also watched. The film was a chiaroscuro chronicle of five young men, including a younger Walid with cropped hair and one of his arms in a sling, bored. At first I was bored too. Not able to get jobs, a lot of the 20-minute film is spent at floor level watching the five of them in Walid's best friend's bedroom play guitars and cards despondently and begin to hatch a plan to get out.

In one scene they are all half naked – bare chests and trousers – leaning against a bedroom wall with something drawn on it that they tell us is a map. The black line through the centre of the wall drawn above their heads is West Beirut's main street. Dotted around the wall are crude squares that represent Beirut's embassies. The rest of the film follows them on their unsuccessful visits to each of these embassies. They have dogs set on them, and on the visit to the US embassy a week after 9/11 they aren't even allowed to pick up the application form. People like them, they are told – on camera – by a surly member of the embassy staff, won't be visiting America again.

At one point one of Walid's friends reads out the Requirements for Visa form: 'They say to me these are the things you need: savings account, bank account, international credit card, job statement, have been to university or school, confirmed reservation at a hotel in host country, invitation from host country, flight reservation and medical insurance. Well, I can get a flight reservation but that's about all. If I had a job statement then I could work right here. I wouldn't be trying to leave.'

This schlep round Beirut's embassy district is the nearest Walid and his mates get to a world trip. Ordinarily, I'd think them wasters but by the end of the film I found their position quite heartbreaking. 'No word' adverts, ubiquitous video-clips and no possibility of a visa would make me *hyperactive*.

4

Virgin in Beirut

Beirut

Walid's second film would pick up where *Spleen* had left off. If people had to stay in Beirut then things would have to change – hence his calls for revolution. If I seem too sympathetic to him and more generally obsessed by the music of the region – like I think all of youth culture lurks in a recording studio or garage somewhere – it was because I'd also had enough of the ubiquitous, over-produced prostitution of video-clips and *Superstar* – no innovation, just reheated old classics in dodgy microwaves – why hadn't I seen the local indie music?

On that first night in Gemmayze, when Xiad's sister had driven us all back to West Beirut, Walid had wanted us to be let down at the Virgin Megastore, so 'we should all go shoplifting from Virgin'. That it was a citizen's duty to do so, 'in order to undercut the leviathans and support the local independents'. Of course Marie had driven straight past the store, telling Walid that if he wanted to go shoplifting, she wasn't going to drop him at the shop door. But it stuck in my mind.

I went to Beirut's independent music store. Walid was right that Virgin was killing off the local start-ups and ergo the local bands. Was it the Nescafé of the Arab music industry?

'It's difficult to say if he's right,' said Paul, the guy who worked the tills.

Paul had a wan, shield-shaped face, a French accent, and wore a sack-like woollen black jumper. All very rustic and it seemed appropriate when he said that he had a flat in Mount Lebanon surrounded by cedars, where he lived alone. It's supposed to be unthinkable that young Arabs live alone – they're supposed only to leave their family when they marry. But the war had cracked that tradition in Beirut. There were those who clung on to their extended family to keep the tradition alive, but there were those like Paul who lived with just a grand piano. Both his parents were dead or 'killed' – this was most probably during the war but it could have been a car crash, cancer or suicide. I never asked outright because I'd learnt not to.

That morning Paul played me a few of the local bands' CDs while I relayed Walid's thesis about Virgin.

'I can see where he's coming from … but really it's a bit, er, paranoid. I'd say what he's got right is that at the moment, if you talk about the wider Arab world then, yes, it is true that everybody gets their albums as bootleg cassettes from shops on street corners. This *does* mean no money goes to the artist and that becoming a musician is not a proper job. So he's right that musicians need help. But that's where shops like ours come in,' and then he smiled. He knew that he'd entered the territory of the hard sell and was hopefully going to retreat. 'OK, even though they are our competitors, Virgin does play its part. I'd say what your friend doesn't seem to understand is that it's only with the arrival of big companies like Virgin in the region that we'll get a copyright law. Until then musicians will make no money from their art.' Paul, the kind of young man who looked like he'd lost the path through the woods back to the monastery, was a free-marketeer.

'Becoming a rocker has never been a proper job,' I put to him. 'Pete Doherty doesn't care now and John Lydon didn't care back then.' No one has ever done it for the pension, holiday pay and silver clock, have they?

'There are heavier responsibilities for someone choosing their job over here – you're expected to be making money. And give a lot of it to your parents.'

It made sense to me but I wasn't sure it would wash with Walid: people couldn't afford to be rebels at the moment, and it was only with the advent of international labels that indie kids would find champions. What about those who decided to let mum and dad survive on their own, didn't they exist? The baby-booming professors needed them to be emerging to get their Arab revolution.

Paul came out from behind his till and fetched a few CDs down off the shelves. Tapping the cover of one as he handed it to me he said, 'One of the best, he's one of two in the region who have a contract with EMI Arabia.' The CD's cover was a study in urban cool – a cartoon rendering in red, black and grey a man, arms contorted into a zip in front of his body with the microphone dangling from one hand, wearing sunglasses like sun-bed goggles. Rayess Bek was Beirut's best rapper. 'The rest? They make their CDs themselves … and pretend they're not interested in being signed. Maybe it's those guys who would steal from Virgin.'

Paul made some phone calls and then scribbled on the back of a flier. Handing it to me he pointed into the air, indicating the music playing.

'Give Zidan a call. Of the six songs on this compilation Zidan was responsible for three. He'll be able to answer your questions.'

One track seemed to be Zidan in his one-man-electronica guise – half like the demo on a Casio keyboard and half Daft Punk – it was called 'Lebanese People'. Let's call it ethno-techno. Another was the Portishead-like band Zidan formed and played bass in. Bathypelagic triprock, with lyrics that, even in Arabic, were pretty damn close to 'I'm so tired of playing with this bow and arrow'. This was the outfit for which Zidan was most famous and I remembered Jad talking about them as one of the bands with which Zen TV did a lot of work. (He'd said they were like the Holiday Inn, another Beirut fad. As if it were a uniquely Arab or Lebanese phenomenon that pop stars, skyscrapers and television might be trends that come and go. Judging by the number of CDs they were still putting out, they were hardly a 'passing fad' anyway.) Walid had also talked of Zidan's band as rare examples of fellow fighters in his revolution. Zidan's third track was a hip-hop act that he managed.

'You won't find any of Zidan's outfits on the covers of magazines and definitely not inside,' Paul said. 'You won't see him advertised on billboards. And you won't hear his tunes playing in shops around town. All because he doesn't have a record contract. He doesn't have a contract because he's not a video-clip artist.' The arrival in the region of Virgin and shops like theirs could change all that.

◈

That afternoon, when Walid and I were talking about *Spleen*, I decided to tackle him on some detail. I reminded him of his exhortations to shoplift and put Paul's argument to him, that maybe it is only with brands like Virgin that a proper premium would be put on the arts.

'Sheeet. This is sheeet. This makes me mad. Who was this guy? He is the bourgeoisie,' hands in pocket, kicking his boots against Xiad's skirting board, his head forward like a rag doll's. (The shaking of his head was in time to the track's beat. Unintentionally. He was such a curmudgeon that he would not have let himself succumb to a beat.) We were standing in the large drawing room and I'd put on the CD Paul had given me.

'But I suppose it is typical,' Walid said, snapping up straight. 'They don't even know that they *need* revolution. And this,' he said picking up the CD I had stupidly rushed to play him, thinking he'd be keen to know of Zidan's new work, 'this is very bad news. Zidan used to be such a genius. He was signed by a Paris label. But they went bust and it seems he has too. Now he has written a track called "Lebanese People". I mean. Question: Who the fuck are "Lebanese People"?'

OK, it wasn't mellow trip hop, it was pretty repetitive and if you worked for *Rolling Stone* magazine you'd probably think it was pretty poor. I knew it was pointless but I said it anyway – that maybe Zidan was trying to say, in as much as you can with the funkier end of electronica, that for a country split like a plate into 18 different sized bits, it was now – post-civil war – united. Or *could* be united. A sentiment not dissimilar from his own call to revolution.

'Comoaunnn, don't be a moron – it's "Lebanese People" in *English*. If you're fucking poor and can't afford lessons to learn Arabic let alone French and never mind English, then this piece of electronic keyboard synthesized sheeet of Zidan's ... it's not going to do anything for you. You won't even understand the title.' It was for the rich over from the Gulf wanting a piece of 'funky Beirut', for the expat Beirutis back from Paris, London or Madrid. It was for people like me. But it is a free compilation, I retaliated, following him as he walked diagonally across the room. No one was making any money from it, I said as he ejected his tape from the machine.

Fatima was still working on her posters, drafting pencil outlines of graffiti letters. Walid paced round the room.

'And what is he doing managing the ultimate fucking sell out – a hip-hop act? He's not just become bourgeoisie. He's become a bourgeois pimp. This is what my new film will expose.' His perambulation stopped next to the TV and in front of an open window. He lent out as if looking across the sea that, while very close, was not within vision. He looked right, left, and then he went.

There had been only one other witness to this strop and because she was stifling a laugh, Fatima's face was puckered. Did she agree with him?

'With which bit?'

Walid was *persona non grata* at Xiad House. In retrospect, the drink they'd kidnapped me for seemed to be a freak outing. Perhaps the trio's awkward relationship had been *why* I'd been invited. They needed the diluting effect of someone else. Xiad found Walid's revolutionary talk tiresome, preferred him not to be there and was wary of my friendship with him, saying that 'Lebanese are not allowed to sleep in Xiad House.' He'd obviously got the wrong idea but still I blushed when he took me on one side and said this. It was a function of Walid's sporadic film-maker's timetable – near unemployment – and that his film's subject was unemployment, boredom and eventual revolution that Walid had oodles of time on his hands. So though we did spend a lot of time together, I had a boyfriend back in London and he had a 40-year-old girl-friend back in Paris. He was material; I was someone to show off to.

But the slight prudishness Xiad revealed on this matter, plus the Nescafé, confirmed that the House, though it was a beautiful paradise you could walk into off the street, wasn't a commune. Xiad was shrewd and careful, preferring well-behaved female guests like Fatima, a nice, demure, creative creature, who now gave me her verdict on Walid's film and the picture of Lebanon life it gave .

'I don't know whether he's right. My friends know him. They say he's, how you say?, "*hyperactif*".'

'I know he's hyperactive. But is he right about Arab hip hop? Did you hear that music we were playing? Did you like it?' I pressed.

'Why not?' she asked. It was infuriatingly passive.

The building I was looking for was a sleek steel-and-glass apartment block with not a ledge, hanging basket or balcony to hide under in the pouring rain. After half an hour a knack-ered Fiat pulled up, so weighed down with bodies that its underbelly touched the road. Four guys got out swaddled in clothes and hats and ran under the pouring rain, whooping and yowling, from the parked car to where I stood. Once inside in the small lift downstairs they shed their hoodies, beanies, gloves, scarves and jackets. As it all came off the smallest and oldest of them introduced himself as Zidan – the famous Zidan – and led us out of the lift to the small door in the corner of the basement car park. This was the crew's recording studio. The other three guys with Zidan were The Three Esses. As they cannonaded around the room, firing up amps and testing machines, Zidan talked to me.

'The thing you should know about these guys is that they used to be double.'

He was referring to the urban legend circulating Beirut that the last time the crew did a gig in Paris half of them never came back. The others were now supposedly on the run in France and would send shouts back to Lebanon on pirate radios. Zidan had discovered them as he was lying in bed and heard, through his sleep, 'beats like I'd never heard before wafting in through my window from the car park'. Getting up on his bed he looked out and saw something he only used to see when he travelled abroad: a group of ten guys a bit younger than him free styling in a car park. He said this was really rare for Lebanon. 'Normally, you'd be arrested for disturbing the peace.'

Zidan was in his late twenties and small with a large head, thick black hair and light black stubble. He wore a silver neck chain and the shortness, smallness and furriness of everything about him made him seem animal-like. The boys he was with were all over 6'2" and they filled the small basement music room. I'd got myself out of their way – and out of feeling like an idiot groupie – by finding a hole against the wall in between a piano that wasn't being used and a drum kit still covered. They all had a gig that Saturday – Zidan's own band with The Three Esses supporting – and Zidan had brought a poster just off the printing press. The boys rolled it out on the floor at my feet. It was a picture of Zidan and his band – The New Government – with their band's name at the bottom.

Zidan's own band hadn't always been The New Government. It had changed members and names a handful of times over the ten years that he'd been playing – bassists, drummers and singers lost to university scholarships abroad. The one constant was Zidan. The poster showed him standing with his band dressed in suits, looking like cops from a 70s TV series, lined up at the base of the statue in Place des Martyrs. The square was once a rectangle of landscaped lawns and boulevards of palm trees, named Martyrs' Square towards the end of the Ottoman period when the first Lebanese nationalists were executed. It's them sculpted on the statue and this statue, situated in the square's west near the Virgin Megastore, is the only thing left, its four figures studded with moth-bite bullet holes. On any given evening Beirut's skater kids would be flying off the ramped enclosure of the statue, and sitting down on the benches inside it to tighten their wheels. If I asked these guys would probably have been into Green Day. I didn't.

It was an easy bit of politicking to say that Martyrs' Square lying empty bang in the middle of Beirut symbolized the vacuum at the heart of Lebanon but Zidan went for it anyway.

'The government has no legitimacy, 'he said, darting round tinkering with knobs and levels to create a swelling instrumental that The Three Esses were beginning to beat-box to. 'We haven't got a government like you have, Allegra – people don't pay taxes, they don't look to the state to do stuff. So all the government does is make statements in your name ... and on that basis it might as well be a rock band as the set of middle-aged men we currently have,' he said. He explained the name of his band. 'And these guys,' he said of The Three Esses (MC Stress, MC Fess – as in 'Fess up or Confess' – and MC Mess), 'well, the government would like to pretend they don't exist. They're poor, no university education and there is no way they'll get a job. And there are millions of kids like them. The only platform they get is when they rap on stage. The government is responsible for the fact that the crew you'll see on Saturday night is only half the group... it's certainly a break from all the video-clipping.'

I relayed Walid's point to them. That Arab hip hop was just taking a medium from commercialized America. 'Why don't you do something new with Arab music rather than American music?' I was trying to find an alternative youth culture to the adoration of video-clips; need it be Eminem?

'Arab music is wonderful,' Zidan countered, 'but a bit of a how you say it? – a one-way street. It has always been very hierarchical … you can only do it if you have X amount of knowledge and for this reason it is not something particularly welcoming. But hip hop is something Arabs can add to. Those guys over there in America have gone crazy with bling. But we've got real grievances. The Arab world could reshape hip hop if it wanted to. OK, look at them,' he said, pointing at his three, 'they're old enough to have been in the army but, you know what?, they're not allowed to vote. What's that about?'

He explained that there had been talk of lowering the voting age from 21 to 18 to let people like The Three Esses vote. But it's been knocked on the head. 'Do you know why that is? Because Lebanon's young Muslim population is younger than the population of Christians. So they killed the idea.' I was stoned, Zidan was stoned, The Three Esses were stoned and their beat-boxing was soothing. There was the gentle tapping of Zidan's beats and conspiracy theories inside and the gentle tapping of rain outside.

'But they'll shove them all in the army. They're very happy to do that,' he continued. The music segued into a soothing riff and Zidan asked if I knew that The Three Esses were the only hip hoppers in the Arab world. I said I thought there were some Palestinian hip hoppers and his eyes widened in outrage: 'They're just doh, ray, me, A, B, C.'

I then said, thinking of the one with the contract whom Paul had mentioned to me, that I'd heard of other Lebanese rappers. MC Stress, the tallest of the three with his dark hair braided close to his head, who had been sitting on a drum next to us listening, then asked Zidan a question in Arabic about a rich guy from Paris whose name he couldn't remember. Looking round for help, he clicked his fingers when it came to him. His name was Rayess Bek – that name again.

'He's got a job in advertising. Lucky him,' Stress said, amplifying this last bit into the microphone that he seemed never to let go of. Through the bass line there suddenly came a loud crash from outside. They leapt up, one of them scuttling across the room, cradling the gear in cupped hands to the toilet where they flushed it down. As Stress did this he knocked 'Fess who poured pineapple juice all over a keyboard. We had smoked a small potted-plant's worth of hash that evening and if caught it was punishable by six months inside. We stayed in silence waiting to see if anyone was coming down and after five minutes began to relax again.

Zidan spoke: 'The hash flooding the Beirut market at the moment is cheap. Too cheap *not* to smoke.' Grown in the Bek'aa Valley it is controlled by Syrians who apparently also control the price, in what Zidan and The Three Esses agreed was a cynical attempt to control the street. At the beginning of the 1990s, in response to American pressure, growers were forced to reduce their cultivation of opium poppies and cannabis. Instead, they turned to the production and marketing of heroin and cocaine. As well as the hash, this heroin was everywhere in Beirut. Zidan said that 'the money made from drugs goes to Syria and is one of the reasons Syrians were so keen on staying in the country.'

This might be true. Certainly, everyone I'd so far met did a lot of drugs. It crossed my mind that Walid and others I'd met had a chemical imbalance or three.

'Walid, I found you some proletariat who want revolution,' I said when I found him a few hours later.

'Ah, I remember. You've been with Zidan's hip hoppers. Rappers. Hop hippers. They do not count. They do not want revolution, they are halting it.'

'But these guys have no job, no *wasta*, no university degree, no years spent abroad, just years spent in the army,' then I paused before being purposefully bossy. 'I hope you'll be interviewing them for your film.'

Predictably he lashed out: 'Were they *very* boring or just a little? Don't tell me. They're unhappy with the status quo, so they think to themselves, I know, let me rap. Fucked over by the government. The best thing for me to do is say words too fast into a microphone. They are the bourgeoisie, or worse, wanna-be bourgeoisie. They create music to make people feel better about being bourgeoisie.' If he wanted to initiate a revolution and break the stranglehold of the bland *Superstar* then he might have to accept some bedfellows he didn't fancy.

We were walking east, out of downtown, on our way to a party. Walid had wanted a cigar but the only shop nearby that sold them was in downtown – which Walid hated so he'd made us run through it. He couldn't bear the plazas full of Khaleejis smoking hookahs. A word I'd first heard used by Zen TV's Khalid I'd since learnt was a term of abuse. While Khaleejis *did* technically refer to people who came from the Gulf, it was actually a jealous term of abuse used by people in resource-light Levant countries for their oil-richer Gulf cousins. Loaded, idle and spoilt. Strained relations between Saudis and Americans meant not only that they were taking more of their holidays in Lebanon than before 9/11 but also that they were investing in the Levant more than America, and it was supposedly Khaleejis who owned quite a few of the apartments in the downtown area.

'The plastic surgery done to downtown,' Walid said, 'is something I'll probably never be able to forgive Hariri for.' On reaching the party, we journeyed up in the lift to the eighth floor and I asked who he'd know. 'The same one hundred people lurk behind every door. The bourgeoisie.' He said that I'd love it, while he'd have to throw himself off the balcony for entertainment.

An American-Lebanese man opened the door and Walid pushed past him, heading for the flat's open patio doors: 'I need to get some fresh air and smoke my cigar.' The man at the door palmed me off on to a friend of his, also called Walid, because the doorbell was ringing again.

It was a 'moving party'. A group of people, this second Walid explained to me, had joined together to hold a party every fortnight in one of their flats with the same guest list. You had to pay, quite a lot, for your drinks but benefited from the vetted clientele. At that moment a guest dropped two glasses of punch on the floor at our feet and we scrambled about clearing it up. It was at this point that it got clumsy calling him Walid II with Walid careering in and out of the picture and so Walid II suggested I call him by his stage name, Rayess Bek.

He looked just like his cartoon on the front of the CD that Paul had shown me: arms contorted, mike in hand and small glasses giving him a geeky chic. Rayess Bek worked in advertising during the day, playing gigs and working on the album he was due to deliver to EMI Arabia at night. The pop stars of the 1960s had had day jobs to sustain their nighttimes on stage. He made adverts. And he *looked* like he worked in advertising not rap. His very fine French features worked best on his album cover as a cartoon: he didn't look very hard. A small woman had appeared at his side and put her arm round his waist. There was, he said, despite his EMI Arabia contract, not much of a living in being an alternative musician in Lebanon.

'There are only four gigs you can play in this country: Beirut, Tyre, Sidon, and maybe Byblos. Maybe you can then go to Egypt or Amman but your lyrics can't travel with you because they don't understand the dialect. Given I won't stop rapping in Lebanese because that's my base, it means I am also limited in my audience. But I also limit myself by what I want to rap about. The politics in Lebanon are different from the politics of those other places. In Lebanon I rap about unemployment, the draft, the 18 sects, the conservatism of society – we live in a closed society where we feel we have no real opportunity to express ourselves. In Egypt, what would they care? Egyptians agree about their national identity. National identity is constantly contested in Lebanon.'

This pessimism seemed to be the result of Rayess Bek's analytical mind and EMI Arabia being a tad gloomy with him about whether his act would travel the region. Though they'd signed him he didn't seem to have got a champagne-and-flowers treatment. Dialect aside, I imagined that his description of 'staying at home because there are no jobs available and falling into a routine that leaves you with no ambitions' was an accurate description of any Arab's condition.

We talked about The Three Esses and how they obviously perceived themselves as locked with him into a rap authenticity battle. Rayess Bek rolled his eyes at what Chinese whispers had done to his perceived social standing. The way The Three Esses talked you'd have thought his family had fled Beirut during the civil war for the Palace of Versailles. (These elements of counter-culture that I'd so far uncovered would have to stop their Montague-and-Capulet act if they were going to cohere into anything other than music.)

Even I was a bit taken aback at Rayess Bek's reality. His family had spoken no French when they arrived in Paris. When they all returned to Beirut, they spoke bad Arabic. So, after a childhood linguistically challenged, he turned to rap.

'The guys at EMI Arabia have the same criticisms of me as The Three Esses. That I'm somehow too "intellectual".'

That night I left alone without saying goodbye to Walid the First, and the next morning he was at Xiad House at lunchtime, slightly miffed. 'You never once came out on to the balcony where all the interesting people were.'

'No, I had a good time with another Walid. Do you know Rayess Bek?'

'Nope.' Oh. 'Do you know what his name means?' Walid asked. Sort of. Rayess I knew meant 'leader' or 'president' but I didn't know about 'Bek'. 'It's an Ottoman title. They sold official titles like pasha and bek. Rayess Bek is how we address older men.'

'A bit like someone in London would address a boss or a pub landlord as guv'nor? Kind of mock deference?'

'Yeah. Sounds right.'

'That's interesting,' I said, enjoying it when Walid put down *Das Kapital* and started being ambassadorial for Beirut.

'No, it's not. It's making the class war kitsch. It's the definition of bourgeois.'

5

Arab Alex
Beirut

Darah is a very tall girl even without heels, a study in androgynous black style – baggy workmen trousers with flaps for hammers, Timberland boots, a big white-hooded sweatshirt and sunglasses. This builder's look was saved by Darah being very handsome, but if it was easy to see why she'd been spotted by Zen TV execs in a Beirut nightclub then it was also easy to see why the glasses plus the trousers plus the boots equalled what was seen as an ambiguous sexuality. The look earned her and Zen TV, where she had worked as a presenter, condemnation, and in the months before all of Zen TV went belly up, she was one of the first casualties. Of all Muslim countries it is only Lebanon that is attempting to legalize homosexuality but region-wide, which was Darah's TV profile, there was no such attempt. Homosexuality was very *haram* or forbidden. This was why she was now a radio presenter. Her heavy eyelids and, when we sat down, the cloud of shisha smoke she spoke through made her seem like a supercilious Marlene Dietrich and my questions banal. But her answers were always full.

There *was* a problem, she said. First off, she agreed with the others that, as Zen TV had made way for the disco divas, bands like Zidan's, real artists, just didn't fit into the current musical scene of the lone, highly lucrative, commercial artist.

In the rare circumstances that they were able to afford to cobble together an album, at the end of the process they then had to go to the censors who would inevitably persuade them that certain lyrics might offend people. If they *didn't* go to the censors then any radio or TV station they approached would also be likely to baulk at incendiary lyrics or out-of-the-ordinary riffs. What these guys needed was a boat like Radio Caroline bobbing around off the coast of Lebanon broadcasting illicit Rayess Bek or The Three Esses. Maybe the dead-eyed video-clips were an equivalent to the stultifying torch songs of the pre-Beatles hit parade. Back then the music industry was controlled by fusty middle-aged impresarios, who second-guessed youth tastes and churned out singers like Helen Reddy to croon about being abandoned above a treacly slick of bombastic percussion and soaring violins. I put this to Darah, bonding as I thought we were about the region's shit music but she shook her head.

'You've got it wrong,' she said, 'the bigger problem is that a lot of people actually like these video-clips.' There was no Radio Caroline because there was no appetite for this kind of grungier stuff. 'For most people, the video-clip stars are the best entertainers they have ever seen.'

We were now in her car and she was giving me a lift across town. Except she wasn't because it was rush hour and we had been stuck in the same bit of traffic jam for a very long time.

'Have you seen the Saudis hanging around Beirut?' she asked me. Yes, yes. I repeated what Future TV's Khalid had said – that Saudi sheikhs had been closing down things like Zen TV. And then there was Walid's cursing and swearing as we ran into downtown past the Khaleejis.

'Well, yes and no. In fact, probably, more no than yes. That wasn't what I was thinking about. Have you heard of Rotana?' Signing 80 per cent of Arab artists, and bagging exclusive rights to broadcast their video-clips, Rotana was the largest producer and distributor of Arabic music. It has six satellite channels, three of which show music and movies. 'And you've heard of its owner?' He gave some money to New York's Mayor Giuliani for victims of 9/11, she said, and then the next month urged America to re-examine its policies towards the Middle East. Giuliani sent the cheque back.

'He's a Saudi prince, a keen proponent of change in KSA.' And as owner of Rotana a keen proponent of video-clips.

By now I knew my Arab pop stars quite well. I knew that the singer belly dancing in Prague was Haifa Wehbe and that Nancy Ajram had got in trouble for pretending to be a waitress and cavorting through an all male café. Very different from Umm Kulthoum who sang for millions of Arabs in a long-sleeve top. This Prince's aim was, in his own words, to 'have the number-one entertainment company in the Middle East.' Darah's point was that if they weren't popular, he wouldn't touch them. It is difficult to ascertain because none of the companies has to reveal its viewing figures, but the region's 50 million satellite dishes are popularly thought to be tuned to al-Jazeera and other news outlets for five minutes a day and to Rotana, Mazzika and Melody Arabia for as much as five hours.

The full name of the man she was talking about was Prince Alwaleed bin Talal bin Abdul Aziz al-Saud. Or Prince Alwaleed. Worth $20 billion, some estimates put him as the world's fifth or eighth richest man. He has feet in both the first families of Lebanon and Saudi Arabia: his grandfather was a founding king of Saudi Arabia and his mother was the daughter of Riad el-Solh, the first PM of modern-day Lebanon, in whose mansion Future TV's HQs had been located. But he was not core Saudi royalty and instead chose to develop an alternative career. He now has shares in the world's best-known brands: Citicorp, Apple computers, Disneyland Paris, AOL, Motorola, Four Seasons Hotels and Murdoch's News Corporation.

While Darah had cautioned me against thinking video-clips less popular than they were, she didn't seem a fan herself.

'What kind of makes me mad is that he's removed the market from the industry. He can afford to keep flooding it with the pop stars *he* likes.' Plucking them off things like *Superstar*, investing money in their looks and production and making them into stars. Outgoings are massive, incomings not so obvious: each of the video-clips Rotana puts out costs about $50,000 while, unlike most satellite channels in the Middle East, Prince Alwaleed's Rotana is free-to-air.

I checked this out and found that he had indeed said: 'My business model is, you make money by getting exclusive artists, that's my fuel, and you make money through advertising and SMS [the 20,000 daily mobile-telephone text messages that viewers exchange on screen].'

'But I think this is going to get messy,' Darah finished. 'I'm a liberal and even I think there is too much flesh on TV.'

Later I bought the Prince's biography *Alwaleed: Businessman, Billionaire, Prince* is a hagiography as slavish as its font size is big. Chapter Five opens with the author painting a scene for us. Prince Alwaleed is peering out from under his gutra – the name for the 'traditional red-checkered' headdress in Saudi Arabia – at a bank of TVs in front of him, some playing his channels, others CNN, CNBC and BBC World.

'In contrast to the sombre news presenters silently mouthing their scripts, vivid colours and quickly cut shots flick across the television tuned to the Prince's latest interest, the Arabic music channel, Rotana. A popular Lebanese singer, glowing from her heavy make-up, furrows her brow in a pleading manner as her ample figure lounges across satin sheets singing about a lost love. Atmospherically lit shots of a swarthy young Arab man staring into the distance, looking equally lonely, punctuate the rolling shots of the pining maiden who is so softly lit that she looks almost out of focus. In spite of her alluring manner, the Prince is more drawn to the rapidly scrolling "tickers" on CNBC, updating stock prices and displaying the change in value of the world economy minute by minute. "Financial intelligence! It's all about financial intelligence," he finally declares pointing at the screen. The one displaying CNBC, not the singer. Financial intelligence is the reason why this man became a billionaire.'

What struck me about this was both the detailed description of how sexy the video-clip was, and that the Prince was uninterested in it. But here again was Rotana's Beirut-based marketing director: 'the success of the music-video industry is a kind of reaction against sexual repression in the Arab world.' They were quite pleased with the flesh.

Since my first day in Future TV being force-fed video-clips I'd reacted by looking for better music but I hadn't probed the sex and flesh issues: I hadn't investigated what seemed to be an odd acceptance of so much flesh on TV. Future TV wouldn't be airing *What Not To Wear* because it showed too much flesh. Now, Darah said, when it came to video-clips, there were an awful lot of Alices going through an awful lot of looking glasses. Families that wouldn't talk about sex or countenance their kids dating before marriage might sit round the TV watching video-clips with their children.

We were still gridlocked in the traffic. Tapping the window of her BMW, Darah pointed at two girls crossing the street in front of us. They were cigarillo thin and Coco Chanel chic. Both wore black-nylon boot-cut hipster trousers and high heels, carried baguette handbags and wrapped around their heads were black sheer headscarves as tight as the rest of their outfits.

'The result of video-clips are these girls. I call them muhajababes. "Muhajaba" means girl who veils ... but look at them. They're babes. I bet you they watch Rotana, Mazzika and Melody Channel. I'm really glad there was this traffic. They are not so common in this bit of Beirut and you are very lucky we spotted them.' She now reeled off a list of places where I would find these girls in their natural habitat. 'They are the demographic the music and TV execs work to. They're not into bands like Zidan's,' hip hop like The Three Esses and Rayess Bek. With their love of the video-clip 'they keep Rotana going, and Zidan off the air waves.'

Unlike the American University on Bliss Street in central Beirut that was Sweet Valley High, the Beirut Arab University, south of the city, where Darah had sent me, was Sweet Veil High. Here, 90 per cent of the women I passed were veiled. Of this massive majority I'm not sure how many were what Darah would call a 'muhajababe', I was still working out the criteria. If the Arab word for headscarf was *hijab* and it was synoynmous with 'modesty' then a muhajababe might be someone who combined the modesty of a hijab with some slightly less modest piece of clothing. The difficulty would then be defining an 'immodest piece of clothing' – make-up, stilettos, tight and low-slung hipsters, even plunging necklines.

Verse 24: 31 of the Qur'an reads: 'Believing women should lower their gaze and guard their modesty; that they should not display their beauty and ornaments except what must ordinarily appear thereof; that they should draw their khumur over their bosoms and not display their beauty except to their husbands.' The *khumur* – or *khimar* in its singular form – here is taken to mean headscarf and is the word we all should use instead of hijab because hijab is supposed to be a synonym of modesty rather than mean a headscarf. But we *do* use hijab.

If a girl were trendy but also covered, modestly, in the places she was expected to be, could she still be a muhajababe? The original muhajababes we'd seen in the car hadn't had much flesh on show, but it would be disingenuous to say that those girls with their cocktail-stick stilettos and cling-film-tight black outfits were not 'displaying their beauty and ornaments'. They were. The muhajababe definition seemed to be most helpful as a barometer of contradiction.

Although possible muhajababes were ubiquitous here, I'd been instructed to get permission to speak to students first and so I was now waiting outside the dean's door to do just that. A few girls lined up nearby were obviously waiting for a lesson. If their bottom halves were a uniform of the same pale blue stone-washed jeans, then their hijabs seemed to display their personality: the Arab equivalent of the witty T-shirt aphorism across the boobs. Two tied their veils – one fuchsia, the other a lighter pink – at the side of their heads like side ponytails; another's was so loose it was barely a hijab – more a sheer accessory with diamanté studs.

I decided I would do a quick straw poll to test Darah's thesis. Had they heard of Nancy Ajram, I asked, and they coo-ed, one even pulling out from her bag a cassette of Nancy's first album, *Mehtagalak* – meaning 'I'm in need of you'. – the tape cracked through use. It came out in 2000, a couple of years before she became truly famous with that infamous video-clip in the café surrounded by dribbling men. Perhaps their *Mehtagalak* cassette was an early classic it was now prestigious to own. Then I asked if they had heard of The Three Esses, Rayess Bek or even Zidan but I got blank stares. Mention of Zen TV left them looking confused, doubly so when I asked about Rotana: 'But of course, why do you ask?' Then a teacher opened the class door and they left.

Nancy Ajram's director was a woman herself – Nadine Labaki – and some of Nancy's lyrics were not exactly the words of a kept woman. The video-clip that saw Nancy slinking round the all male café was for a song called 'Akhasmak Ah': *Akhasmak* means 'Quarrel with You' and *Ah* means 'Yes'. The song meant 'Yes, I Would Quarrel with You'. Perhaps the video-clips were not the misogynist pornography that Jad, Khalid and even Walid had said. Even though Darah didn't like them that much and had even lost her job because she didn't conform to the stereotype of ladies that video-clips seemed to dictate, she'd been able to see that there must be a reason why they were popular. The video-clip for the title track of Nancy's 'Ya Salaam', translated to mean 'How Fantastic', used a backstage set featuring drag queens. Maybe Nancy was pushing at boundaries more subtly than Darah presenting Zen TV could ever do.

Five suited men interrupted my train of thought as they filed out of the dean's office. I filed in to make my usual vague pitch for young Arabs. As I was asking for formal permission to meet a few of her students, the dean leapt in:

'You should start with my family. I'm a widow from Alexandria and my two daughters live on their own in the only places they could find jobs – Cairo and Dubai – making us a pretty weird Arab family.' A family get-together for them was being on MSN messenger at the same time. In English with a definite St John's Wood lilt she explained her atomized family.

'I'm on secondment from a sister university in Alexandria – these universities are subsidized by Nasser's estate to serve the Arab nation.' Gamal Abdel Nasser, the second president Egypt had ever had, championed Arab nationalism during the 1950s and 1960s before his death in 1970. He called on Arab states to join together – in pan-Arabism – and confront the 'imperialist West'. These universities were one way of doing this.

'Look behind you. You see the hole in that safe?' She was pointing to a safe in the corner of her office: the build of a fridge, it had an apple-size bullet hole in its bottom left-hand corner. 'The Israelis got all the way up here when they invaded in 1982. We think they were after the exam papers.'

If this were a Nasser university then the Israelis would have been very interested in it.

Someone else had entered the room and, still looking at me, the dean held out her hand and took receipt of a manuscript. Her student was a small neat man in his late twenties. Wearing a slightly over-size navy blazer with brass buttons and shoulder pads over a fluorescent-pink shirt – more *arriviste* Chelsea banker than Arab semiotics student – his PhD choice seemed even more unlikely when he opened his mouth:

'Please say I've done enough this time, Professor Ludmilla. I don't think I can spend more time with Alex … I'll never be able to listen to Beethoven's Fifth again,' he pronounced in affectedly dainty English. I leant forward to see better the title on his manuscript, 'A Linguistic Analysis of *A Clockwork Orange*', but Ludmilla had seen me and slammed her hand over it. Too late. I'd seen enough.

This PhD title alone could kill the critics dead. While the Middle East and North African region was supposed to have experienced the largest increase in the numbers of those graduating from university, it was thought to be quantity not quality. The first UN Arab Human Development Report, written by Arabs about Arabs in 2003, damned Arab higher education as too much about rote learning. Outside the gated communities of the American universities in Beirut, Cairo and Dubai, offering American syllabi for Americanized Arabs, this report dismissed universities as nothing more than municipal spaces in which to memorize ensemble. Not quite the sea of *shebab*, the Arabic word for young people, reading and rocking in madrassas, reciting passages from the Qur'an whole … but nearly.

Despite 10 per cent of the Middle East being Christian, the same brute memorizing of the Muslim prayer book, it was argued, was being transferred to the digesting of physiology textbooks and American plays alike. In fact, you could almost say it was applied to video-clips as well, equal beneficiaries of an appetite for passive ingestion. But the PhD of this Tory boy – Ibrahim Nice But Dim – would doubtless have demanded the deconstruction and theorizing that critics of Arab universities said they did not encourage.

'Do you know any Arab Alexs?' I asked him, knowing my time was running out and Ludmilla was going to want her conversation about his second draft with him in private.

'In this neck of the Beiruti woods,' Ludmilla answered for him, 'there are plenty … this is the Dahiya – home of Hizbollah.'

And then she kicked me out. I made my way back to Xiad House in the centre of Beirut and away from what she'd called the Dahiya – the name for the southern suburbs of Beirut where around half the population of the city lives. A dense and sprawling Shiite area that is half suburb, half slum. I'd find out soon, she said, if she'd let me interview her students.

That night we went to hear Zidan DJ in Gemmayze. As soon as Walid realized Zidan was playing his electronic stuff he left me alone in the bar. A small woman just over half my height approached me. In my abandoned state, Aisha was a godsend.

'Do you know that man?' she asked, gesturing to Walid who was standing outside, high and thin as the lamppost he was leaning against and sharing cigarettes with two women. 'Poor you. He's such an asshole.' I felt disloyal and told her that I was pissed off with him. Both because of being abandoned but also because Walid had promised to take me to south Beirut that morning but had cancelled – on account of what he said was a hangover.

While I was waiting to see if the dean would give me permission to interview some of her students, I wanted to go to the refugee camps near the University. I'd seen how video-clip culture was playing with the students in one of Beirut's poorer universities, now I wanted to know how video-clip trash culture was playing in the Palestinian camps in the south of the city. But I couldn't find anyone to take me. I asked Aisha why I was finding it so difficult.

'All young Arabs say that they care about the Israeli–Palestinian question – that that is why they say they hate America and the West – but really they care because it is the one straightforward thing in their lives. It's like environmentalism for you or anti-globalization – a very simple political cause: "Brother Arabs – Palestinians – were robbed of their land. It's unjust and we're angry."

'What's more,' she said, raising her voice and throwing both hands up – a few heads turned at tables around us – 'it is something Arab governments *let* them care about. But,' and she swept forward towards me to deliver a very loud whisper, 'better to look at how they treat the Palestinians on their own doorstep. Very few want to know.' One person listening had caught her eye. 'That's true, huh?' she challenged him, but he had looked down into his beer.

In 2002, the Lebanese government passed a law to prevent refugees from owning or inheriting property, working in over 70 professions, and receiving proper healthcare. Palestinians are prohibited from bringing materials into the camps – even a light-bulb – without permission and the Lebanese army monitors who goes in and who goes out. This is done, supposedly, as a favour to the Palestinians. The half-century-old charade is that the Palestinians will be going home soon. If the Lebanese made life more comfortable for the Palestinians, the argument went, the pressure would be taken off the Israelis.

'But,' said Aisha, 'do you get Lebanese campaigning for Palestinians to have more rights in the camps? No. Do you get them calling for Israel's downfall? Of course. It is pathetic. We know Israel's culpable. But the thing we could be doing something about – the conditions and rights of the Palestinians right here – we do zip.'

Aisha had looked familiar when she'd first approached me but only, I now realized, because a lot of the central Beirut girls wore their hair in the same short Afro. Her mother, she told me, was one of the leading ladies of Arab nationalism who had put on the veil as a marker of regional pride. Now, through the contortions of 30 years of Arab identity, her daughter wore a short black globe of hair. An exiled Yemeni princess who'd paid Xiad House a visit the day before also wore an Afro of the exact same dimensions. Sitting in the bars of Gemmayze right at that moment a scattering of both men and women were wearing their hair Afro.

As Aisha talked knowingly about her mum and her reasons for veiling, I tried to calculate just how knowing she was about her own barnet. I wondered whether she was working on the conceit that an Afro was natural, or whether she'd be honest about the crafting: the backcombing and gelling and scrunching and blowing that must be every inch as arduous as the gripping and flattening and wrapping of wearing a headscarf. Did she want the world to think she was letting it all go? She couldn't. Someone who'd walk up to me and slag off the person I was with, who'd pick a fight about Palestine with a person a table away, for her there was no doubt the Afro was something other than the lazy option. The difficulty was trying to untangle why.

For Aisha's mum the veil was a symbol of Arab pride, but the side-effects have been a boon too. 'Mum says that the only reason women of her generation have made gains in the workplace is again because of the veil. It made women socially acceptable as they entered areas they'd never been in. But, I had dry hair and in my late teens it had started to break due to lack of sunlight. Allah allows you to take your veil off in this instance, but you're supposed to put it back on when the hair is repaired. Before I de-veiled, people told me to prepare myself for men staring at my hair and that I would long for the day when I could put it back on because I would feel more "free".' She said this last bit ironically, bending her arms into wing shapes on either side of her body.

'But when the veil came off, men didn't stare. Or at least they might have stared, it's just they didn't stare so much that I noticed.'

As she de-veiled she also dropped Islam. Aisha, a sociologist now, seemed to have deep-conditioned her way out of

Islam. Her teenage hair had decided for her that religion didn't amount to much. To make her point more clearly she rummaged around for another example. Clicking her fingers she'd got it.

'OK. My friend Yusuf. When he was a teenager he got bad spots. Friends and family teased him and said that it was Allah's way of telling him to grow a beard. Get more religious. Actually, to be more correct, they told him he should join Hizbollah. And so he did. Grow a beard, fair enough … but join Hizbollah. How crazy is that?' She clasped her hands together in a heart shape in front of her and keeled over to her left, the tips of her 'Fro squashing against the back of a man at the next table. 'I love it.' She was delighted that she was able to regale me with a little tale that undermined religion.

Some girls – muhajababes – were embracing tight jeans and five-inch heels with their veil, others like Aisha had binned the veil for the 'Fro. If I thought the muhajababes were Alwaleed's generation then I didn't know what galvanized the Afro wearers. I had a few gos at working out the whys and wherefores: most African Muslims are Sunni Muslims. Aisha was a Sunni Muslim – this much she'd given me as a starter for ten. Did she dump the veil of pan-Arabism for the Afro of pan-Africanism and Islam's African roots? Or maybe it was a tugged forelock to the civil rights movement of 1970s America? Or just black style: Lauren Hill coming late to Beirut. Later I asked Eva, a friend of mine, a Reuters photo-journalist working in Sudan, what she thought. Was I being patronizing for being intrigued by the march of the Afro in central Beirut?

'Darling, I would argue it is far more shallow for the Lebanese. Here in the Sudanese refugee camps I've seen no

Afros – they want to be thought of as Arab not African – so, it does have an African and not an Arab vibe. But this isn't true for young Sudanese hipsters coming back from studying abroad who get that an Afro is fashionable and run with it, to the chagrin of their Khartoum family. But all this Arab vs African thang is of course crap. Same blood, same religion.'

That day I received an email from the dean at Beirut Arab University. She couldn't give me permission to talk to any of her students.

Instead, Aisha insisted I meet Yusuf.

6

Hizbollah Acne

Beirut

I met Yusuf the next day in the Monoprix supermarket on the airport road south after he finished his shift. As I waited for him I watched a supermarket exactly like ones at home: families with children sitting in trolleys, those trolleys ripe with food. Fielding banter from colleagues, Yusuf led me out into the car collection point, past queueing saloons with black-tinted windows. We clambered into one of the VDub vans that function as taxis, and headed south for Shatila. Here we were surrounded by Druze in their brown felt uniforms. As the newly constructed four-lane highway thinned into two pockmarked lanes we hit a bottleneck. We crawled past a cartoon strip of shops. Those not selling Louis Quatorze sofas were chop shops. All the industry along the road's four miles Yusuf said was illegal. The government was trying to get people back to south Lebanon 'now that Hizbollah had pushed the Israelis out and it was no longer a war zone'. But shopkeepers were refusing to budge. Government pledges to rebuild factories or help farmers get the land back up and running hadn't materialized, so they were staying put. I was listening to what he was saying but was relaxing, for just a moment, into being with someone who was not going on about helicopters and revolution.

'What's the matter? You're quiet. Are you scared?'

Like virtually every other Lebanese faction during the civil war, Hizbollah bombed civilians and kidnapped foreigners such as Terry Waite and John McCarthy but it also pioneered the use of the suicide attack, targeting American and French embassies. The US State Department says that the group has killed more than 300 American citizens, of which over 200 were US marines in Lebanon. These murders, alongside allegations of atrocities committed abroad in the years since the Lebanese civil war, meant that when in 2001 America drew up a new list of 'terrorist' organizations that should be subject to financial sanctions, Hizbollah – its stated aim the destruction of the Israeli state – was on it.

'No. My boyfriend says that Hizbollah' – I dipped my voice and leant closer, not massively sure that what I was about to say was correct 'is like the French Resistance during the Second World War. They've got no interest in me – a Westerner. Any more, that is.'

'Who said anything about Hizbollah?' Yusuf had dropped his initial amiability and his tone was now harsh and loud. 'Other people live in south Beirut than an internationally renowned terrorist organization. Half the population of Beirut live in south Beirut in fact. Are you saying half the population of Beirut supports Hizbollah?' he said not dipping his voice.

It didn't matter – the brown Druze, stacked like skittles around us, were hypnotized by the swirling traffic. He was right. He hadn't yet said anything about Hizbollah. He didn't know I knew the beard story – which was probably a sensitive issue. More importantly, in this city where most people don't like to reveal their surnames and you don't ask where and when people lost relatives, I should have known not to talk about political groups as if they were postcodes; never to assume out loud that an area is typified by its world-famous insurgency movement even if it obviously is. I was trying to think of a way to rectify my position but he was now smiling. 'I'm teasing you. Relax. You're right. We're now in Hizbollah heartland.'

In 2000, Israel withdrew from south Lebanon, pushed by Hizbollah, or pulled by enlightened Israeli politicians within Israel, depending on who you believe. Either way, Hizbollah's stock has been high ever since. I now had a quick tour of the Islamist world according to Yusuf. Though Hizbollah – 'Hizb' and 'Allah' or 'party' and 'god' – means 'Party of God', it is not the most zealously driven of Islamic fundamentalists. Similarly, though its stated aim has been destroying Israel and it has expressed sympathy for the activities of Hamas and Islamïc Jihad, it's not quite as militant as Hamas, which in turn is not quite as militant as Islamic Jihad.

'Did you know Hizbollah leaders distance themselves from Osama?' Sheikh Muhammad Hussein Fadlallah – the quasi-spiritual leader of Hizbollah who lives in the area we were now in – was one of the first Muslim clerics to condemn the 9/11 attacks. Hassan Nasrallah, Hizbollah's Secretary-General, was also on record as having warned Muslims to avoid the 'Zionist trap' of believing that they are pitted against Christianity in a religious war. Yusuf was cogent and a good ambassador for his group. He pointed out that Hizbollah leaders have denounced 9/11 and Islamic group attacks on tourists in Egypt. 'But Hizbollah does also express sympathy for suicide attacks in Israel.' I pulled him up. He didn't address that. Instead he dodged it: 'We have eight seats in the Lebanese parliament.'

Then we got on to acne. Most people already knew the story, he said. Personally, I couldn't believe it was true. He had two perfect cheeks of taut plaster.

'It *is* true. The local imam came up to me one day after evening prayer and said that my spots were a sign from Allah that I should pray. Hard. In Hizbollah. Of course there were other reasons. But, ya, Allah, I was ugly,' and then he changed the subject.

Yusuf wanted to know where I'd already been in Beirut and, like most people, he raised an eyebrow on hearing about the *Superstar* auditions. Did I know the history of the Camille Shamoun Stadium where the auditions were held?

'A friend of mine wanted to audition there, but his mother wouldn't let him. When she was younger, before her son was born, she was living in Shatila. In the days before the massacre Israelis moved some of those they slaughtered to the Cité Sportif. They even took some who they didn't actually get round to slaughtering.' His friend's mother was one of these women. Many men she knew were locked into the basement before being either killed or released.

'They've since rebuilt the stadium. Pavarotti has sung there.'

We'd reached Shatila, where Yusuf spoke quickly to the guards in Arabic and the universal language and tone of blagging: emphatic body language and easy *bonhomie*. He needed to see his family urgently and they let us through. His relatives on his mother's side were Syrian and lived in the Palestinian camp because it was the only thing they could afford. Still thinking as a central Beiruti I thought how off it was that while Palestinians had no choice but to live in these camps, Syrians moved *in* as a real-estate decision. Historically, Syrians and Palestinians used not to get on. Back in the early days of the civil war, Syria initially intervened on the side of the Christians. At that time Damascus had little control of most Palestinian organizations and was afraid that the build-up of Palestinian forces could lead to a new Israeli invasion.

But, some 20 years on, the story, Yusuf explained, was different for a south Beiruti. Here Syria's protection against the Israelis and – in Yusuf's eyes – 'pushing of the IDF [Israeli Defense Forces] from Lebanon' was remembered and honoured. If Syria were that selfish, well-rehearsed arguments ran, then what about the Shebaa Farms? That's Syrian land occupied by Israel that the Syrians aren't agitating for. With all this in mind Yusuf said Syrian families in Shatila were, currently, 'royalty'.

Since entering the camp we had been rushing down tight alleys between shacks little sturdier than pig sheds. What felt like about half a mile into the camp, we darted into an empty hut: the least desirable bit of an undesirable rubbish dump. Yusuf clambered up on two crates and rested his hand on the bottom of a square hole that, once I had joined him, he said would serve as a rudimentary window. Here, we were to wait for Yusuf's second cousin to come by after he'd finished prayers. In the meantime Yusuf talked.

Yusuf's mother was Syrian Shia and his father Lebanese Shia. Shia is an abbreviation of words that mean the followers of Ali, the Prophet Muhammad's cousin and also his son-in-law. As the father of the Prophet's descendants, Ali is as near as Muslims get to a holy bloodline, and, when Muhammad died, Ali stepped up as the heir to the Prophet's religious authority. Shias look to Ali and not to the rule of the three Sunni caliphs who jockeyed with Ali after Muhammad's death. The Sunnis, in turn, argue that Muhammad anointed no one to be his successor and instead they were stronger candidates because they were elected by Muhammad's instruction of consultation (*shura*). Probably two-thirds, and maybe more, of the Middle East are Sunni. Around 10 per cent is Shia but it could be more since, in some countries, if the Shia population is very small it may not be recorded. Lebanon, alongside Iran, Iraq, Bahrain and Yemen, is one of Shia's strongholds.

After the acne and the beard Yusuf had joined a Hizbollah phalanx stationed in a south Lebanese valley planted, he described, with huge cardboard cut-outs of Iranian ayatollahs. Iran is estimated to give Hizbollah an annual sum of $200 million and Yusuf himself got a stipend every month of around $20 to $40. Iran, he said, funded his school – something called a Hawza. What did Iran get in return? He laughed.

'To control what we learn.' He was mocking me. 'Not really. Control of south Lebanon. All sorts of things.' Before the civil war, less than a third of Lebanese students went to private, aka sectarian, schools like Hawza. By the time Yusuf left school in 2000, the figure was more than 60 per cent. Lebanon, a bankrupt state, was relying on religious groups to provide basic services.

Yusuf put his index finger to his lips and gestured for me to bring my face closer to the basic square cut in the shack's corrugated iron. The sightline on a building opposite showed two pieces of the same crinkled metal, clipped together, revealing some but not all of what was going on inside. A string of boys passed, all dressed in many layers. They filed inside to join a just visible queue in front of a table, at which an older man stood, and then they left.

'There. Did you see what was happening?' I hadn't. Grabbing my wrist, he pulled me down off the crate, out of the shack and along the alleyway in the direction the boys had gone, stopping, with jolting irregularity, to listen before tugging for us to move off again. On reaching a clearing we saw the boys again, this time in a group at a booth. Now one of them broke off from the group, saying goodbye. We followed him down yet another depressing alleyway – he was apparently Yusuf's cousin Muhammad.

The family shack was on the edge of the camp. Dribbling down the back wall were strings of wires. Yusuf's second cousin Daoud made money by siphoning off electricity from the main Lebanese supply – hence the wires – and charging camp dwellers for its use. The ruse is that Lebanese authorities don't come into the camp, so there is little they can do about this illegality. In the shack, Yusuf's uncle had greeted Yusuf and began talking about Iraq's elections in which the Shia had, in the last few days, emerged relatively victorious with nearly 50 per cent of the some 8 million votes cast.

'This is the best news. The era of the Shia is upon us,' he said, talking to me now. 'Shiites will be freed from Persian paws,' making a silly scooping action for my benefit. Muhammad, whom we'd chased for reasons Yusuf was yet to explain to me, was sitting in the corner of the shack watching

TV. He hadn't really acknowledged our presence and was instead staring like a sentinel at the video-clip now playing.

As Yusuf's uncle got more and more loquacious about his hopes for Shia Islam relocating to Iraq away from Iran, Yusuf threw a few questions his cousin's way about school, Iraq, the camp and football. Muhammad's answers became ever shorter. On the TV that was so transfixing him, a girl was singing a song about her teacher, an older man who at first rebuffed her amour then returned it. The denouement was the young woman getting a spanking. Muhammad was engrossed and unwilling to be distracted. I imagined that these satellite channels were illegal and thought of Jad exasperated at people who didn't even pay for subscriptions wanting Zen TV terminated. Maybe this lot hadn't liked Zen TV and had agitated for more video-clips and less chat. I couldn't, however, imagine surly Muhammad agitating for anything.

❖

'What was the point of that, Yusuf?'

Yusuf was visibly enraged. 'I'm always angry when I leave there.' He was mad about his cousin's thesis that soon the Shia would start to take their cue from Iraq not Iran. The Iraqi Shias have so little money he said, Hizbollah would be doomed without Iran paying up on time. 'But I'm angry you missed Muhammad being paid.'

Was that what he'd taken me to see?

'Yes. That's why he queues up with those boys. He gets paid by camp imams to be religious. He gets that money for going to a camp mosque, not just five but many more times a day. The more he goes the more he gets paid. OK, I don't know if that is strictly true. But, certainly, he and his friends get a wage from filling the congregations of the camp's prayer meetings.'

Which bit did he have a problem with? Yusuf was in Hizbollah or at least 'had' been in Hizbollah ... it was unclear whether he was still active. But Hizbollah wasn't exactly an irreligious outfit. What was the difference between the two cousins?

'The difference is that I believe, and that he spends his free time watching video-clips. Now, since the Israelis' withdrawal in 2000 and what some think is Hizbollah's job done, the next generation is idle.'

'But isn't your job done?'

'No, there are still the Shebaa Farms.'

Israel's occupation of 14 farms, in an area where the borders of Syria, Lebanon and Israel meet, is used by Hizbollah to justify the notion that Israel still occupies Lebanon. If Israel is still perceived to occupy Lebanon then Hizbollah can continue to define itself as a 'resistance movement' rather than the 'militia' to which the UN Resolution 1559 refers. The sticking-point is that the UN defines the Shebaa Farms as Syrian territory. Hizbollah, and Lebanon, insist they are in Lebanon. 'Our job is not done. Muhammad should be in Hizbollah. It is a serious part of government and this election we will surely get more seats. Its battles are only just beginning. The answer is not to sell yourself to the first jihadi group with the highest price, grow a beard and go to mosque ten times a day because they tell you to.'

By jihadi he meant al-Qaeda. The animosity between the two groups was allegedly strong, Hizbollah being Shia, al-Qaeda being Sunni and its radical Wahhabi strain regarding Shiites as infidels. But despite the theoretical reasons for rivalry and both the Lebanese Shiite cleric Muhammad Husayn Fadlallah and Nasrallah speaking out against 9/11 and random acts of al-Qaeda terror, American and European officials are supposedly not sure the division is that wide.

'It doesn't matter how many times a day you go to mosque, it is all wasted if you watch video-clips.'

'So you'd ban them? Hizbollah would ban video-clips?'

'No, I'm not saying that. I'm using them as a way to prove he doesn't believe in this jihadi stuff. We're not about to ban video-clips. Fadlallah himself is so forward thinking on women's rights he gave a lecture at the American University in Beirut. AUB. Yes. *AUB.*' He was referring to the AUB, the gilded central Beirut university.

'Do you want an Islamic republic like Iran? Surely that's what Iran wants? That's why it gives you all this money?'

'The Iranian Republic requires the consent of the people. Can you imagine the Lebanese consenting?'

I couldn't.

7

Palestinian Red Bull
Amman

When a car pulls up and someone has to get out to let you get in you know you've got the worst seat. The fifth person to be picked up by the taxi to Jordan, I wouldn't be getting a window seat in the four-person saloon but was going to have to sit between two girls. It's one thing to inflict this on the youngest sibling in your own family, another thing effectively to incarcerate a stranger. There was little elbow room, no view except the unmarked road ahead, and a hump in the car's chassis robbed me of leg room for the eight-hour journey.

This seating arrangement did, however, have the effect of breaking the ice with these two girls. The man in the front seat – a Jordanian businessman – remained an even more perfect stranger, saying and doing as little as a marked man, the entire journey. On the back seat the girls didn't deem my presence between them a block to their conversation. They'd just finished their university term and this holiday now beginning was casting their minds back to the last one. Did the older and plumper girl remember, the younger, smaller girl – I suppose about 18 or 19 – was asking, that it was the last holiday when two girls at their university had had plastic surgery? She did and she took up the reminiscence. When they had all returned to college – neither girl knowing the other had had a nose job as well – a teacher remarked when she saw them together for the first time that they had bought exactly the same nose. Bad enough when it's the same T-shirt, said the younger girl without feeling the need to finish her sentence; worse when it's the same T-zone, I thought, doing it for her. Now the two girls spent a few minutes checking and affirming how strong each other's resolve remained never to have plastic surgery.

They swiftly moved on to other trends that had gripped girls in their class that term. Those who had recently decided to veil. What did Mona think was worse 'or more sad' the slighter one asked, refining the choice: 'Veiling or plastic surgery?'

'Plastic surgery,' the older one said, 'just.'

'Why "just"?' the smaller one tested.

'Well, I'd say they are quite similar really. It's a physical thing you do to change your appearance. But, with veiling you're not meant to unveil but you can if you really, really want. With plastic surgery, once it's done. *Khallas*.' Khallas means enough, finish, end of story.

I had been moving my head to look at each of them when they talked. Their conversation had been in a doggerel mix of English and Arabic. But I'd obviously been included in the conversation all along. These girls were neither veiled nor letting it all hang out like Aisha and her politics of the 'Fro. They wore the normal uniform of 20-year-olds everywhere: tightish, bell bottomy, denim-lycra-mix jeans with hems frayed at the back like mine, tatty fashion trainers, fitted jackets and as many layers as they could fit under that jacket while balancing fashion with freezing temperatures. They were as familiar as my own sisters so I waded in.

I was a bit knocked, I told them, that they were talking about veiling as even possibly in the same bracket as plastic surgery. One is devout, the other is the extreme choice of societies more self-obsessed and, more likely than not, *not* devout. I'd seen the ladies of Beirut with bandages on their noses promenading along the boulevards of what the postcards called the Middle East's Paris. They were not at all embarrassed by the white gauze strapped to their faces like they'd been mauled by a dog. I could even spot a 'rhino' without the telltale bandaging: detachable noses plonked there like they weren't meant to stay. Some were even recognizable as being Gwyneth Paltrow's nose. The vogue at the mo was for girls to go to their plastic surgeon with a picture of Paltrow. The girls both leant their heads back against the car seat to look at each other behind my head, I don't know whether sharing a moment about my ignorance or innocence.

'You're talking about people who veil because of religion,' clarified the slightly better-looking younger one. Now she spoke as if there were another category. 'We're talking about some of our friends veiling because it is now – how you say? – trendy.' It seemed there *was* indeed another category.

'It used to be that a veil meant baggy material everywhere else. Now it doesn't,' older Mona said. 'The friends of ours that are veiling are doing it because a tight headscarf and a tight outfit is a good look, they think.' Little one agreed. They were talking about Darah's muhajababes and I was about to ask them about Prince Alwaleed and his Rotana channel, responsible according to so many for sexing up the region, when they got in there first.

'We blame one middle-aged guy,' they both laughed, presumably at the fancy of an idea that saw an old man influencing their mates. 'Absolutely bags of money: pop-star friends, internet sites, television programmes. People – both girls and boys – are so into him he's like a heart throb.' Money, pop-star friends, TV: check. But Alwaleed hadn't been making the girls veil, had he? He'd been changing the rest of their clothing but surely the veil was the one thing he hadn't been responsible for, give or take a more gaudy colour choice or diamanté pattern?

'A lot of people we know have practically fallen in love with him. So if he suggests they veil, what do you think they are going to do?'

It wasn't Prince Alwaleed but someone they called Amr Khaled. 'He doesn't have a beard and he doesn't go on about Palestine. This was why he was popular.'

Then some music came on the car radio and they both leapt, pleading for the driver to turn up the track, a melody I remembered from my afternoon watching video-clips in Zen TV. Now I thought back to first sighting a muhajababe I realized that I'd thought the veil came first and the tight outfit second. But maybe the veil was the recent thing. Something these women and girls had decided latterly.

The girls were Palestinian. In fact 60 per cent of Jordanians are Palestinian. King Abdullah's wife, Queen Rania, was born in Tulkarm, central Palestine. When the state of Israel was created in 1948, Jordanian cities obviously – being within spitting distance of Palestine – became overspill sites, with some sheltering up to 80,000 refugees. In the 1950s a law was passed enabling these refugees to become citizens with the same rights and responsibilities as 'real' Jordanians. They pretty much had to take this citizenship if they wanted to go to school, work and get a birth certificate. So perhaps it followed that now these girls, like Aisha and her controversial, contrarian and kind of cruel doing-down of the Palestinian situation, were *over* the Palestinian problem. They were certainly attributing the success of a superstar to his, in their words 'not going on about Palestine'. Perhaps it was what we'd call in the UK compassion fatigue. Or maybe it was just moving on. So did this guy Amr Khaled do it for them? 'Are we veiled?' the little one almost snarled at me.

'But do you have to veil to follow him?' I asked Mona, with whom I was actually getting on quite well.

'What about the other stuff?' She just shook her head. For all her cool demeanour, I could imagine littler one falling for things but it was evident that kind but quite serious Mona just didn't. 'I do think that he is an improvement on other preachers. But at the end of the day it's not my thing.'

'I'd rather go to a Three Esses gig than a mosque,' added the younger one, burnishing her aptitude for being a walk-on part in *The OC* and Mona agreed. We spent the rest of the journey talking about Beirut's music.

The next stop should have been Jerusalem but I hadn't been allowed across the border by the Israelis so was forced to stay in Amman. Hamdi was a businessman, the son of a Palestinian minister and a friend of a friend of a friend I'd emailed. I was keen to meet him because (a) I was dejected (b) I wanted to probe the Palestine fatigue and (c) it was raining and he had a Mercedes. A few days later, stepping into his car out of the February funk was like entering a warm department store. Hamdi dressed like a young businessman: as an older businessman. He wore a wool-lined leather jacket and turned the collar of it in on itself – it brought the coat a couple of inches above his frame and made him appear more burly.

I'd spent an entire 16 hours – up at 8 am and back in Amman by 11 pm – trying to get into Palestine and during this time I'd battled with the name of the place I was trying to get into. The physical location was a flower bed of different sized territories including the West Bank, Gaza Strip and East Jerusalem and names included the 'Palestinian Territories', 'Occupied Territories', 'Occupied Palestinian Territories' and 'Judea, Samaria and Gaza'. The UN opted for the penultimate one: 'Occupied Palestinian Territories'.

The route I'd chosen into the Occupied Palestinian Territories was the shortest between Amman and Jerusalem. Though the actual border was little more substantial than the distance of a shuttle bus between a departure lounge and a plane it took an age and you could eventually be refused.

'I do that journey two or three times a week,' Hamdi said. 'It's not ideal ... but I need to for work. I mean, can you imagine, relying on the journey you've just done to make money?' Hamdi asked me, leaning sideways in the car so his body was hovering above the gearbox and his head was near mine. He navigated the deep puddles that had developed on Amman's roads with just one hand on the steering wheel and the other hanging limply at the end of his arm that rested on the window ledge.

'But we have no choice but to travel between the two places. Palestine is an emerging market.'

Hamdi was a senior Palestinian politician's son so I was taken aback by his camaraderie over border-crossing travails. Palestinian VIPs were supposed, in exchange for good money, to be able to fast track their progress over the borders.

'I've just returned from Palestine today but on my way out there was a huge traffic jam and I was late for a meeting. I got out of my car and at first jogged but, then, forgetting myself, I broke into a sprint. I was sprinting towards an Israeli soldier holding a gun.' I suppose I didn't get it, so he took his eyes off the hillside roads of Amman and turned to me in the passenger seat, saying it again, louder. 'I mean, I was sprinting towards an Israeli soldier with a gun.' Pause. 'I still don't know what I was thinking. I had to stop immediately and put my hands in the air to make sure they knew I meant no harm. I just wanted to know whether I'd make my business meeting or not. That would be so typical of this place. Shot for trying to be on time for work. Now, where shall we go?'

I'd been walking everywhere across Amman's seven hills or jebels. He'd just driven us past a bridge being constructed that would join two of the jebels and it had taken enough shape for its support structures to be clearly in the form of the letter Y. They called it the Y bridge as in: 'Why do we need this bridge?' It was kind-of odd to be asked which restaurant we should go to. He was the local. Wasn't this his job? The two girls on the car journey over had mentioned their favourite restaurants and I suggested them. He raised an eyebrow.

'What's the matter? Aren't they nice? Would you like to go somewhere –'

'No, it's fine. You've obviously been hanging out with some prize-A Ammanis.'

'What are "Ammanis"?'

'It's a name for the wealthy of Amman, playing on the wealthy label Giorgio Armani.' He didn't look any higher or lower class than they did. There were some off-class dynamics in this car.

The restaurant recommendation was on an bare and undeveloped hill in the Abdoun district, near a Starbucks and a McDonald's, and the nearest buildings were some newly built LA-style villas almost a football field away. It wasn't exactly Mayfair. When we got out of the car it felt like *I* was taking *him* out for dinner.

We sat down and he explained. He didn't know restaurants in Amman because it seemed he didn't really spend much time in Amman, in turn because he didn't seem to like the city that much.

'The reason I have trouble with the border crossing is not the Israelis. Oh, no. It's the Jordanians letting me back in. Have you been told about the card system?'

The hundreds of thousands of Palestinians who fled to Jordan following wars with Israel were initially accepted. But soon they organized into resistance groups that began to pose a challenge to the Jordanian ruling monarchy. Open fighting broke out and reached its apogee in September 1970 (Black September): the crushing and expulsion from Jordan of Palestinian fighters. Now the Jordanian government put a kind of filter on Palestinians. They had brought in coloured cards – yellow for absolute residency and access; green for only temporary visits. Hamdi's paperwork was healthier than most but still every time he returned to Jordan he had to make sure he had the right bits to secure re-entry. He didn't understand why the Jordanians made returning so difficult. Or he did, but he didn't like it.

'You see,' he said, shuffling the ketchup, mustard, BBQ and even piccalilli sauce around on the table looking for his condiment of choice, 'if this government just chilled out people would move away from Jordan to Palestine. People know there is more money to be made in Palestine than in Jordan. And Palestinians would rather spend the money they make in the country they love: Palestine. If Palestinians can get into Palestine then the Jordanians shouldn't make it so difficult for them to get back.'

So, he was not a fan of the Hashemite Kingdom of Jordan. A monarchy installed by the British in the 1920s, it was easy to see why eighty years later young Arabs thought it anachronistic. The one concession he made to the Jordanian government, alongside the Egyptian one, was therefore an odd one: their peace treaties with Israel.

'The thing that is smart about the Egyptians and the Jordanians is that they have understood foreign investment is the only way to go.'

In 1951, Arab countries boycotted Israel and any companies found to trade would be blacklisted. So commercial links with Israel withered on the vine. Now Israel trades with Egypt, Jordan and Turkey. Qatar, Oman and Bahrain are dipping their toes into the Israeli market partly because a desire to trade with America necessarily requires a willingness to trade with

Israel. The resulting goods may not, however, feature a 'Made In Israel' sticker.

'Israel is a big regional player in a foreign-investment sense. They've done this because they recognize that economic reform should not be tied to political reform.'

If the girls on the car journey were depoliticized Palestinians, despite being the son of a Fatah cabinet minister, Hamdi was also a *new* Palestinian. Though his dad's party, Fatah (the Palestinian establishment), was founded by Yassir Arafat and had dominated Palestinian politics for decades, it was now losing popularity due to a series of corruption-scandal waves that kept hitting it. Instead, the whole meal he spoke of Palestine the emerging market, Palestine the smart person's investment, Palestine the country to invest in. Hamdi was also a new Palestinian because for him, it was both the homeland and big bucks: utopia.

'Now, Ramallah – that's where the business is – it had a multi-million-pound nightly turnover – all from the foreign support sent from all over the world.' Palestine had so much money as a government, he said, it employed the second largest number of people after the French government. These were statistics that didn't stand up to close analysis but his consumer confidence was refreshing. His particular business idea was a 'telecommunications venture'.

'When Red Bull wanted to crack the Jordanian market they hired the prettiest girls in town and, wham, bang, guess what's the number-one drink in Jordan? Red Bull. That's what I'll do for my business. Of course Red Bull was popular for other reasons, but pretty girls were important.'

'Why is Red Bull popular?'

'Because it's not alcoholic but it's, you know,' and then he made the awkward little movements of a man who can't dance, miming dancing.

'So you don't drink alcohol?'

'Pretty much, yup.'

'Because of your religion?'

'Yes.'

'So would your pretty girls selling Red Bull be veiled?' I asked, not really taking my own question seriously.

'Maybe.' I was expecting a ticking off at making such a simplistic link. 'Maybe they will be veiled. He elaborated: 'I mean, the thing is, really, maybe it is religion that's going to save this region. I wouldn't mind voting for the Muslim Brotherhood in Jordan, if I voted at all. I like some of their conservative views.' If my preconception of Hizbollah in Lebanon had been kidnappings, the Muslim Brotherhood wore their beards curlier and their robes longer, and so I was shocked by Hamdi, friend of a friend of a friend, schooled in America, driving a BMW, and talking about pretty girls advertising the business he would set up when Jordan and Palestine had embraced enough of the free market to let him work unhindered. He'd told me he'd thrown a US election-style party for the best night of his life – this January's Palestinian elections. Beer had obviously been replaced by Red Bull.

The Muslim Brotherhood, often simply known as the Brotherhood or the Ikhwan (*ikhwan* is the Arabic for 'brotherhood'), was founded in Egypt nearly 80 years ago by a schoolteacher called Hassan al-Banna. He wanted a return to an 'original Islam', uncorrupted by Western influences: to see the Qur'an and the Sunnah – laws, in his view, passed down by God – organizing everyday life and government. In its original form the Muslim Brotherhood sought to protect workers and provide for them hospitals and schools. Membership went from a keen but meagre 800 to half a million by the 1950s, whereupon some Brothers carried out a failed assassination attempt on the president of Egypt, Nasser, and the organization was banned.

Now the Muslim Brotherhood runs something of an informal franchise around the Islamic world. Hamas in Palestine is supposed to be Muslim Brotherhood in all but name and in Jordan the Brotherhood is called the Islamic Action Front or IAF and it is actually licensed: it's Jordan's sole authorized religious party in parliament *and* largest opposition party. Hamdi's words had been: 'I wouldn't mind voting for the Muslim Brotherhood in Jordan'.

Compared with its brothers around the region, the IAF has co-operated with its ruling regime – the Jordanian monarchy – more than others. And it is popular. At the last elections, 17 June 2003, the party won 20 out of 84 seats. It had been 'their conservative views' that Hamdi had said he liked. In the 1990s the IAF had talked of an end to co-ed schooling, banning alcohol on the national airline and nightclubs – the stuff of Western headlines warning of the perils of Islamists running the Middle East.

But he explained: 'You see if I lived in America I'd be a Republican, and if I lived in the UK I'd be a Conservative . Things have gone too fast here, we are getting all of the bad things of globalization: drugs and prostitution, and soon a big casino in a hotel in one of the circles (the large roundabouts that dominate Amman's road system). But none of the good things of globalization. I want to resist some of this stuff, while the Jordanian government want to encourage it because it preoccupies people. Because of this I'd vote for the Muslim Brotherhood. They would slow some of this stuff down for me.'

I got what he was saying and was even sympathetic but I computed the corollaries of what I was hearing. Hamdi's dad was a senior Fatah politician. The IAF that Hamdi was possibly, maybe, considering voting for, had strong links with Hamas, Fatah's sworn enemy and competitor. I put this to him.

'But I don't vote here. I vote in Palestine. And, yes, you're right, I wouldn't dream of voting for the far right over there. In Jordan, for me, it is a more feasible proposition.'

8

Badly Drawn Girls

Amman, Jordan

'He said that? I knew Palestinians thought like that but I'd never heard them actually say it.'

I was sitting in the office of Firas, director of an art gallery called Makan. My feet were resting on a joist on his desk. He had a large heater pumping out scalding air into the room's elegant dimensions that, despite the equally elegant canvases on the walls and delicate tiling, was white and cold as a meat fridge. Having stood up to close the shutters on an erupting thunderstorm, Firas was now remonstrating with both of his hands up on either side of his body as if he were carrying and shaking a box.

'The IAF pour money into the Palestinians in Jordan to ensure their support inside Palestine,' Firas explained, more to himself than to me – trying to understand why someone whom I had described as a knowing, urbane young man, Firas's own age, was giving the IAF credibility. Firas was now busy developing another point. Maybe, he said, Hamdi was able to make such a remark because in Palestine conservative politics was all about the homeland, whereas in Jordan, for liberals like him, it was about women not driving and covering up: that is if Hamdi were 100 per cent Jordanian he'd think like Firas on the Muslim Brothers.

'No, he was quite clear,' I said. 'He hadn't been talking about Palestine but about how, when he sees the drugs and the prostitution on the streets of Amman, he's very tempted to vote for the Ikhwan.'

Makan means 'place'. Situated halfway up the steep hill of one of Amman's seven jebels – Jebel Weibdeh – an orange sign with black letters marked steps down off a sloping road that led to double French windows. I'd found Firas online during email contact with an Amman film co-operative, and we'd struck up a friendship. As we talked a woman kept popping into his office and it was only when she left for the day that she came into the room properly to say goodbye. Firas waited for the door to click shut before asking if I knew someone called Xiad who lived in Beirut: Lana, who had just left, had been in a long relationship with Xiad and after they split up she set up Makan. I then saw Xiad's hand in everything around me. Firas was listing people he knew who formed a cat's-cradle of artists and contacts that strung between the two places. The keyboard in the corner of Firas's room he'd played with Rayess Bek. So Makan was Xiad House in Amman and to be used accordingly.

Cosy? A bit claustrophobic actually. Although bouncing from one art commune to another, sitting by their heaters, drinking their coffee and meeting their friends was very 1968, it didn't feel like journalism. On the other hand, maybe this network was important as effective opposition to the ageing and unpopular Arab regimes. Groups like this *were* one of the region's counterbalances to, for instance (with Firas still chuntering about Hamdi's Islamist comments), the Islamists. Firas was now rolling through his phone looking for a number.

There was someone I should meet, he said, Daoud, an artist who would make me understand the folly of Hamdi's breezy admission that he could possibly vote Muslim Brotherhood.

The Jordanians were over the moon about the rain. That morning's front page had even announced that people shouldn't despair: though the rainy season was drawing to a close after a pitiful performance, the current downpour meant Jordan's reservoirs might be full in time for summer. The hills on which Amman was built meant the city's roads swerved like Alpine footpaths and steps from one street level to a higher one were near vertical. When it rained this game of snakes and ladders was set to water. I'd found the past few days particularly frustrating. Friday – their Sunday – is anyway eerily silent for a non-Muslim. But these past few days taxi horns had beeped a few decibels quieter and the clocks downtown, all telling the wrong time, differently, had tocked louder. Even the enormous Arab flag flying from Jebel Amman seemed stilled, almost bombed into submission by the rain. It's the tallest unsupported flagpole in the world – its flag visible from 20 kilometres away in Amman's poorer suburbs – designed to withstand earthquakes and, according to a Royal Palace official, bad weather.

Fantastic mascot of modernity that the flagpole is, during these days of rain I'd been ringing people who didn't pick up their mobiles, unable to send emails as the internet was down, and pressing doorbells that didn't seem to buzz. I'd tried Makan twice but it had been locked up and in darkness with an ankle-deep puddle as a welcome mat.

I went back to Makan for the third time and found signs of life. A party of six was sitting on the covered balcony: three people with rugs on their knees and three Dalek-like heaters. They'd had quite an easy time of it, they said. Firas had packed in his work a few days ago when he realized even the guy selling milk next door had shut up shop. In weather like this, he said, without a car – in fact even with a car – you couldn't really go from A to B. At that first meeting with Firas he'd given me Daoud's telephone number to ring but I hadn't been getting any answers to my calls.

'Where is his studio, Firas? I'll just go and knock at his door.'

'Nooo, don't,' he said getting up from his snug chair. 'I wouldn't. We must wait till he comes to us.' Later that day, as the sun dried the rain out, Firas took a call from Daoud. Apparently, he'd taken one look at the rain and gone to sleep for three days.

Daoud had been sleeping in his studio, where he also lived, he said after he collected me from Makan and walked me there. Three loops of the road up from Makan we passed the grand gate of the Darat al Funun, a kind of Royal Academy of Amman. During one thickening storm I had rushed inside the gallery's complex, made up of three nineteenth-century houses in suburban jungles of jacaranda, built when Amman was still a village. In one of the houses T. E. Lawrence is supposed to have written some of *Seven Pillars of Wisdom*. When I asked if they knew any young artists I could inter-view, a woman sticking ornate Arab-calligraphized addresses on invitation envelopes said, without looking up, 'Young artists aren't our thing.' But I wasn't asking for the city's finger-painting supremo or Queen of Drawing In Between the Lines – what about the woman who made the Bridget Riley-esque optical illusions out of Arab patterns, hanging on the wall over there, was she a local artist and was she, by any chance, young? She didn't even bother to reply. Daoud now told me that Darat al Funun had said they wouldn't exhibit his work.

Daoud unlocked his own less ornate metal front gate, and after we'd entered, locked it behind him. Ascending a damp staircase we got to the second floor where he paused under a blue light-bulb and looked for other keys on a loaded key ring. Once inside he locked this door.

'Welcome to my home and gallery.' He raised his arms then, turning, walked away along a narrow corridor. Off it were six doors, round which were crammed canvases of all sizes. They were all nudes. Everywhere you looked was daubed flesh, open legs, stand-alone breasts. And they were all very bad.

I followed the sound of coffee being ground. Because this house was on the side of a jebel, the rooms to the left of the corridor gave out on to the valley bottom and those on the right looked on to an upward-sloping street. The valley windows were bringing in a mountain chill that, mixed with turps, nearly succeeded in masking a musty smell of BO and tobacco. As I walked along the corridor I peaked through each door. In the front room, those windows not open were blacked in, the floor was lined with newspapers and there were many skulls – all the pieces in this room were musings on skulls. A central table was piled high with plaster-cast craniums and the pieces on the walls were thick oil renderings with holes cut out in which skulls were inserted. The next room was smaller and returned to the major theme of nudes. On the floor string was thrown, apparently discarded.

'I found some string and couldn't decide what to do with it,' Daoud said coming to find me. 'Go and sit in the sitting room. – this way,' and he redirected me back but through his studio.

Yet more nudes, this time with alien heads. On his main easel, a large wooden thing taking pride of place, was written in English a quote straight out of a W. H. Smith diary: 'You never step in the same river twice', an aphorism that would meet his eyes wherever he was working.

Eventually, in the sitting room, I relaxed a bit. This room's windows were also blacked out but with red crêpe paper. The sofas, chairs and paintings – still nudes but at least with human faces – were all blue, orange and purple. A large red umbrella, hung upside down under the light as a chandelier, was the most artful thing in the flat.

'You might have guessed that the human body is my concern, Daoud said entering with two cups of coffee. He was small with close-cropped black hair, grey flecked at his temples, though he was only in his mid- to late twenties. His look was tight black jeans and a black Chairman Mao jacket.

'Yes, but there are quite a lot of aliens' heads, aren't there?'

'Who says? It's not an alien. It's a human. I call it figurative art. With the human body I want to go to extremes. To you they may look like aliens but to me they are a representation of something inside all of us.'

It all started when he was a law student at Jordan's Yarmouk University in Irbid, north of Amman. A decision not exactly forced on him but, with his father dead, one that the men in his extended family had helped him make. At this point he'd heard of da Vinci and Picasso but thought of art as pretty pictures not a livelihood. From law he got distracted by poetry and from poetry by art. By the end of his degree he was graduating in law but knew he wouldn't use it. He had decided to become an artist. Puff! went the idea of a pay cheque home every month. His family went mad.

'No, I don't send any money home. Instead, any sales of paintings go towards the rent of this place.' Firas had already said Daoud made so little money he could barely keep himself afloat, let alone his widowed mother, and he was now in the doghouse.

'One term we had had an exhibition of Italian paintings. I had never seen anything so beautiful. I bought the catalogue and tore out a picture that I hung on my wall. My cousin came to visit me in the holidays and as soon as he entered the room he jumped up on the bed and ripped it down telling me I should be ashamed of myself. He said it was two-times *haram*: that it was sinful but also that I had "sisters" in the building.' He meant there were women also living in the building.

'The man in the picture on my wall was only half naked … so imagine the anger when I started to draw fully naked people. I was strongly criticized and it wasn't just my cousin who objected, at university I was always quarrelling with people who saw me sketching bodies. Now I am an estab-lished artist this has only got worse, and that is why I had to have my own gallery. With locked doors. The Muslim Brotherhood think I'm attacking them. So I hide away.'

Ah, that would explain the locks and bolts on the internal doors. He said, however, that he wasn't scared. Because the Muslim Brotherhood think all art is *haram* their beef wasn't so much with a nude painter but with all painters, he said. But something recently had caused him to worry again.

'Here in Amman there was a sculpture of figures holding a book, made for the roundabout in the sixth or seventh circle. The Muslim Brothers complained and the artist had to change the design by making it half abstract. This worried me greatly. But I like to think that they objected because it was in an open place. If it is just me, in my gallery with my walls blacked in, then it is OK. I like to think they can't get me here.'

I remembered that Musa, the TV producer in Beirut who ran *Superstar*, had said that the Muslim Brotherhood had called for *Superstar* to be banned in Amman, calling for an end to be put to what they called a 'sad comedy'. Hamdi didn't like the drugs and the prostitution maybe. But if the Muslim Brotherhood curtailed a harmless TV series and drove Daoud to black in all his windows, surely he'd rethink?

Daoud put down his coffee cup suddenly and went crawling under the large worktable, banging around at the back of it and eventually emerging with a book.

'But they are wrong about Islam and depictions of the body. It has been found depicted in many Islamic works of art, it is just it is open to interpretation,' and he was now showing me a page from a large book so heavy that the spine was groaning as he handed it to me open. 'Look at that ornamentation very closely. There are erotic shapes and some of these guys in the mosques don't even know it.'

I looked very closely at the Islamic artwork – a detailed sketch of something that eventually appeared on the side of a mosque. I was on the hunt for penises and bosoms, but I didn't find them. So I rescanned the image hunting for even more abstract non-specific curviness of a woman and column-like shapes for penises. It was a bit ridiculous. I still couldn't see anything but he swore they were in there.

'They go to mosques for two things: religion and politics, and I laugh because I think of them praying and not looking closely at the patterns. But they are there.'

I would later look around for his Islamic sanctioning of the portrayal of the human body in Islamic ornamentation and not be able to find it. Even if he were right – that Islam had space for the depictions of the human body – it also called for modesty in how women carried themselves. Would any definition of modesty include women posing for nude portraits?

Now that I was holding the big book he got up and brought down off the wall a large canvas, just a fraction smaller than him and he struggled with the weight of it. She was a naked woman and the centre of the work was her bum. He sat back down on the stool opposite me with the canvas resting on his open legs.

'The Ikhwan are winning and they don't know it. *They* think people are becoming more liberal, too liberal, but, actually, as Adonis has documented, even modern people who hang out in Abdoun [the district where Hamdi and I had eaten] want life to be simpler.'

Adonis, as the author of more than 20 books, is the Middle East's Philosopher King. Unlike Daoud his artistic leanings were fostered by his family. Though he was raised as a farm-hand, it was his father who also made him memorize poetry, and when Adonis recited one for the then Syrian president he was awarded a scholarship to the University of Damascus. An Adonis poem used traditional Arabic poetic styles to express very modern feelings, so it was easy to hear him speaking to dyspeptic Daoud.

'They too, like the Ikhwan, want life to be decided by God not themselves,' Daoud continued. He was talking about people like Hamdi. 'It's easier that way. Only the other day I was in Darat al Funun with a friend and we were standing in front of a painting.' Only now did he point to the woman on the canvas that had been resting on his knee like a ventriloquist's dummy: 'The painting was of a woman's bum – it is this view – but the woman has trousers on and I said to my friend, "Oh, what a shame. Why didn't he go all the way?"'

The skulls were in a room not visible from here. Sitting where I was, all I could see were nearly fifty renderings of the naked female body. I wondered whether, because it could sometimes seem that almost everything was taboo in the Islamic world, those who tried to wrest things from the land of taboo were seen as heroes even if those things shouldn't be wrested. This guy, with his naked woman sitting on his knee, was not a very good artist. Instead he was endangering his own life and leaving his widowed mother unsupported, while he knocked off another badly drawn girl.

'I do not want democracy, because if we got it – we'd get the Ikhwan. *But.* One of my paintings was declined by the Jordanian Culture Ministry. It's not just the Muslim Brotherhood. Everyone is viewing art and culture in terms of Islamic laws.'

9

Designing the Revolution
Cairo

The station manager had stopped the coach rolling out of the station to get me aboard but as I clambered on there was a short silence before everyone else seemed to file past me and get off. If it weren't for the only one left – Faisal, a round 20-something, who looked like Garfield – I might have been worried. Faisal annotated the fight that broke out by the coach's front window, wide as a widescreen TV. The fracas was developing in the Egyptian port of Nuweba. We'd all just crossed, by ferry, the Gulf of Aqaba from Jordan. This was a private coach, he explained, taking an extended family to a special football match. Khaleejis, as both Walid and Future TV's Khalid would have called these Saudis, off to spend their money and leisure time in Cairo.

'So your problem is that you have party-crashed. But you're unlucky two times. These people have just received some bad news – that someone important has been killed. Have you heard of Rafiq Hariri?'

That day 1,000kg of TNT had been detonated as Hariri's motorcade drove past the St George's Hotel near the Beirut Corniche. My first thought was of how Walid would react. Would this help precipitate his revolution, or set it back? Walid couldn't even walk through Hariri's downtown, even if desperate for cigars, but the politician's rags-to-riches biog should technically have saved him from Walid's firing squad: his family was not one of the brands that produced most of the country's politicians. Then there was the Hariri-owned Future TV, surely feeling decapitated. And Yusuf's Syrian cousins. In the last months of his life Hariri had said Syria should leave Lebanon. Did his position on Syria mean Syria had the perfect motive? And how would those Syrians living in Lebanon be treated?

When the Saudis were eventually placated they got back on the coach and we set off. Faisal was not unbothered by Hariri's death and since I couldn't talk to Walid, he turned out not to be a bad second. A Saudi Sunni, perhaps he also spoke for Lebanese Sunnis.

'I am a business student ... on my way back to university in Cairo. If you ask my parents who they want me to be like, they might first say Alwaleed but it would be more likely that they would say Hariri. Alwaleed inherited his money. Hariri didn't and I haven't. So it's more realistic that they want me to be Hariri.' Did I know that those two didn't get on?

'Alwaleed is half Lebanese – his mum was Lebanese. He'd like to have been Hariri: to have been prime minister, I mean.'

At an opening for a very large hotel that Alwaleed funded, the Prince addressed the assembled guests with a criticism of Lebanon's economy:

'Can any one of you, brothers and sisters present in this gathering, tell me what the expected debt figure will be in the next four or five years? Will its size continue to be 170 per cent of GDP at the end of that period?'

Hariri wasn't there at the time, Faisal said, but President Emile Lahoud and parliament speaker Nabih Berri were.

Faisal said it was, in the circle of business students, an infamous speech. Hariri had acted with good grace, hearing the comments while he was on a foreign trip and issuing an announcement that I later found: 'We accept such statements from anyone who wants to build a hotel in Lebanon.'

I didn't know any of this. Jad and Khalid at Future TV had said that social-commentary youth programming had been scrapped for more of Alwaleed's video-clips because of bonds between Hariri and Saudi businessmen. If this were true, the Saudi chum couldn't have been Alwaleed. I asked Faisal what he knew of Hariri's relationship with Saudis. Alwaleed's main regional-media rivals – Orbit offering 24 pay-TV channels and ART with seven – were also owned by Saudis. What was Hariri's relationship like with them? Was it this close? Faisal paused. He said he hadn't spent much time in Beirut but had heard that a sheikh had wanted to give money to Beirut to rebuild a famous mosque.

'The Omari mosque?' I asked. This was dovetailing with what Khalid had said. Maybe. He wasn't sure. Actually, he'd heard that Hariri had upset Saudis by *not* wanting their help in rebuilding the mosque. Supposedly, so the desert myth now circulating in KSA went, he didn't want a great big mother ship of a mosque slap bang in the middle of postcards of Beirut sent around the world. Maybe Zen TV hadn't been killed by conservative Khaleejis after all. Maybe Hariri did it because of the bottom line. Because it wasn't very good.

Faisal brought his luggage over to sit next to me and spent that bit of the rest of the journey he was awake talking Hariri. It was a premonition of Hariri's canonizing. Though the tales I'd been told about him, while he was alive, weren't complimentary – debt, debt, disgusting renovations and more debt – now you couldn't find a cynical voice. In the next few days my hotel's TV would be tuned, along with most TVs, to coverage of the assassination. Within a couple of days, Hariri was buried, his coffin paraded in a three-mile procession round Beirut. Mourners chanted slogans like 'We Want Syria Out' and 'We Don't Want Bashar'.

After most of the hundreds of thousands who attended the Martyrs' Square funeral went home, a sizeable number bedded down in the area near where Hariri and his seven bodyguards were buried, lighting candles, drinking, smoking, playing music and effectively maintaining a vigil. This was a spot in Martyrs' Square near Virgin Megastore and the statue where Zidan and his band The New Government had posed for their gig poster.

Most of the demonstrators wore red T-shirts and many had the flag of Lebanon painted on their cheeks. In the days that followed one thousand of them staged an anti-Syrian rally in front of Lebanon's parliament, calling for the pro-Syrian government to resign as a prelude to free and fair elections due in April and May. They unfurled a 30-metre-long banner with the word Resign written in French and Arabic and signed by thousands. In Damascus, President Assad replaced the chief of military intelligence who commanded Syrian agents in Lebanon with his brother-in-law. If that were a sign that Assad had dug in, then the protesters did too, erecting five tents. Their line was that they would not leave the square till Syria withdrew its troops from Lebanon.

They marked the one-week 'anniversary' of Hariri's assassination by marching from the spot in Beirut where the bomb exploded to their base camp and his burial site, where they resumed the whistle-blowing, animal-skin drum banging and drug-taking. This was almost too much for me. If the professors of baby-booming, calculating the changing size of the Arab youth bulge and the probability of their precious revolution being precipitated, weren't excited, then I was. Except I was travelling on my own, watching a television in a hotel, so there's only so much excitement you can exhibit. It was possible, certainly some of the TV presenters were billing it as such, that we were watching television pictures of a revolution. Revolution as directed by Bertolucci – except he'd have banished the colour-co-ordinated red and white T-shirts that were to go down so well in Washington for being too un-French and a bit Coca-Cola to be the authentic markers of an organic uprising.

Some of the faces were oddly familiar, largely reminiscent of those I'd met who'd been vitriolic in their indictment of Hariri's political class, but because most of the shots were fleeting it was difficult to know for sure whether they were the same people. Except for one scene that the cameras kept returning to. A group of 20 dancing in a circle into which each of them took turns to step. Here, jerking like a shaman, was Walid. In death, evidently, Hariri was to become more than in life. He was now a martyr to Lebanese autonomy when perhaps before he'd just been another rich old man. For this reason, were I to bump into any of them that second, it would have been churlish to remind them of any specific Hariri bile they might once have expressed.

Up close the Lebanese flags – a cedar tree on white and fringed in red – looked like the tasteful Christmas

Decorations section of a New England department store. But from a distance it was a lagoon of red and white that unless the camera stopped, was quite trippy. Khalid had said that the university course in Beirut with the largest uptake had been graphic design. It struck me that this uprising was a vindication of Beirut's graphic designers – their careful calligraphy was finally being put to good use.

Fatima, who had been designing posters on the table in Xiad House when Walid showed me his first film *Spleen*, had been drafting pencil outlines of letters in the space left in the middle of some artwork. More particularly, she'd been writing in Western not Arabic letters. When Zen TV had first launched, their senior graphic designer told the press that there would be no 'tacky' Arabic calligraphy. It was this department that produced Zen TV's logo, in the corner of all programmes I watched, which looked like a cartoon rendering of a TV but was a slice of DNA. I thought the banishing of Arabic calligraphy particularly self-loathing but now it seemed like their painstaking design of posters for gigs and exhibitions was transferred to politics.

If Lebanon got red, white and a Christmas tree then Egypt got red and yellow. Elections were due in Egypt within six months and a group called Kifaya had been formed, composed of people opposing Hosni Mubarak. In his late seventies, President Mubarak had been in power for 24 years, re-elected four times. His presidency had been on perpetual replay. Before him had been Anwar Sadat for a not unauthoritarian

11-year stint. During the Second World War Sadat had fought alongside Nasser against the occupying British forces and in 1952 their rebellious forces defenestrated King Farouk I. When Nasser died, Sadat replaced him and his reign was popular until, in the mid-1970s, he made Egypt the first Arab country to recognize Israel's sovereignty. The rest of the Arab world felt betrayed by Egypt, their figurehead of pan-Arabism. This was the kind of realpolitik of which Hamdi in Jordan approved. Hamdi would also, I presumed, have approved of Sadat's Intifah policies or 'open-door' economic reforms, ushering in private investment. But apart from among cub-businessmen in a Middle East of the future, Sadat was unpopular and, in 1981, when some key men in his security operation went on Hajj (pilgrimage) to Mecca, he was assassinated.

Mubarak's re-election was partly due to the Egyptian constitution stipulating that the People's Assembly play the main role in deciding who should become president of Egypt. As such this year's elections would be his fifth cakewalk to victory and that's why the opposition movement's resentment of Mubarak was effectively boiled down to an exasperated 'kifaya' ('enough'). The regime reacted with poise and panache, allocating hundreds of riot police to any one gathering and throwing Kifaya supporters in prison.

In my early days in Cairo the newspapers talked about a Saudi-British young woman having been arrested at one of these demos. She'd served a short stint in prison and by calculations was due out around now. After two bungled attempts – she just didn't turn up – we met.

It was the morning before the next demonstration, the last one being the one at which she'd been arrested. I sat in the

124

internal courtyard of a Khedive-period building, squatting on the doorstep of a restaurant. The building was a minor classic of the type built 140 years ago in this quarter, modelled on Paris when the Khedive attempted to make Egypt part of Europe. It was near the HQ of Al Ghad, or The Tomorrow Party. After three failed applications the Al Ghad had finally been given legal recognition by Egypt's Higher Political Parties Affairs Committee (the body set up by Mubarak less than six months earlier to decide which parties are allowed to contest elections). In the committee's 28-year history Al Ghad is the first serious opposition party to gain its approval.

Eventually, a very small person carrying a haversack stuffed with rolled-up posters looking like rockets careered into view.

'The first thing I want to make clear is that I won't be coming this afternoon, it really would be very foolish of me.' But she would be putting up posters for the demo, that she was allowed to do. 'The second thing to make sure is that you know I am talking to you because I enjoy talking – not because we want the West to help us with our campaign.'

She had a pointy face and wore her hair in a ponytail that gave her face lift and emphasized a *retroussée* nose. Fayruz and two friends had been arrested when handing out leaflets at the Arab world's book fair.

'I am a secular intellectual … the beginning of my troubles. We got caught on a Friday – any other day and we'd have been fine. But because we were leafletting on a Friday before midday – none of our friends was up.' On a Friday, she seemed to be implying, holy people pray, intellectuals sleep off the effects of the night before. 'So it was jail for us.'

Fayruz had never been to prison before but her female companion had been arrested four times since her twentieth birthday in 1999.

'She told me all you have to do – all you need to do – is scream and scream and the police usually let go. So from the moment we felt the tap by the police to, I don't know, when we screamed. But it did no good – in the end we were put in the car screaming.' Fayruz leant forward. 'Don't worry, it wasn't *sad* screaming. I suppose better to call it *shouting*. We practise it because an arrest is going to happen to all of us at least once.'

In the police station they underwent a Russian-doll-style interrogation: one set after another of policemen asking questions. When they sent in the fifth guard, 'We refused to answer any more. So he sat down in front of us and began to write a story that he said was our statement. It was a fantasy, a lie about how we were supposedly giving out socialist propaganda.'

'Which you were, weren't you?'

'Yes. But you should always deny everything. Unless you want to make a political statement, you always deny every-thing. Our story was that all we had was eleven leaflets about a socialist workshop that I'd printed off the internet. They said we were inciting demonstration against the regime. Which in some lights you could say we were. But we had to kill the story. Just telling people about socialist events is very different from revolution.'

'How had you got your story straight?'

'We do that every morning in case we're arrested,' she gabbled, wanting to get to the more interesting bit of her tale.

'They started to tell us that Ibrahim [the journalist friend of theirs who had also been giving out leaflets] had beaten up a policeman. We got really mad.'

'How did they think they'd get away with that?'

'Because he did.' Oh. 'He needed to hurt them, to make them realize he wasn't going to take this lying down.'

'But won't they be able to prove that he did beat up a policeman?'

'Technically, yes, but we knew there were people there who weren't supposed to be, from the secret service, and that doesn't look good. They hadn't been videoing for that reason, so we knew that while they could get away with quite a bit, so could we.'

Because Ibrahim was a journalist, he had been let free when he showed his union card.

'Had he not showed his card they would have had no proof he wasn't Ikhwan and they'd have taken him off and tortured him. They can give you 4 or 15 or 45 days … and they can carry on doing that for six months, and even after that they can rearrest you. That's what happens to the Ikhwan.'

When the girls were waiting in line to go into the court they were seated next to Muslim Brothers who were up for the renewal of their sentence. The girls, Fayruz said, had the light handcuffs on but the guys they waited next to had on the heavy ones, 'the kind that can break a bone'. They'd talked to these Brothers who'd told them that they weren't expecting release.

Egypt was the epicentre of the Brotherhood. Banned there since some of their number attempted to assassinate President Nasser, for 50 years it has still managed to be Egypt's main opposition. No one knows how large it is. *Al-Ahram*, the government newspaper, estimates there are now 750,000 members but the Brotherhood will neither confirm nor refute this figure since they don't want to deliver lists to the intelligence services nor be seen goading the government. For that reason they also fielded fewer candidates than they could do at the last elections 'to avoid being provocative' said one senior official. 'In 2003 we had a march against the war. It was beautiful – the first time the Muslim Brothers had joined up with the government, almost ever.'

The Egyptian government had been against the Iraq war and so had, more predictably, the Muslim Brothers. In a rare act of political unity the government and the Muslim Brothers had been present at the same anti-war demonstration. Demonstrations before this time had been rare but now they proliferated with one journalist pointing out to me what she saw as a 'delicious irony': out of these government-sanctioned demonstrations against the war, first would come demonstrations against Israel and second demonstrations against the Egyptian government.

'At that stage,' Fayruz continued, 'the Brothers' leadership didn't even take the opportunity to say we want the release of our political prisoners. How bad is that?'

In the short time we spent together – we had three *citrons pressés* each – Fayruz was most animated on the subject of bread subsidies. That day, the subsidies had been lowered yet again and 'while I was in prison, the shits added another tax to regular fuel'. She paused to light up a fag: 'There's already a tax on the cheap oil that microbuses and taxis use.'

In her line of fire was Gamal Mubarak, the President's son, whom people were sure was being groomed to take over when the elder Mubarak died. Gamal Mubarak is the President's eldest son, a former investment banker and a fierce champion of the free market. It wasn't at all certain he would inherit power but he had been given a position as head of his father's policy committee, a pretty important position. This committee's importance was confirmed when, in 2004, a new cabinet was announced featuring a lot of Gamal's staff. If he were to succeed his father, he would be the first president of Egypt not to have come out of the army. Fayruz was not a fan of such a Pharaonic succession.

'If the people owned everything, this would not happen.'

While this was international socialism, it was also, I put to her, the socialism of the Muslim Brotherhood – with its welfare-state provision of social services. Was she sympathetic to them? She had certainly been sounding like she was. The Brotherhood and secular intellectuals like Fayruz seemed to be shoulder to shoulder. This was obviously very different from Lebanon, where the secular elements of society seemed ranged against a government that had the support of the country's Islamist group, Hizbollah. The Brothers' current batch of MPs – the 'Group of 15' – had campaigned to ban books, rid state TV of video-clips, and they spoke out in support of female TV presenters who wanted, in a secular country, to be allowed to wear the veil. They'd called for a ban on drinking alcohol punishable by 30 lashes and 20 lashes for those who operated drinking establishments. They'd been voted down on this. But, still, odd bedfellows for an intellectual who can't get up to pray on a Friday because of vodka necked the night before. Didn't Fayruz find it odd that she was a chain-smoking, unveiled Julie Christie, shoulder to shoulder with the Muslim Brotherhood?

'Don't you fear them – banning alcohol and music, enforcing hijabs?' I asked.

'No.'

'But sharia law?' The Arabic for Islamic law, sharia is a body of laws that had an opinion on most bits of a person's life. As a self-professed secular intellectual, sharia law should be anathema to her.

'So what? Sharia law is already the basis of our constitution. You should go hear them speak: it's a low priority for them these days.'

If a Palestinian businessman whose father was a Fatah politician had been an unlikely possible Muslim Brotherhood supporter, then wasn't Fayruz just as odd? For the last half-century, the noisiest and most popular forces in Egypt had been the ruling regime and the Islamists. Arab liberals like Fayruz had been pushed to the sidelines and this camp's secular democracy activists had enjoyed no solidarity with any established Muslim institutions.

But now I was at the demo in front of Cairo University, attending the demonstration Fayruz had helped organize, but didn't dare attend. The line of riot police followed the grand landscape of mangy palm trees in front of the university and penned in both left-wingers and Muslim Brothers. I broke through and after a few pleasantries did what Fayruz had challenged me to do. I asked a few of the Muslim Brothers whether sharia law was a low priority. They all – four of them – batted me away with the exact same line:

'Our priority is political reform.'

Sitting on the monument's pedestal was an older man with a staff and a Merlin beard dressed in an indigo-blue dishdasha with a plum-red turban. A Sufi veteran of such demonstrations, his day job was meteorology, and he refused to be drawn on political predictions. After taking the 'political reform' line from the four Muslim Brothers I was weary and for a moment this Sufi meteorologist made me think that asking people about democracy in the Arab world was like talking about the weather, both because discussion of it was all around you, and because no one had any say in determining it. Now a cheer went up as a delegation of teenage boys in football shirts, down from Alexandria for the day, shimmied up the monument and tied a red and yellow Kifaya banner round its girth.

10

'I Need a Right'
Cairo

Central Cairo was fly-posted with a striking image of a young man – head thrown back and mouth open, either screaming or yawning. A hand beside his face held a cigarette lighter with a flame. The caption, in English, read: 'I Need a Right'.

In the corner of the posters I noticed a credit: the name of an art gallery Firas had told me about: Townhouse. When I went in search of it, I found it situated at a little crossroads, a large Khedive building with geranium foliage tumbling over the sides of its balconies. All the windows were open and my target demographic (I had long been creeped out by the sound of my own voice asking for 'young people') were visible moving about on all of its four or five floors. Its basement was occupied by car mechanics and the tables and chairs of the coffee house or *ahwa* across the road blocked one of the crossroad's through-roads. Was the 'I Need a Right' as overtly political as it seemed – a poster in the tradition of Lebanon's red and white revolution and Cairo's red and yellow Kifaya movement? I asked the curator – a Canadian called Michael – he nodded and said he had just the person for me.

Was this gallery a Xiad House full of Fatimas drumming up posters for art exhibitions and democratic uprising as well? Michael was now talking to me about someone called

Hisham. Hisham was the real thing, he said, walking out of his office, on to the landing and through into the next room.

'German collectors are very interested. You know, of all my artists I am most proud of him.'

He asked people if they'd seen him – as if he were the gallery cat – and one person pointed out of the window at the mechanics opposite. Squatting next to a body half emerging from beneath a car was Hisham. Michael called out of the window to him and then sent me down.

Michael had met Hisham when he'd advertised for Townhouse's security guard. A Cairo company, Care Service, sent along what they thought was their least employable 21-year old. They'd had him on their books for a while and he'd ended up walking out of every security job they put his way because of his tendency to get into brawls.

'But things got really bad when they made me do mornings – that would mean turning up at 7 am when I don't rise till midday.' Care Service realized that perhaps the only place he could realistically secure was an artists' colony. Here, Hisham's sloth could be circumnavigated by him living on site. 'But, no, I didn't stop losing my temper. The difference is that at Townhouse, they didn't seem to mind so much. Now you could say I am the strong man of this place.'

Hisham graduated from security guard to artist quite quickly. A few playful sessions with other people's material and soon Michael was encouraging the strong man to reminisce about his days as a car mechanic and bus driver's assistant.

'I work with the scrap metal from cars because it is like me: it doesn't do what you tell it to do very easily. Only fire and

133

hammering will get it to bend. And even then it is into shapes you can't determine.' His early work was a big hit. Metal sculptures of street characters in action: one of a derelict car with sheet-thin metal figures.

Hisham was stocky, good looking and fancied himself. He talked about himself in the third person – everyone addressed him as Ustaz Hisham, or the Professor. I told him I thought he seemed quite popular. That wasn't true, he said:

'Many people think I'm rude … I'll explain,' and we went back upstairs to the room with computers so he could do so. 'This was one I did about an Iftar [the break-fast or first meal of the day after fasting during Ramadan]. All these men,' he said, pointing to a group of fifteen gathered around a trestle-table, 'are the kind of people I would hang out with when I was a street kid. He works in the *ahwa*,' he said of the man in the centre, tall and thin as a ladder, 'and that guy's a mechanic who works downstairs,' he said of one of the smaller men standing to one side of the table. They were clearly arranged to resemble the Last Supper.

'I brought the table into the Townhouse's main room. Then I added a feast – the kind of food you'd eat at an Iftar: bread, sweets, Coke. And then I got all my friends from the streets to come in and I set a video camera up and recorded them for a few hours.' The aim, he said, was to see the dynamics of his friends round the table.

'Like, for instance, this man,' and he jabbed a finger at the screen. 'He doesn't talk very much and we had all always thought he was very shy. But now look. When he eats he stretches across four people to pick up some bread when there is a loaf much nearer him. This is not shyness.'

Hisham was talented. Though a skit on the Last Supper was not very original, his piece was. From a small village near Sharqiya, kicked out of school at 16, barred from taking exams because he'd beaten up a teacher with a birch, unloved by his father, he had reinvented the Last Supper.

If you were making a film you'd put a camera up at a vantage-point of the crossroads and leave it for a few hours before taking it back to the edit suite. There you'd speed up the shot and get a dizzy Brownian motion-effect – lots of people using all the different buildings at that crossroads. Hisham's work of art had brought the men who hung out on the street inside the big Khedive building. The mechanics seemed to amble, quite often and quite aimlessly, into the gallery for a chat; artists would amble over to the *ahwa*, tea boys (*ahwagis*) from the café darting round all the buildings keeping people's caffeine high. Haight-Ashbury had been a crossroads. It was an Arab Haight-Ashbury.

'You like it? Huh?' Hisham asked me. 'Well, the government didn't.' First he knew of this was an article appearing in a newspaper alleging that his piece was a threat to national security and to Egypt's reputation because of its disrespectful depictions of citizens. They meant the poor. Then, the next week the security services raided the gallery and confiscated it. They took the work. And Michael had the deleted items on his hard drive checked by the ministry. 'He says it's just that they're jealous. Never been asked to exhibit themselves and then someone like me gets a go. So do you know what we do to drive them mad? We make sure that we always send invitations to the Ministry for our private viewings. They never come.'

Hisham left me to photocopy his press cuttings. While I waited I asked Michael if I could meet the artist who did the 'I Need a Right' poster. And he obliged. This guy was a photographer called Said and though less in love with himself than Hisham, less of a talker as well: 'Oh, that?', Said shrugged. 'Well, actually people thought it read, "I Need a Light".' As in a cigarette lighter. That was a let down.

Feeling deflated, I went outside to sit on the stairs and wait for Hisham to return with my photocopies. I watched the *ahwagi* come and go two or three times: arriving slowly, concentrating on the see-sawing water levels of the full cups. This was a job Hisham had done, he'd told me, but would this guy become an artist? Next thing up to entertain me while I waited was a prayer. A clattering sound from on high and then five of the building's more devout artists running down the steps past me to the base of the stairwell where the first one there took out a large green mat and unrolled it before bending to take off his shoes. Others arrived, shedding shoes, glasses and mobile phones, before they assembled in a line and crossed their arms in front of them to pray. I watched through the railings ten foot above them. One of the guys was praying to his mobile. Still no Hisham.

I got bored. I picked up an old newspaper. There was an article by a young professor of law about how the hooting of football fans kept him awake at night. He dreaded football matches, he said, because the morning after the match the night before if you weren't into football then you'd got nothing to talk about.

'Umberto [Eco] had it right: I am not scared of football fans, I am only scared of their conversation.' But what he said next diverted me. 'The popularity of football is just another sign of the death of politics in Egypt. Cairenes choose one of two teams, it is that simple. Instead of a different political party winning the elections, power is circulated through the Egypt Cup tournament. Forcing the coach to resign if your club loses the tournament is the alternative to getting rid of a cabinet that has failed to deliver. The transparent rules of the game by which a club wins when it plays better replace the more complex procedures whereby a party rises to power by popular vote. And foreign observers who determine whether elections are fair and orderly are likewise replaced by referees to ensure an impartial attitude towards both big teams.'

Hisham never did return with his photocopies. Or at least he didn't within the hour. If the artists and mechanics at this crossroads were creating their own classless utopia (even though they didn't quite have the chat perfected yet), then sports club were also at it. That's where I went next.

Cairo's two main clubs were Zamalek and Ahly, founded in 1907 and 1911 respectively. From the start, the two clubs each attracted a discrete clientele. Zamalek allowed and encouraged Westerners to join and became seen as royalist and imperialist. Ahly was considered the nationalist option – Ahly, after all, means national – and it was even headed at one point by jazz-age prime minister of Egypt, Saad Zaghlul, who led nationalist forces demanding independence from Britain. The metaphor extended to the very colours they wore: Ahly – Kremlin red; Zamalek – white (Zamalek were recently rebranded The White House). Following the peaceful coup of 1952, Nasser abolished all political parties and, the argument ran, the two institutions of Ahly and Zamalek became the only institutions in Egypt that Egyptians gave a damn about ... and, it has been said, the only institutions the Egyptian government wants them to give a damn about.

For both sport clubs in central Cairo – a mixture of drinking club and gym – their most successful faces are their footballers. Ahly was named Africa's Club of the Century in 2000, and Zamalek is the only African-Asian football club to ever top FIFA World Club Ranking of the month in February 2003. That week there had been a derby between the two teams that had attracted hundreds if not thousands of riot police. Ahly – at the top of their game, with a 21 match-winning streak, the longest undefeated streak in the Egyptian league – had won again.

I walked along to Zamalek first. The walls of its enclosure were covered with election posters with slogans like: 'Ideas for a New Zamalek ... vote for Ihab Mustafa, sports journalist' and, maybe in reference to their defeat that week: 'For the principle of Zamalek returning to the golden days vote for Muhammad Zaid, Candidate Number 21.' Another election-seeker was a tax inspector. All of them detailed their personal phone numbers. I went inside and asked to speak to the manager. The political accountability wasn't total: Zamalek's manager was away.

Ahly's grounds were attractive and wooded. Men tall as trees lugged sports bags to and fro, while mothers with young children left: the evening was turning from after-school games to bathtime. It was probably not quite as classless as the townhouse crossroads … but a lot seemed to go on within these clubs. From inside the club there was an orchestral arrangement of games whistles, shouts for strategic attention on pitches and the delighted sounds of crowd approval. As I went in, the sun was setting and a muezzin sounded from the club mosque. Those in the middle of a floodlit game went to the side of their pitch, while others who weren't tied up in practice or match walked over to the little mosque to the right of the entrance, picked up a green plastic mat and prayed. This group included one young man in a karate uniform. I waited for prayers to finish before approaching him.

'It's not a karate uniform, it's martial arts. There's a difference,' he explained, before going to walk off.

'But is it Islamic?' I asked his back. He stopped in his tracks and then retraced his steps. One of the number of jobs my younger brother Alex has done is sell karate lessons on the doorsteps of London. His tales include being berated by Christians for asking them to consider buying his karate lessons. Didn't he know they couldn't possibly? That they already had a higher spiritual authority? It was thinking of Alex that had made me call after this man. 'A lot of people think not,' he said, coming back to where I stood, 'that because we have to bow to the sensei it encourages submission to a master other than Muhammad, peace be upon him. It's called *ruku*' [bowing down during Muslim prayers in respect to Allah] even though it is not worship but respect … It's still not clear what the answer is as lots of senior imams rule that if it is worship then it is impermissible. But we get round this by not nodding.'

139

His name was Ahmed and he said that he didn't do karate anyway, that his martial art was something called silat that originated in Malaysia.

'Chinese Muslims used silat as a means of bringing the inner jihad [holy struggle] into self-development. But for me, the best evidence in defence of martial arts is that the Prophet was a wrestler. The imam in the club I used to belong to, a very learned man, he said karate was not *haram*. And that was good enough for me. Of course it's contentious. But they've got rid of him now.' He told me the name of this imam and I recognized it as the one the girls in the car over from Amman had mentioned. Amr Khaled.

I found Ahly's chairman, Hassan Hamdy, ringside in the basketball court watching his B-team in a friendly, sitting amid a phalanx of suited sporting executives. So this was Arab democracy. According to Hassan al-Mestekawy, a sports journalist writing in *Al-Ahram*, the number of people who voted in the last parliamentary election in the Qasr el-Nil district (where the Ahly headquarters lie) was half the 12,000 who voted in the last Ahly elections. The management of both Ahly and Zamalek buy players annually and sometimes twice to thrice a year to fortify their squad. If this man in front of me bought a bad player, he'd be toast. If he embezzled money – money that has come from club membership – and was found out? He'd be toast. Eventually the teams broke for half time. The president, a squat man who looked like an armchair, approached. I needed his permission to roam around Ahly's grounds and talk to the players. This was a powerful man, but if he bought bad coaches and the team started to lose, he'd also be toast.

As he got nearer I decided that I wanted to interview one of the players and to do this I'd have to pretend I was a sports journalist, making a mental note *not* to mention politics. The coach saw no problem and pulled a guy called Kaidar off the bench. I watched Kaidar swap his white trainers for a red and yellow – Kifaya? – pair and lumber over to me. They were Adidas.

'Ahly won "Club of the Century", you know. Real Madrid visited us but soaked up too much sun – they went to Khan el-Khalili, the pyramids – they got ill and so we beat them.' He'd been a member since he was 14 – when he was 13 he'd already reached 6'1".

'One day that coach,' and he pointed to one of the pairs of shoulder blades facing us, 'was driving in the car behind my school bus and he said, "I've seen a giant." My head and shoulders were twice as high as those sitting next to me. The coach followed the bus all the way to the school and when I got off, he bought me.'

Now Kaidar said he earned $400 a month, which is 'one of the good things about the job'. But there were, he admitted, those at the club who were trying to raise it to $20,000 a year. Did he want a twenty-grand salary?

'Well, I say to them that they must be careful. We don't, it's true, get the best pay around, though it is not bad. But what we have to be really grateful for is the management. I could get more money at another club but Ahly's is the best managed. The elections that Ahly has are the best in the Arab world. A lot of members are in the business world and they wouldn't stand for any embezzlement or cheating. You know, the club even gives tickets and year-round membership to people from poor areas. It puts on trips for members ... Sometimes they let everybody into the club for free and you can be watching a match and turn around and find somebody very dirty behind you.'

The armchair returned wanting Kaidar to put his Typex-white trainers back on. In his place I was given Hazem who wanted to discuss the US Lakers.

'I'm just back from a six-month scholarship to the US to play basketball.' In front of us Kaidar was now joining the rest of the team for the next quarter. They formed a huddle and Hazem nodded towards it:

'We may play basketball but we're still Muslims.' What?

'They're praying.' He seemed to be saying their huddle was a prayer and I chose not to remind him that every basketball team huddles. Instead I asked how successful he thought his club was.

'I reckon that 60 per cent to 70 per cent of the people in Cairo support Ahly because, well, let's see – it's so easy to be a member. Clubs [like Ahly] are safer to hang out in than *ahwas*. Families can hang out there too ... you can't do that in *ahwas*.'

11

The Cairene Sensei
Cairo

Karate-kid Ahmed's old sports club was near Ahly. It was called The Shooting Club, and Ahmed had been a member from the age of 10 till about 20, when his dad had pulled the family out to save money. His dad came to think the club was a rip-off.

'I remember them being so stuck up. I mean. People actually spend their free time shooting clay parrots.' Parrots or pigeons? 'Yes, pigeons.'

But he had nicer words to say about his preacher: Amr Khaled, the guy I'd first been told about by the two girls in the car coming over from Beirut to Amman. I was curious about this man, and I wasn't sure why.

I asked the club's guards if I could speak to someone about Amr Khaled. They looked at each other and laughed. A man carrying a sports bag in one hand and a briefcase in the other passed me at that moment and said, without stopping, 'They will not be able to help you,' and so I followed him.

'The subject of imams is not an Open Sesame kind of topic for those boys over there,' he said, reaching his car and opening the boot. 'Some of the more notorious of this club's imams,' he was now using his elbow to point in the direction of the club, 'have been so bad that even I considered moving my family from it. But I didn't,' he slammed the boot shut and walked round the car. 'The other clubs wouldn't have been much better.' He folded his body into the front seat and gestured for me to get in the other side.

'One second the clubs were about working out and seeing friends ... and then crash. The people got religion quite badly.'

He was now not really talking to me but to his dashboard and the many levers demanding his attention. With one of the guards having moved away from their post to get a better look at what was going on with us, this stranger offered to give me a lift back into town.

'It looked posh, didn't it? Well, when my family joined it was really quite cheap.' He'd been a young doctor with three children and The Shooting Club had been all he could afford. Around that time the large number of people who had been making money in the Gulf returned to Cairo to enjoy it, 'but with the Gulf's money also came the Gulf's religion.' Members of Islamist sects arrived and those that joined his club took over the mosque. So if Ahmed had been there then, if he'd have wanted to take up karate, he wouldn't have been able. Religious lessons replaced swimming lessons.

'I hated it, my family hated it and the club's president hated it ... but, mercifully, it didn't last long.'

The Islamists went too far by installing a former Jama'a al-Islamiya member as the imam of the club's mosque and were ousted. Jama'a al-Islamiya, meaning 'The Islamic Group', occupied the beyond-the-pale bit of the Islamist spectrum. They were formed, as were Islamic Jihad, in the 1970s when the Muslim Brotherhood renounced violence. Their aims were the overthrow of the Egyptian government and its replacement with an Islamic state. Their imprisoned leader stands accused of attempting to bomb the World Trade Center in 1993 and as such they are hated in equal measure by the American and Egyptian governments.

'And *that* is why you shouldn't ask about the club's imams.'

When he pulled in to a lay-by of a very wide road about ten minutes away from where we'd started, he took an old receipt from the dashboard and wrote in Arabic a couple of sentences over two lines.

'Get out here and ask around for this mosque. It's where Amr Khaled started.' What was the point of the Islamist story?

'Is this man, Amr Khaled, an Islamist?' I asked.

'No. That's what they say is his "beauty".'

The district was one of Nasser's suburbs: Medinat Mohandiseen or Engineers' City, created for Cairo's emergent middle classes, and where their roots had twisted and curled in the soil during Sadat's open-door policies of the 1980s. Nasser's socialist suburb was now the place you'd go to buy Mercedes, muffins and make-up. On Mohandiseen's main road shoes were king – shop windows were filled with every shoe imaginable, clustered in similar colours, suspended by fine wires for ultra-visibility.

The doctor's Arab calligraphy appeared to be illegible. Those people I showed my scrap of paper to mostly frowned. Asking in two of Mohandiseen's biggest mosques – large and municipal with inelegant after-dinner mint-green lighting strips lining their form – I began to feel a bit foolish. Above the ground-floor shops, cafés and restaurants seemed to offer the best opportunity to regroup.

For each of the eight customers there seemed to be one member of staff. I chose a table away from the window next to a girl my age wearing quite a bit of make-up, a flower-patterned headscarf from which peeped a fringe of high-lighted hair. Though she had three books piled on her table including *Death of a Salesman*, she was reading, not very seriously, a local free paper. She was doing a lot of looking around – and chain smoking.

I showed her my scrap of paper with the name of Amr Khaled's mosque on it.

'Why, of course,' she laughed, smiling at and with me. In slight mockery she repeated how I'd been mispronouncing his name. It was easy to do so, she said, if you're a tongue-tied Westerner. The correct way was Amr as if it rhymed with Charmer and Khaled with the 'kh' very guttural and an 'ed' at the end. This girl was now on her feet and at the window asking a table of tourists to move aside a little. Pointing to a small road leading off the main thoroughfare she turned her head back to me and said with great excitement: 'He preached near here. His first mosque was down that road.'

Now standing up it was apparent that her tight trousers were so tight she couldn't do up the top button and the trousers were in danger of giving up completely. She wasn't fat, it's just she was one size bigger than her clothes. And these trousers made her a muhajababe. As did the headscarf and, most importantly, the make-up. I had already noticed that Cairo had the highest concentration of muhajababes after south Beirut. The same tight garments indicating loose interpretations: plenty of fuchsia as in Beirut, sheer fabrics, diamantés, feathers.

Zina was a local. She had sat at the same table every Monday night for six years – it had become her desk. 'At 17, this,' and she gestured around her, 'became my club. My parents went to Zamalek club – my dad is on the management team there – but I preferred to come here and read books.'

While for a lot of people, their home away from home was the mosque, the *ahwa*, or the sports club, for a new generation like Zina there was now the muffin shop as there was the art gallery for Hisham. 'Henry James. I was reading a lot of Henry James back then and,' she said, pausing to suck inexpertly on her cigarette, 'if it was Henry who persuaded me to read English Literature at Cairo University then I'd say it was Amr Khaled who got me into photocopying.' She wasn't joking. It didn't strike me as a great tribute but I got her I point – and later discovered she ran a photocopying (or as she calls it, a 'Xeroxing') business. Amr Khaled was a very big figure. As big as Henry James.

'I still have the notes I made from his [Khaled's] lectures, most of which were copied down sitting on the pavement outside the mosque because I was never early enough to get a place inside. People would arrive hours ahead of the sermons to get a spot, causing heavy traffic congestion.'

Khaled was in his late thirties, from a solid middle-class background and 'as famous as a superstar. Have you seen a picture of him?' I hadn't so she started to describe him. He didn't wear a beard preferring to be close-shaven and instead of a white dishdasha or jellaba he wore a suit and tie 'and he speaks in Egyptian dialect Arabiya, not classical as most preachers do'. This new *modus operandi* extended to the manner of preaching.

'He doesn't shout at us. He talks,' and then she leant nearer and blew smoke out, 'softly.' I obviously didn't look sufficiently impressed. 'It's no good. You don't get it. I shall have to play you some tapes.' Zina now waved at the waiter for the bill, took out some cash to pay and scooping up what had been spread across the table said her goodbyes and left with me in tow.

Going with Zina to her family's small Mohandiseen flat was where and when I realized how big Amr Khaled was. On our way over, as Zina talked about a relationship that was just coming to an end and one that she hoped would take its place, I asked what Amr Khaled had to say about this:

'He doesn't say, "God will damn you," if that's what you mean. He *does* talk to us about boyfriend-girlfriend relation-ships. But he advises us it's better to be married. Perhaps, I don't completely agree with him on that.'

She left me in the living room – empty because her family were at the club – and returned carrying a sheaf of notes, of which she read out snatches.

'While he never tells you to veil, it is clear from his lectures,' and then she proffered the papers, 'that he'd like you to.'

When Darah had first introduced me to muhajababes in Beirut, tapping on the window of her car to draw my attention to a pair of girls, she had talked of the sexy clothes and blamed Prince Alwaleed's video-clips. But now I was sure that she paid insufficient detail to their reason for veiling, perhaps she had taken it as given that there is a constituency in her region that just *will* veil. Were those girls instead Amr Khaled followers? Beirut was obviously a very different place from both Cairo and Amman. But the types of girls who would be sophisticated in their taste in music and clothes would need a pretty class act.

Now Zina was showing me a lecture with sentiments that would have inspired karate-kid Ahmed: 'Khaled is also a real sportsman,' she said, adding her own commentary to his sermon on football that she was reciting to me. 'He used to play for Egypt as a teenager. Sometimes he would end a session early if there was a football match on and that is why he often gets footballers to appear on his shows.' So there were 'shows' as well as lectures.

Certainly this chatter-box zeal was of a different hue from that of Al-Azhar – the home of Egypt's official Islam and where all religious preachers ideally had to have been trained. The cousin of Ahmed (a man who was accompanying me to quite a few of Cairo's mosques to translate and speak to them when they didn't want to speak to a woman) was an Al-Azhar student and when I met him he was on holiday from the university. His homework was to finish his memorizing of the Qur'an. He was halfway through but worried like any student on holiday with a huge workload: 'It feels like everything new I'm learning is pushing something older out the ear on the other side of my head.'

Al-Azhar was seen as yesterday's news: hopelessly co-opted by the government. Leant on daily to issue pronouncements on what is Islamic and what is not, its verdicts are often seen as a little too convenient for the government. An example of this was a proclamation about usury, supposedly one of the biggest stumbling-blocks to foreign investments. Al-Azhar decreed companies that make interest on their money no longer to be *haram*. Businessmen may have rejoiced but most people saw it as confirmation of Al-Azhar's poodle status.

Zina told me that Amr Khaled was marked out as different from the start because he was not trained at Al-Azhar but as an accountant. And she meant this made him a good thing. Now she was sifting through papers in a box to find her favourite bits like they were holiday snaps. At the bottom of her box were videos.

'This is old Khaled. *Words from the Heart.*'

The opening credits featured Amr Khaled alongside young men and women, praying, crying and giving hearty, healthy belly laughs, as if they were in a vitamin-supplement advert. The opening titles segued into a studio discussion. The colour scheme of the set reminded me of *This Week*, the TV programme I worked on – purple and mauve plasma owing a lot to lava lamps and sure to look outdated. In fact I wasn't even sure whether it didn't look out of date already, a self-parody of a television studio for a post-modern age.

But the colour scheme was the only similarity with *This Week*. Now we were into the realms of *Kilroy*. A man I didn't recognize, Khaled was sitting in the middle of a studio of young people. He had a moustache and held lecture cards.

'There will now be a discussion about the love of God,' Zina was speaking over the top of Khaled who was doing some pretty smooth TV-presenter moves, walking over the set like Simon Schama navigating ruins. The studio audience handed round a microphone to answer Khaled's call to give him, and us viewers, proof of God's love. Like Alcoholics Anonymous they each proffered their quite personal stories, some a little nervous, others cocksure, and a proud Khaled, coaxing and cajoling them through their stories, glowed with pride. Zina's favourite, which she fast forwarded to, was about a man who survived his car being spun over not once but seven times – seven having an added resonance for Zina and the audience because it is a supposedly lucky number. This was evidence of God's love because Allah had given him a stay of execution and with the extra time on this earth he went on the Omra, or lesser pilgrimage.

'It's this bit here coming up,' Zina was saying. 'What I find so great about him is that he could have said that this man was very lucky to be alive and that we should all be grateful, but instead Khaled tells him that if it had been God's will to take his life, then that would have been fair too. He is fair.'

Later a girl would talk about the time when she was due to be at a cinema that burnt down. She is ready to believe that God has been kind to her and spared her life even though he knew she was about to go into something *haram*. But Khaled corrects her and says that movie-going is not *haram*.

'It is the unpredictability that we respect. He's something else, isn't he?'

What was her Top Ten of his lectures? She bit her lip and sank back into her parents' marshmallow furnishings.

'Well, he lectured a lot about how we owed it to ourselves and our communities to work hard. To make as much money as we could. If we are rich we can spend our money doing things Allah would approve of.'

I checked up on some of this later. On wealth Khaled said:

'I want to be rich so that people will look at me and say, "You see, rich and religious," and they'll love God through my wealth. I want to have money and the best clothes to make people love God's religion.' He also said, continuing in a similar vein, 'One of the proofs of God's love is that it encourages you to be ambitious, to raise yourself ever higher in society.'

Zina had thought about it some more and had decided: 'One of the best things he has done for us is address the unemployment problem Egypt has.' How? 'Well, he has been one of the first to say that one should work for any amount of money – sometimes, in fact often – people don't work if they can't get a really well-paid job. They think, I am educated, I must hang on for the best job. Well, it doesn't work like that. Sometimes you must settle for less to be able to get more. Amr Khaled has told me that the only way to change society is by changing yourself first. And he was right. By changing myself I got into the photocopying business.' Khaled sounded like he'd been on the phone to the baby-boomer professors. He certainly had a journalist's ear for a 'line'.

It was also her 'Xeroxing' company that had earned Zina a place at one of Gamal Mubarak's business hothouses. One of the ways that Gamal the Liberalizer got his message out there was through these business schools, voluntary organizations that tackled unemployment and housing problems among young university graduates. I later looked at his website, and his themes were the same as this Khaled man. There was even a poll Gamal Mubarak asked people to take part in. The question was 'Why Are Youth Away From Politics?' and the polling options were (a) don't personally care (b) weak political awareness and (c) no trust in regulations. And this from the son of a man who had ruled his country for nearly a quarter of a century. Zina now talked the talk.

'I have no problem with Gamal. He's what we call "well fed". He doesn't need power and that is why he should have it. Take the bread-subsidy scheme: this is run at a great cost to the government and, really, for Egypt to take off, should be taken over by private companies that would be able to do it better. Energy prices have just gone up making the bread even more expensive to produce. This should be cut free from the government.'

It was true that energy had got more expensive and the government had kept the cost of bread down by using cheaper ingredients. Zina's was not an uncommon world view. Hazem, the Ahly basketball player, had saved money from his contract to set up a company making sports equipment and told me, 'I can tell you one thing Mubarak should do tomorrow – taxes for a young person like me starting a company are high. Slash them.'

Zina agreed. 'Yes, I think the taxes should be done away with. If people are supported in setting up industries then they will be able to feed themselves and won't need bread subsidies.'

Was Amr Khaled then, with his talk of why you owed it to yourself to make money, the religious wing of Gamal Mubarak?

Her parents were about to come home and Zina now set about tidying the A4 sheets of paper with the proficiency of someone who deals with hundreds of sheets of A4 for a living. She'd been smoking in their front room and flung open all the windows and repeated a little open-shut motion to waft air in and out.

'My mum and dad don't know I smoke … it's a problem.' She'd smoked a packet so I thought her concern a little late.

'Zina, do you mind me asking why you smoke?'

'Because I like it.'

'But isn't it *haram*?'

'Maybe.'

What was 'maybe' about? Surely if you cared enough to veil, you cared enough to not smoke. So I asked why she wore a headscarf and she grew a bit more frosty.

'Why do you think I wear my headscarf?' she threw back at me. I had actually got no idea. We carried on like this for a while with me not knowing my hijab from my elbow and her standing at the window of her parents' flat wafting it to and fro. I had thought that those who veiled wouldn't smoke. So eventually I just said that.

'That's not what we think. *They* might think that. But that's not what we think any more.'

'Who's they?'

'The Ikhwan. If I smoke and wear the headscarf you know that I'm *not* one of them. You know that I'm Islamic. That I am devout. But I'm also different.'

The headscarf, Aisha had reminded me in that small Beiruti bar, had been a symbol of Islamic awakening in the 1970s – signalling a rejection of the West. Now Zina was giving me a reason I hadn't heard before. It seemed that for Zina – if not for the secular intellectual Fayraz – the Muslim Brotherhood had replaced the West in the hierarchy of things to which to signal opposition – and that opposition was being fought through puffs of smoke and florid hijabs.

'If you know what you're looking for then you'll see being a Muslim these days is a different thing,' Zina said.

I left Zina's and went back down on to the main street. She'd already said I wouldn't find Khaled there, that he'd moved into a bigger out-of-town mosque with more parking spaces, but now I was here I might as well check out the old mosque. How small was it really? How uncomfortable was the pavement outside that muhajababes like Zina sat on, furiously scribbling notes? Were the loudspeakers still there?

I crossed the airport-runway-size main road and took the thinner side road off it that Zina had pointed at from the bakery's window. I followed this down and round a few times through shack-structures until it widened out slightly on to a residential, more modern road with the mosque straight ahead. If there'd been hundreds of cars they'd only have been able to get down a one-way system.

Immediately opposite the mosque a BMW car showroom was open late. This was fitting. Khaled seemed to preach an Islam that ushered in the kind of entrepreneurial spirit that an Egypt under Gamal Mubarak would like to see. Together they were titans of the free market, self-help and muffins.

Gamal showed every sign of following in his father's footsteps on Israel, negotiating with it with a view to making money from trade deals.

Khaled's line on Palestine was similar: 'The Palestinian [situation] and the Iraq war were Arab tragedies born of the spiritual shortcomings of the region.' It seemed right then that these two were in alliance against the Muslim Brotherhood that Zina pinpointed as the 'enemy' and that Khaled's first mosque be opposite a BMW showroom.

Though the black-and-white stone mosque had a commanding entrance, the upstairs floors were the same layers of balconies and windows as the adjoining residential buildings. I stood under a tree looking at the mosque and tried to imagine the pavement full of Cairenes like Zina, sitting on the ground alongside those that had come from further afield to watch Khaled. Where was there room for them all? The pavements weren't that generous with the buildings quite near to the road.

'You here to meet the new imam?' said a voice behind me, from the BMW showroom's ramp. 'He is a doctor, a very famous geologist and scholar of the Qur'an – he has spent his life studying how geology and the Qur'an, er, how you say?, suit each other.' I asked if people crowded the streets when he delivered his sermons and the man raised an eyebrow.

'Khaled isn't here any more' – he patted a car parked on the small patch of tarmac he had been allocated – 'so now there's more space for my cars.'

12

The New Eve
Cairo

The publisher's was next to a large Ikea-like furniture shop covered in billboard adverts for showers and gardening equipment. A shop nearby was still selling Valentine's merchandising days after the event. Big cushions in the shape of hearts, cuddly teddy bears stuck together by their snouts, kissing in among an old harvest of limp red roses – they seemed odd objects of the West to be sold so near to the office of the Muslim Brother I was there to visit. In Saudi Arabia a fatwa had been issued against Valentine's Day on two accounts: imitation of the West for starters *and* celebrating the birthday of a Christian saint. The religious police would confiscate roses from flower shops and eventually florists opted to close on every 14 February. Here in Cairo, not only had the florists pedalled Valentine's Day but also kept it going a few weeks longer than necessary. Perhaps the liberal secularists with whom the Muslim Brotherhood were now in informal coalition were beginning to have some influence on the Brotherhood. Political reform really was all they were concentrating on.

Yellow department-store lighting dazzled me as I waited inside the publisher's office looking at shelves of their product. Selim was small – when he stood to greet me he reached little higher than his desk. His jacket was a light sage-green thing over a white shirt and he didn't even have stubble let alone an overgrown fundamentalist's beard. As I went in a man and woman nipped in on my tail as the door swung to, as if late for a meeting. We all sat in armchairs with Selim behind the desk. A telly next to us and in his direct line of vision was still on and quite loud. He didn't dip the sound and when he talked it was always with one eye on al-Jazeera. Like many of the nearly important people whose offices I'd sat in recently this man had arranged his stationery like rare butterflies. Boxes of staples, rulers still in shrink-wrap, unopened tubs of elastic bands all arranged primly on a massive desk surface.

'Here they are,' he said of his two employees who'd nipped in with me, his response to my request to meet two young members of the Ikhwan, 'but I can't see why you might be interested in them. Everything they have to say, I can say.'

The woman curled her lip to indicate that last comment had been received with good humour and then spoke for herself. 'But none the less, we are happy to answer your questions,' she said.

'It's just I will answer them too,' Selim added.

I was interested in the Brotherhood because Zina had spoken with such venom about them – she even seemed to have taken up smoking to spite them; the feminist Fayruz had seemed in happy coalition with them. In another country Hamdi had surprised me by contemplating support for the Muslim Brotherhood, and though Daoud had been scared of them it was actually no more than that felt by a wider, unsympathetic Arab public.

Selim was a big man in the Ikhwan. Essentially, a politician but for the fact that members of the Ikhwan weren't able to enter politics. Instead they operate in a parallel political world of syndicates and unions and rarely use the word Ikhwan but Independents instead. Since Egypt's constitution bans *religious* political parties the Ikhwan's strategy has been to gain political power of the professional unions. Inside this alternative Egypt this man was a player, senior in the Journalists' Union and, described as 'Ikhwan-lite', had been suggested to me by a retired general – Colonel Muhammad – whom I had befriended in what was intended to be a perfunctory visit to a think-tank to beg some contacts but turned into a deep and meaningful debate about how Egypt was 'getting more religious'. Colonel Muhammad had given me contact details for this Brother in front of me now and he'd warned me that at no stage would he confirm that he was a member of the Ikhwan. Instead, I would have to pay particular attention to the not very subtle subliminal politiking he would use. The direct question 'Are you a member?' Colonel Muhammad said would only embarrass me. But I asked it anyway.

'This is not the right question,' Selim said, finding the remote, turning up the volume to make more audible a report about the continuing pressure on Syria to pull out from Lebanon. All our heads turned to watch the report but it didn't keep his attention for long and soon he was leaping around from channel to channel. Us 'kids' looked back away from the telly and towards each other. I asked them whether they were in the Ikhwan. I'd heard that joining the Brotherhood isn't easy. You get recruited by your local group when young and undergo tests before you become an 'active' brother. The woman, Hassana, smirked to show that I'd misunderstood something and shook her head.

'We are not members of the Ihkwan.' OK, does the Ikhwan exist?

'We believe in the Ikhwan's ideals.' But does it exist?

'It is a noble organization.' So are you a member?

'It's not for me to say, but what if I was?' If you were, I'd want to know why. She then surprised me by nodding. This seemed to be a question she was going to be able to answer.

'They believe in greater respect for Islam in this country and I think this is an admirable thing.' So you're a member?

'I support their attempt to make Islam more respected in this country.' Why?

'It is a spirituality that we are lacking and the Ikhwan seeks to reinstall. Besides, surveys show the mosque is the most respected thing in Egypt.' When, in 1992, bits of Cairo were destroyed by an earthquake, the Muslim Brotherhood gave every homeless family $1000. Selim's remote had clattered on to his desk and the TV was now off.

'*Khallas*, Hassana!' he shouted. Then to me: 'This is incorrect. Our priorities for the time being are not sharia.' But she hadn't mentioned sharia. 'Where once our main slogan was "Islam is the Solution", it now calls for reform and democracy. We will let people live how they like: Christian or Muslim.' Hassana's head was bowed and nodding. I was uncomfortable but I didn't think he was bullying her. His tone seemed to be didactic. He was explaining to both me and her.

Colonel Muhammad had, being a Colonel, 'briefed' me beforehand that while the Brotherhood had only ever been a mainstream Islamist group – that is to say seeking a state based on Islamic law that would allow Egypt's Christian population (the Copts) to continue to live in Egypt – and never an Iranian-style theocracy, it now wanted to emphasize its role as competitive provider of public services and downplay its positions on personal morality. When Colonel Muhammad and I talked about this later we concluded this was possibly why Selim flipped when his employee began to lay out the Ikhwan's position on religion. The Ikhwan's line change had been recent and perhaps dissemination had not yet happened. That was why Selim insisted on staying in the room while we talked.

The publisher picked up the remote again and returned the news coverage to its status as nearly the noisiest and most opinionated guest in the room.

'We can not say easily that the Ikhwan exists. But we can say that our publishing house exists,' said the young man, Marwan, speaking for the first time and exhibiting great political dexterity. 'Let me show you some of our publications.'

Marwan, who was tall and wore jeans and a long-sleeve T-shirt decorated with an aborigine pattern, was the firm's graphic designer. He did have a short beard, but it was more designer stubble than pious. Looking at the range of their recent issues, it seemed he was responsible for the various front-cover illustrations on display out in the waiting room and around the streets of Cairo, redolent of children's colouring-in books. He leant forward and flicked through the books for me.

After her scalding, Hassana was sitting back watching us both, effectively hiding in the snug black and burgundy fabric of her jilbab, a fabric that went all the way to the floor. The plural of jilbab, jalabib, lurks in the Qur'an within verse 33:59: 'O Prophet! Tell thy wives and daughters, and the believing women, that they should cast their jalabib over their persons (when abroad): that is most convenient that they should be known as (such) and not molested.'

Because there are no pictures from the time of the Qur'an no one could say whether Hassana's jilbab was the garment Allah intended but in the 1970s Muslim Brotherhood women were convinced enough to adopt them, as was Hassana. Because of this distance she'd put between us and with only her face visible, her concentration seemed quite foreboding. She had a sharp jawline with no podge in it and I thought how well the veil suited her and how crap I'd look. We were all a bit awkward with their ogre of a boss guarding us and so we looked into the books that Marwan was zipping through.

A face caught my eye. I put out my hand to stop Marwan and asked him to flick back. By now I knew Amr Khaled's name better than his face, but this was unmistakably him. He was in this Muslim Brother publication, and frozen in this glossy colourful magazine page. I got a better look at him than when I'd been watching Zina's tapes. He was everything Zina supporters said he was: clean-cut, with pomaded hair and buffed, clear skin embalmed in after-shave and moisturiser. To me he looked a little 1950s, with a Nasserist moustache and possibly a little boss-eyed.

'You know him?' Hassana asked me. The pair had done a Question and Answer session with Khaled, Marwan said, before flicking on to get to a page and graphic he was prouder of. Hassana was now moving forward in her chair to add her head to ours bent over the magazines. 'You know that Brother?' she asked me, jettisoning her attempt at stonewalling, and made her colleague return to the Amr Khaled feature. 'Brother' was a normal term of reference for a fellow Muslim, but being in a Muslim Brother office, there was an ambiguity about what she meant – 'brother' or 'Muslim Brother'. She was now unrestrained. 'In his introductory quotes he says that there is no doubt that human beings have achieved great success in material things, but advances in the past century have been at the expense of other matters ... like women's rights.' The article saw Amr Khaled lay out in a, b, c, d form the rights of women because 'women are the most important people in the family'. Domestic violence was wrong; daughters should inherit as much money as sons; women should participate in elections and so on.

With Hassana continuing to translate the Amr Khaled Q&A I zoned out, concentrating on how to encourage her new-found enthusiasm. If this wasn't extraordinary then it was certainly very important. I looked at the publisher who was now intent on an *Al Arabiya* news package. If he re-engaged with what we were talking about would he shout at her like he did last time or be unbothered? I had no idea. Zina had signed up to Amr Khaled partly because she saw him as in opposition to the Muslim Brotherhood. She said he was a new kind of Islam and that she saw him as preaching what I thought amounted to a get-rich-and-get-religious piety sympathetic to Gamal Mubarak's vision of Egypt. In the offices of a Muslim Brotherhood publisher, Hassana was suggesting Amr Khaled's reach was wider than just the upper- and middle-class Egyptians that had first been his base.

'You know that Khaled became too popular, don't you? The government kicked him out a couple of years ago. It was too much for them: he started with 200 to 500 people attending his sermons and then went higher.' Eventually, his numbers had reached 40,000. As Egypt was the heart of both Nasser's pan-Arabism and pan-Islamism, I had been thinking, post-meeting Zina, that Egypt was the heart of pan-Amrism. I thought he was intellectual bedfellows with the third most important person in the presidential household – Gamal Mubarak. (Mubarak's wife, Suzanne, was by all accounts the formidable second.) Yet he'd been kicked out. Obviously not.

Khaled himself told a newspaper down a telephone line from the UK, where he'd gone to study, that he had been asked by 'certain' authorities to give up *da'wa* (preaching) including satellite-channel broadcasts, for having 'allegedly tackled issues that recently caused problems'. Khaled called these claims 'slanderous', arguing that his sermons 'are all there on tapes to prove it'. Ten thousand Khaled supporters signed an online petition – possibly Egypt's first ever such campaign – asking the Minister of Religious Endowments to lift the ban. Hassana said the Egyptian government saw Khaled as a threat and an Islamic one at that, but their banning him was pointless.

'His tape sales went up when he was banned,' she said. And his appearances on satellite channels and his internet site continue as before this time from Lebanon then from the UK, where he'd gone to do a PhD on comparative religions at a university in Wales. Later I found quotes indicating that the Ikhwan top brass were as aggrieved by Khaled's enforced exile as Hassana.

At the time, Muslim Brotherhood MP (obviously, offi-cially termed an Independent MP) Hamdi Hassan had sent a written question to the Egyptian minister responsible asking him to explain why the young preacher was banned, saying that Khaled used 'a straightforward, moderate discourse that appeals to the young', and that banning him at a time when 'Muslims and Islam are accused of terrorism, just seems illogical'. He sent the question three times, 'but [I] have yet to receive a response,' Hassan told an Egyptian newspaper. Maamoun El-Hodeibi himself, the Muslim Brotherhood's head at the time, was also quoted as saying that 'stifling peaceful Islamic voices is shortsighted'.

All very vociferous, but how had Zina got the wrong end of the stick? How had she thought that Amr Khaled was in opposition to the Ikhwan? Because the support didn't seem to have always been there. At one stage the Muslim Brotherhood *had* criticized Amr Khaled as promoting 'Air-Conditioned Islam'. So what had changed?

Hassana, who liked me now we had bonded over what she thought was a mutual love for Amr Khaled, the weird sorority of teenage girls with a crush on the same bloke, gave me the magazine to keep as a present. A few pages after Khaled's Q&A was an article entitled 'The New Eve and the Battle of the Hijab'. In 1955 the magazine *The New Eve* had been launched, the piece said – it was the first Egyptian women's magazine with the first female editor to match, and it ran campaigns on things like replacing sharia court with a normal court. Hassana's magazine here reprinted a summary of a three-page article that had appeared in *The New Eve* about a woman called Huda Shaarawi. The magazine's front cover in the 1950s had been a picture of a girl, not veiled, wearing full make-up, with the headline: 'We Want a

Feminine Revolution'. So a babe, rather than a muhajababe. Huda Shaarawi had done something *The New Eve* wanted to remind its 1950s readers about, and this 2005 magazine now wanted to remind its current readers about too.

In early twentieth-century Egypt you wore a veil and belonged to a harem, only if your husband was wealthy and could afford the paraphernalia of guarding a harem or the Sudanese eunuchs. Huda Shaarawi was well-to-do but nonplussed by the wearing of the hijab, the idea of sharing a husband and more generally her wealth – as a younger woman she visited Alexandrian department stores to buy her own clothes rather than have them brought to her home. Fortunately for her, greater political events conspired to help her. After the First World War, Egypt stepped up its efforts to free itself from British rule and women broke out of the harems to join the effort. In 1919, Huda organized the largest women's anti-British demo and when British soldiers tried to stop it the women sat, in silence, in the hot sun until they dispersed. Huda became famous. Her line was that women in ancient Egypt had had equal status to men and it had only been under this foreign domination that they'd lost out. In 1922 her husband had died and a year later, returning home from an international women's conference, she removed her veil as she disembarked from the train at Cairo railway station. Silence was followed by applause was followed by a few others de-veiling. Within a decade only a few women remained veiled. 'Freedom is something you have to take,' *The New Eve's* editorial had said, praising the gesture as 'a jihad', claiming she had 'unique courage': 'Huda Shaarawi has broken the barriers of primness and has brought light to Egyptian women.'

But this magazine I'd been given didn't like the Huda Shaarawi tale. Huda herself had paid a big price in her personal life, the magazine commented. *The New Eve* hadn't, this modern magazine thought, emphasized the context of her de-veiling or 'the need to hold on to Eastern traditions'. The Qur'anic line on the headscarf (verse 24:31) is confused. Veiling began as a custom in pre-Islamic Arabia, where the hijab was considered a status symbol (supposedly only women who did not have to work in the fields had the luxury of wearing a veil). In the prophet's lifetime all believers, men and women, were encouraged to be modest with a ruling being passed to guide any man visiting the home of the prophet: 'When ye ask [the wives of the prophet] for any article, ask them from behind a curtain, that is purer for their hearts and yours'. But the veil didn't become widespread till later. There is no explicit refer-ence to the hijab in the Qur'an, let alone the burqa or the niqab.

The third key passage in the Qur'an that deals with the correctness of women's clothing is 7:26, a verse that reads, 'O Prophet, tell thy wives and daughters that they should cast their outer garments over their persons when abroad, that is most convenient, that they should be known and not molested.' None of them mentions the head or hair. Over the centuries, various Islamic scholars have come to interpret these words as directives to cover everything. The most strict would like at least one eye covered. In 1994 a Harvard-educated Egyptian judge, Chief Justice in fact, Said Ashmawi, wrote a book that gathered all the above and concluded that Islam does not oblige women to cover their hair. Now he receives death threats from Egyptian Islamists and has a guard in the lobby of his building.

Despite Ashmawi's efforts, in contrast to the early twentieth century, many women are now veiled. The veil seems incredibly popular. Hassana was veiled, and Zina was veiled. The news agency AFP even reported that Huda Shaarawi's own granddaughter had recently veiled. Seeing whole teams of Ahly girls playing volleyball, some with no headscarf, some in tight, plain, bandex hijabs (made by Nike, it kept hair from the eyes and it seemed quite sensible), I'd trained myself not to think the headscarf remarkable. Instead of just being sold outside mosques as used to be the case, Zina now said whole boutiques were now devoted to the hijab.

I'd even done headcounts to check the stakes of the hijab. At 3 pm one Wednesday the number of women wearing headscarves was massive – 85 of the 100 women who passed me standing at a busy intersection, where Tahrir meets Talaat Harb: the equivalent of Piccadilly Circus. I knew that the high proportion of women veiled in central Cairo might be because it was just that: a public space necessitating public clothes. So I did other counts. The proportion wavered around the 80 mark in most places. It had been an impression of these massive headcounts that had made me think veiling unremarkable. Now I had semi-scientific corroboration.

But one of the last things Hassana said to me was this: 'Amr Khaled says in one of his TV programmes, "A woman in a hijab on the street is like a Qur'an." This is a beautiful saying, isn't it?'

Amr Khaled was OK by the Muslim Brothers because, among other things, he believed in the sanctity of the headscarf.

13

The Problem with Being *Rewish*

Cairo

But, beautiful sentiment or not, Amr Khaled had left the country and that seemed the end of that. I was anyway a bit suffocated by endless chat about the headscarf and I wanted to find something a bit more fun. Those artists I'd met in Beirut didn't seem to be very childish after all, occupying the square in central Beirut and trying to effect serious political change. One of my possible children of the revolution, Rayess Bek, had dampened my hopes of him being a region-wide success when he talked in Beirut about how difficult this would be – that to become a region-wide star he'd need to change his lyrics from Lebanese to wider concerns. Which, while not few, didn't trip off the tongue – for him – so easily. So were there any Rayess Beks here, articulating an Egyptian ennui? I looked around and found a promising candidate.

While those in Beirut had rapped in Arabic, the form was very much recognizable as 100 per cent nicked from the West. But in Cairo there was a young artist, Mahmood, talking of hip hop being a homegrown phenomenon: that the pre-Islamic Arabic poets using rhyme to talk to each other had been locked in one of history's first rap battles. The strongest resurgence of such pre-Islamic Egyptian life seemed to be Pharaonic philosophy – drawing on the Pharaohs to explain something in contemporary Egypt. One student politician I spoke to invoked the Pharaohs and their cronies to explain why there was, and would be, no revolution in Egypt: 'because the Pharaohs were patient. The peasants have been on the land for 5000 years – we are used to things moving slowly.' I wanted to hear more from the hip hopper, about which particular antediluvian Egyptian era had yielded the first Arab hip hop, and someone suggested I try the American University in Cairo, reputedly stuffed with braying Arab pony-club kids.

The 'I Can't Get You Out of My Head' video had just finished playing on the big telly in the university's student-union reception area – a large rectangular cruise-ship lounge with a low ceiling, under which beige divans were arranged to create a kind of sprawling bed of meeting areas. But now the TV had stopped pulsating with Kylie and something more soothing had taken over. A tall handsome man with light stubble was standing in front of others, similarly sombrely dressed. The group looked like a polished boy band but there was no choreographed routine, instead they stood straight as bollards. On either side of them were heavy red-velvet curtains and staggered into the background were medieval candles and candelabras. It seemed a very Christian spread and the sound was like Gregorian chants. The video ended and the artist's name appeared. This was Sami Yusuf.

In terms of column inches, poster inches and music-channel inches Sami Yusuf was as big as Kylie. His current album was on sale on every street corner: the abstract violet and white image on the CD's cover and posters was in a different league from other stars' branding. The violet background was actually a night sky, and the glowing white box in its centre seemed to be a holy place at the top of a hill. The camera appeared to be positioned at the bottom of the hill looking up at its apex, presumably in some religious anticipation. This was clever. To me, you and a number of Egyptians the glowing light box would look much more like a big party kicking off in a *Goldfinger*-designed conservatory at the crest of some top-secret privately owned hillock. To Muslims it looked like an alcohol-free cube of worship to Allah. The ambiguity was intended.

The university's press officer came out to meet me. He hadn't heard of, and was pretty uninterested in, Mahmood the Pharaonic rapper but he looked into his mobile phone for an answer all the same.

'Try Amira,' he said plucking a name beginning with A from near the top of his address book. 'She might be able to help. She teaches the university's ballet and opera lessons. In her headscarf.'

Back to the veil. To go from rap to opera and ballet seemed the desperate *non sequitur* of the out of touch but I took her number anyway. Later Amira nodded that it was indeed true: she gave ballet and opera lessons in her headscarf. 'I have to shut the door and lock it to prevent men entering.' So she didn't really. She took the veil off when the door was locked. Nothing that unusual, despite the spinning of the university's press officer.

Like Zina, Amira loved her veils and she talked about them as if they were Philip Treacy creations. She hung them on a hat-stand in her bedroom and spent anything between 5 and 200 Egyptian pounds (between 50p and £20 in British currency) on them. Her favourite type was a white one because of how it 'illuminated' her skin but she didn't think Spanish style suited her (supposed to be worn with big hoop earrings, the headscarf is tied to one side of the head), preferring the ponytail-under-the-scarf look.

But my plan in searching for this rapper had been to take a break from the veil. So I refocused Amira back to the rapper. She didn't know of him but, latching on to his talk of 'pre-Islamic Arabic', suggested I meet someone back in the Union who ran the Egyptian Folklore Club. I feared that my search was too far gone down a worrying folk-dancing cul-de-sac when, back in the University by the end of the day the chair of the club interrupted her society mid-meeting to write, in Big Dipper handwriting, dotting letters with circles, the name of someone called Karma. Karma was probably a student who did a good line in Cleopatra impressions.

When I knocked on the door, I heard music being hurriedly turned down. Someone in what sounded like a dance studio was having to unlock the doors, as I suppose Amira had to do whenever someone arrived late for one of her lessons, and as I imagined Daoud had to whenever a potential customer came to view his nude portraits. These locked doors showed up the idea of 'the Arab Street' for the whopping misnomer it was.

The vault-like door, thick for sound-proofing, now opened on a tall room pleated with black fireproof curtaining – possibly a theatre without a set. It was Karma herself who opened the door.

In the room beyond her were more than a dozen men and women and all their kit sprayed across a shiny floor: big bags with clothes hanging out, drinks bottles, stacks of CDs and mobiles: *Fame, circa* 1980. In front of a wall of mirrors five girls were waiting, one of whom must have been Karma's twin. The twins were tall girls with thick hair down to their lower backs: Karma's in a plait and her sister's loose, just like the girls I'd shared a taxi with over from Beirut. Karma, whose facial muscles had the kind of droopy look you have after exercising to within an inch of your life, gestured for me to sit down and then rejoined them. They formed two lines, the music was turned back on and they started again. They were, according to someone sitting near me, an R&B band.

I looked at the people I was now sitting among. Chewing gum, sucking on straws, one was braiding the hair of the girl in front. They were all staring straight ahead at the routine, a little more cool than Jennifer Beals in *Flashdance*, a little less cool than extras in a Grandmaster Flash video. A short boy with a body like an oompa-loompa had now walked from what was obviously the boys' row at the back of the studio to start spinning on his head in the middle of the casual circle the girls' dance routine had brought them to. After an impressive couple of orbits his centre of gravity went and he collapsed sideways. The music was killed and the dancers parted, slinking away from the centre.

Karma came to sit next to me. She didn't know the guy I was looking for. She asked around. A smaller girl pulled up a chair to sit next to Karma. Nor did she and then she launched into a complaint about a pair of jeans she had just lost and had to replace: they would now be more expensive because of the new taxes. She wanted to know if Karma knew about this.

'The new tax on jeans?' Karma did, nodding while elaborating for my purposes. 'We have taxes on everything. They go up periodically. They are, how you say?, "Stealthy taxies [sic]". Every time they say it is to fund some project that has gone on for years, like the Tuska project that would send water from the Nile to the desert. Taxes rose to fund, what was it?' and she stopped, looking for help around her, 'A £50-million project over 11 to 12 years. I'm 19 years old. It's been going over a decade. That's almost all of my life that I can remember.' Another girl had joined us. She was wearing bike gloves that covered just her palms and revealed her fingers, maybe she was a breakdancer too. None of them said anything but Karma looked at her feet and the girl with the gloves seemed to be slightly pursing her lips, selecting her point of view.

'You mustn't be taken in by the headscarves,' a fourth girl over the other side of the room, nearly upside down with bending over a big canvas holdall, shouted over to us. Emboldened, the girl in gloves took up her point:

'Girls who wear the veil are the sluttiest women I know. *Taabyaah*? ['So why do it?'] These girls dress worse than us but think they're much more pure ... they're snobs: just because they're wearing a headscarf they think they can go round in slit skirts doing really bad things that we'd never do.' OK. It was back to the headscarf, but at least there was a bit of kick.

I thought of Zina. It hadn't been her muhajababe tight black trousers that didn't fit that had made me a bit confused, but the smoking. And the talk of one boyfriend being despatched for another one. All very liberated, but if I know my basic Qur'an, a bit inconsistent. More people had sat down with us and there was now an empty dancefloor.

'Our religious culture is falling down,' Karma said. 'Either it is what I call extremist and hijab wearing … or nothing. Zero in between. But what if you want to be in between?' I told them about Zina's line that the hijab worn with style was her way of showing she *wasn't* extremist.

'Yeah, I've heard that line,' the girl wearing gloves said before turning to the others and asking them a question.

'Who's that guy … the one who is on TV all the time?' Karma knew who her friend was talking about and so did I. It could only have been a matter of time. Whoever else I might try to track down, I kept finding Amr Khaled instead.

'Yeah, he's really popular. He started telling girls that if they don't veil they will go to hell. After he gave a sermon saying this, the number of veiled girls in my class, doubled.'

'I watched one of his programmes and he talked about heaven as if he'd been there,' the smaller girl said to what was by now a group of more than ten of us, sitting in one corner of the empty theatre like a picnicking party. This girl got a laugh. It didn't seem that they were fans.

'Yeah, I think he makes people do religious things out of fear not love,' another one was agreeing.

'Did you hear he wanted to change Valentine's Day to Muhammad's Day recently?' a third person chipped in.

'I thought that the best thing the Egyptian government ever did was get rid of him,' another one said.

'Until he sprung up on Saudi and Lebanese satellite chan-nels,' Karma rejoined, sarcastically.

Zen TV had folded because what went down OK in Beirut didn't wash further afield. This was because, according to another of Future TV's executive producers, the only thing that unites the Arab world is 'language and the Qur'an' (other than that, he said, it was all rivalries and that was why his programme *Superstar* was so successful). Following that reasoning, religious satellite television would probably be pretty popular. People, it seemed, were preferring to get their religion from satellite TV; even, in some cases, turning directly to Mecca instead of the local mosque for religious instruction. At the beginning of this year's Ramadan, the Saudi religious authorities had announced – a day earlier than expected – the start of the Muslim lunar month of Dhu'l Hijja. Normally, governments would have ignored the Saudi call, citing their own astronomers. But because the Hajj is now broadcast live, millions of Muslims scrambled to change their Eid plans. Every Muslim country apart from Indonesia felt obliged to follow the Saudi line.

Was Amr Khaled surfing this wave too? The Egyptians had kicked him out, but to all intents and purposes he was still in the country. In the days when the state held a monop-oly of TV and radio the government could be in control. Now, with satellite channels, things seemed to have changed.

One of the young men who'd remained on the boys' bench while almost everyone else had joined the cluster, now clambered down from sitting on top of his bucket chair. He reminded me of Eric from *Dungeons & Dragons* and now he broke into the girls' circle. From the way he smirked it was obvious he was used to sticking a spanner in the works.

'I think you girls have got to stop this. You're sounding a bit paranoid.' A chorus of high-pitched disbelief ballooned above the group of dancers but he toughed it out. 'If the Amr Khaleds out there have bad effects I think it is, unfortunately, because of the girls not because of Amr Khaled.' Now he was being clobbered with shoes and drained, plastic water bottles. 'Of course he shouldn't force young women to do things, but veiling is in their – your – best interests, and he is just encouraging them – you – to realize that.' Karma wasn't having any of it. She told him to shut up and listen.

'OK, one typical Khaled story,' she insisted. Two young women head to the mall, she said, but the more religious one insists on visiting the mosque first. As they listen to the sermon, the unveiled woman starts to cry and asks for a head-scarf. Later that day, she is killed by a car. Moral of the story? Thank Allah, this girl renewed her faith. 'Frequently, girls on his shows who aren't veiled are cast as depressives, you know – like something is missing. Sometimes by the end of his show, girls will actually decide to veil there and then on camera.' One of the girls grabbed her towel and draped it over her head in a mock act of veiling. But her mates didn't laugh and instead recalled another of his lectures in which he coached women on how to continue wearing the hijab during summer.

Later I found Egypt's liberal newspaper commentators were on Karma's side. One pointed out that Amr Khaled based the 'integrity of society ... on the integrity of a woman' and that the integrity of a woman came down to 'her hijab' because 'one woman can easily entice one hundred men but one hundred men can not entice a single woman'. Amr Khaled, the commentator said, thought the erring Muslimah, or female Muslims, were not Muslims at all. 'Even if you do not understand,' he is supposed to have said, 'you must obey.'

It was when the daughter-in-law of unveiled Suzanne Mubarak (Hosni Mubarak's wife and the first lady of a nominally secular country), veiled – supposedly after listening to one of Amr Khaled's tapes – that the camel's back broke. Amr Khaled was chucked out of Egypt.

'The problem is that a lot of girls who veiled after listening to Khaled,' Karma said, 'later took it off because their conviction isn't strong enough. And taking the veil *off* is the real problem. That's when you're in trouble.' Why? 'Because of what your community thinks of you.'

I remembered the way Michael, the curator at Townhouse, had talked about a young woman who had come to one of his street-kid workshops one day wearing a headscarf, the next day not.

I went and checked out one of the lectures that Karma mentioned. Called 'The Youth and the Summer', it was quite a good read and begins like this:

'*The Youth and the Summer.* This is not the latest hit movie. It's the title of our lesson today. I usually repeat this lesson at the beginning of every summer. Summer for many of the youth means: How many girls am I going to know this year? Will I be able to have a girlfriend this year too? Why can't I have a girlfriend while all my other friends have done it so easily? This year I will definitely make a girlfriend.'

I could understand his popularity. People had emailed in to him their worries about the summer and instead of a lecture he had boiled down the 12 'most recurrent' email queries. The first was from a boy: *'Things become so difficult for me during the summer time (you all know why), what do I do? I'm afraid of temptation and I don't want to fall into sin'.* Amr Khaled advised practising a sport and suggested fasting and quoted Allah's apostle as saying: 'O young people! Whoever among you can marry, should marry because it helps him lower his gaze and guard his modesty [i.e. his private parts from committing illegal sexual intercourse, etc.], and whoever is not able to marry, should fast as fasting diminishes his sexual power.'

The next question was from a girl: *'I'm afraid of getting carried away with romances, what can I do?'* Amr Khaled said that when Allah ruled on this in the Qur'an it was as a 'rule specifically directed to women, not men. Because it is the girl who actually holds the reign [sic] of whether to go on or stop the relation.' His advice is 'don't have a mate from the other sex, don't have a boyfriend because this is absolutely forbidden.'

I supposed it was stuff like this that drove Karma et al. mad: 'Imagine a girl coming on the Day of Judgement with a flag on which is written that she betrayed her father. I'm asking all the youth to cut off their love relations with the other sex now. Never enter a home from its window, or through the internet or telephone, or without the permission of the father.'

But back in the theatre, Karma was now developing her point in a different direction and wanted me to pay close attention.

'I'll give you an example,' she said. 'I don't wear a head-scarf. But I know sex before marriage is pretty bad. Like, if someone has sex before marriage, they are going to hell. God is merciful, but Egyptians are not. So these veiled girls who follow Amr Khaled have what they call a Gawaz party. OK, do you know what that is?' A Gawaz party was for an *urfi* marriage: an informal arrangement whereby people get married temporarily and then it is lawful for them to have sex. Urfi is a term that refers to a definition of a legal issue within Islamic law. If the sharia is silent on it then the urfi definition is the next best thing. It used to be common among the widows of soldiers who had pensions that they would lose by officially remarrying. Now it was for teenagers who couldn't afford the circus of a proper marriage – nor particularly want it.

'But a lot of the women get tricked, 'she said, and by this she meant that they think the boy loves them and will do honourably by them, which he invariably doesn't when she gets pregnant. The last thing he wants is his casual dalliance turning into the kind of financial involvement that the urfi marriage had been a way around. And so, typically, he bolts. 'They get married in front of their friends, have a big party and then get to go and have sex. Girl gets pregnant and the father, who is often about 18 years old, can't look after the kid. A girl's reputation is like a match. Once lit, you can't go back.'

I heard what she was saying and thought of the muhajababes with their tight trousers, plucked eyebrows and make-up. The point of veiling was modesty but these other elements were immodest. It seemed they were also taking part in urfi marriages. Could Amr Khaled be blamed for his followers bastardizing his teachings? I now looked at the contrarian in their group who they had thumped for suggesting they cut Amr Khaled some slack and, sure enough, he was rolling his eyes.

'Even if women are veiling more because of Amr Khaled's preaching,' I put to Karma, 'it doesn't necessarily follow that they are also sleeping around more because of him, does it?' She wasn't beaten but she was frustrated and some of her friends now fidgeted, with a couple even unfurling limbs and preparing to get up and go. I'd killed the moment.

'I can't prove anything,' she said, 'and I suppose it's just a hunch,' she continued, 'but what I do blame him for is the confusion. He talks about what to wear at the beach and football and all that, but really he is actually very conservative at a time when Egypt is more sexually aware than ever. At least that is what my mum and dad say.' This last bit was sweet. I looked at her quieter sister who nodded that their mum and dad did indeed say this.

'Rotana, Melody Arabia, Mazzika,' the girl in the bike gloves listed. 'And Amr Khaled on the other … it is making people who are, how you say?' and Karma clicked her fingers looking for the word, '*rewish*, anyway, even more *rewish*.'

A colloquial word, *rewish* or *al Rawshana* has meant hipness but also means distracted or confused. A magazine that wasn't particularly fond of Amr Khaled had described him as the Sheikh of the Rawshana. Karma continued, 'As an R&B band, we are caught in the middle.'

'Take these girls who wear the headscarf,' said the girl with the gloves. 'A lot of them are wearing make-up, huh? And often they wear a fringe? Hair highlights? All these things, by drawing attention to the female face and features, they are *haram*. Who is closer to Allah? The girl with blonde highlights, bangs and a layer of make-up all under a head-scarf … or me?' she asked, eyeballing me. She was wearing a dancer's top – spaghetti straps with in-built bra – and flared grey tracksuit bottoms. No headscarf but no highlights and no make-up either.

'People are scared of talking about sex. Parents are still pushing for young girls not to talk to guys. Some of my friends got periods without their mothers telling them what it was,' the girl with the gloves continued.

'And yet whole families will sit around the television set and watch clip after clip after clip.' Karma was back. 'People bitch at us for dancing the way we do so bad that we have to lock the door when rehearsing. When I was walking home the other day I was harassed by ten policemen. They didn't leave a part of my body untalked about. And I was wearing a tracksuit. Just because they know I'm a dancer. These people think the dancing we do is sexy when it's actually sport. They watch clip after clip after clip and think we are their prop-erty.' Her eyebrows rose in emphasis before she was off again. 'Because of their attitudes if we want to become professional dancers – proper dancers rather than video-clip dancers – we'll have to leave the country.'

I was reminded of Safa in Future TV and her reason for not airing Trinny and Susannah in the Middle East. Safa had said, 'We wouldn't get away with it. Any more.' 'Any more' implied that it was becoming *more* difficult to show flesh, not less. Maybe Karma and the girls were suffering for the same reason that Trinny and Susannah had lost out and Zen TV had been closed down – sexy flesh fine, real flesh not so fine.

The man who'd been on the TV when I'd first arrived at this university was called Sami Yusuf. The reason his performance had been so starkly different – more restrained – from the preceding Kylie video was because it wasn't really a music video, it was a *nashid* (religious chant). Muslims practise two types of prayers, the biggies to be done, ideally, five times a day but also little moments, like daydreams. These are called Supplication and this was the name of Sami Yusuf's latest single, the one that had been playing in the student union. The idea was that listening to a Yusuf song was, in effect, praying. A Sufi custom originally, in the 1970s nashids – stripped of all musical instruments – became tools of political Islam, adopted by university students to criticize the state. Later, during the first Palestinian intifada, nashids garnered tambourines, drums and Bontempi synthesizers and two groups emerged in the region. With their steady bookings to perform at weddings, out went themes of war, injustice, claret skies and terrifying gods and in came love and happiness. By the millennium there was a market of more than fifty bands and samples of jazz and rap helped them compete with pop.

Sami Yusuf's nashids were something else again. Though he stripped the form back to vocal harmonies and minimum instrumental, his accompanying video-clips were as well produced as most other clips, with more clothes on and more pious themes. Before Yusuf the nashid and pop industries had been distinct. Now he straddled the two. He deliberately chose to air his videos on mainstream Arabic satellite music channels rather than religious channels like Iqra'a and his distributors had made sure that his albums were stocked next to popsters Haifa Wehbe and Nancy Ajram rather than next to the lectures of preachers. His arrival was well received. A popular Egyptian weekly put him on the front page with the headline 'Sami Yusuf against the "Porno Clip Devils"', and the article described Yusuf's *Al-Muallim* video as an *'amaliyya fida'iyya'* (resistance operation) against the semi-nudes that normally hog the limelight.

While the video on at that moment had been a bit subdued, nigh gothic, others of his featured the wide marble staircases and brass fittings of a *nouveau-riche* Cairene suburbia. It wasn't exactly the keeping-it-real urban authenticity of American performers that Karma and her group aspired to, but didn't they find the presence of Yusuf on video channels, albeit sprinkled in among the usual tits, arse and amour, to be bringing *some* change?

There was silence. The girl with the gloves was the first to break it, jerking her head and pointing her gloved hand – all very Ricki Lake:

'You remember we told you about Amr Khaled?' Her eyebrows were raised, 'Well, he's his friend.' An outburst of laughter seemed to imply approval at how she'd punctured my idea. They were now all competing to recall Yusuf's worst videos. One of them mentioned Yusuf saving a blind man from tripping over a pebble when crossing the road outside his mansion. Yusuf's brand of religion was certainly Khaled's type: trendy personal piety.

I later checked. Khaled had aired Yusuf's videos on his television shows; several tracks from Yusuf's *Al-Muallim* album as well as an advertisement for purchasing the CD appeared on Khaled's website, and the two participated in a joint lecture and concert in London in 2004.

An Egyptian admirer, Aida, posted a note on Yusuf's website, 'I love youre [sic] music I think you are such an inspiration to all muslims an u are the one who got me to put on the hijab you and amr khaled thank you so much for being a good inspiration to my life.' One of Sami's new songs – "Free" – dealt explicitly with the hijab:

> What goes through your mind? / As you sit there looking at me / Well I can tell from your looks / That you think I'm so oppressed / But I don't need for you to liberate me. My head is not bare / And you can't see my covered hair / So you sit there and you stare / And you judge me with your glare / You're sure I'm in despair / But are you not aware / Under this scarf that I wear / I have feelings, and I do care / CHORUS: So don't you see? / That I'm truly free / This piece of scarf on me / I wear so proudly / To preserve my dignity.

'Don't you get it?' Karma said to me that afternoon in the practice room, I hope not meaning to be as aggressive as she sounded. 'Soon there will be no more middle in the Middle East'. I'd touched an entire dancing troupe's raw nerves, and Karma and the girl with the gloves at least were determined to leave their mark. This last sentence was immediately effective and affecting.

I will be veiling soon, but I'm not going to do so because of some guy in a suit selling me religion.' Karma told me that in order for her to get really close to Allah, she knew she'd have to veil. 'But not yet. I would be faking it if I said I was fully convinced right now. That's why I don't like Amr Khaled and his lot. Because they rush us.'

I hadn't found the Pharaonic rapper – someone whom I could cast as an Arab Allen Ginsberg – but, by sheer frequency of mentions, I'd decided the Amr Khaled phenomenon, or the man himself, was really important.

14

Daddy Comes Home
Cairo

For the couple of months that I'd been in the region there'd been a Cairo story rumbling along that had made the papers of the neighbouring countries. The story always led with a big picture of the protagonist turning the other cheek to a battering shower of paparazzi flash photography. Her name was Hind el-Hennawy and she'd just become the region's most famous single mother. After I met Karma and her crew I decided to visit this woman. She'd had the urfi marriage that they'd warned of and when she'd had the baby the father had bolted, but she didn't seem to be the *desperado* they described as going in for these ceremonies. I was told to make my way to a bakery in the Muqqattam Hills, an outlying Cairene suburb located so far out it was in desert. Journeying through the lunar landscape I saw the type of LA villas that I'd seen in Amman and also on video-clips when the narrative is set at the artist's make-believe home. These suburbs' names translate into things like European Countryside, Dreamland and even Beverly Hills. Arriving in Hind's suburb, it seemed she lived in an LA mansion too.

'Let me set a few things straight,' Hind's mother said as soon as she had picked me up and we were in the car together. 'The press have been implying that because I'm a psychology professor I'm OK with the situation my daughter is in.' She was shaking her head like a windscreen wiper.

The press had indeed made much of Hind's parentage. Indeed, it seemed to be something that Hind herself had encouraged. When Hind and her brother were little, their mother had got a job in Saudi Arabia. Traditionally if one spouse had to relocate both would do it but not Hind's parents. Hind's father refused to accompany his wife and play the part of *mihrim* ('male guardian') so her mother went on her own leaving daddy to raise the two kids. By Egyptian standards Hind's dad was a paradigm-smasher. Accordingly, papers reported that the two initials in the family's front gate were her parents'. I expected them to be loved-up renegade hippies.

'I'm not going to pretend it is not a nightmare,' her mother was saying, clawing back some conservatism. 'Her reputation is, well, her life has been ruined. When Hind was little she used to cycle to school. She'll cycle nowhere now.' The girl with the gloves in Karma's crew would say that the match was spent.

Hind had been putting her baby to bed and the first thing I saw of her were her ice-pick stilettos descending the central spiral staircase above the sofa I'd been left on. But it was just the shoes that were whiplash. Now sitting down next to me, she wore no make-up, a plain black wipe-clean gilet and a nose stud. And no headscarf, so whatever she was, she wasn't exactly the model hijab-hussy Karma and her friends had so derided.

In December 2003, Hind had graduated from university with a degree in Fine Arts and went on to get a job working for Egypt's Nile Media Centre designing costumes for a new series of a sitcom called *Daddy Comes Home*. The lead of this programme was to be popular young actor Ahmed el-Fishawy who, three years younger than Hind, was already famous as the host of a pious new television programme about young people and religion. Hind described the early days of working on the programme. She said she was more excited that it was a 1940s period sitcom than by the fact she'd be meeting the famous Ahmed – son of two of Egypt's best-known film stars.

'At the first sitting he was wearing a close-fitting T-shirt and I took it from the sides and stretched it across his chest and I remember thinking his stature was perfect for the high-waisted trousers men wore in the 1940s. He pulled back and said the only woman who touched him like that was his mother, and I asked him to swear that was true on his mother's life.'

That she was anxious to play down any attraction she might have had for Ahmed before meeting him, and play up her professional credentials by saying how much she liked clothes from the 1940s was, I supposed, no surprise. But though she was very straight, and very articulate, the inflection and emphasis of her story had the creaks of a story that had been used many times. I had to scribble to get it all down but also to avoid the cringiness of it all. It didn't stop with Hind's dewy words: the necklace Hind wore with her daughter's name, Leena, written in Arab calligraphy, had been sent by a famous Egyptian jeweller. One of Egypt's best-known documentary filmmakers, already talking screenplays and film rights, was Leena's godmother and had been present in the hospital at the birth. Even *Daddy Comes Home* was perfect and waves of cynicism occasionally approached. But I pulled myself together. Upstairs her five-month-old baby was sleeping with no surname. Without a surname she had no Egyptian ID, which meant no immunizations or school enrolment. Particularly sad was Hind's worst nightmare. It was of Leena being kidnapped: she'd have no way of proving she'd been stolen since there was no proof of her existence in the first place.

Hind and Ahmed fancied each other but Hind said she knew her sociology-minded parents wouldn't allow her to marry the son of a wayward actor. Ahmed's dad was a lothario and ridiculed by intellectuals like Hind's parents. And they'd already rejected three of Hind's suitors and I saw that she still wore their rings on her fingers. Ahmed, Hind says, came to her with an idea. Unable to countenance just having sex because Islam forbids it outside marriage, they had an urfi marriage. What Karma and her crew had said was sex without marriage – 'there's one being held every weekend in this university' – Hind insisted was a 'secret, religious marriage'. What Karma had said was seen as an occasion to 'get their friends round, get some drink in and do the ceremony before going off to have sex', Hind insisted was very private and intimate: just her, Ahmed and one witness – a friend of Ahmed's.

Which is where the problems started. After they had married and spent the night together – Hind had been a virgin until then – she became pregnant. I didn't ask why they hadn't used condoms. When she told Ahmed, at that time staying with his father in Beirut, he asked her to have an abortion. Hind refused.

'I rang Dar al-Ifta – you can ask them whether something is right and wrong – and they said abortion is *haram* even if I were married.'

Dar al-Ifta is Egypt's highest religious authority and it was funny to hear her talk about them as if they were a quaint little do-gooder helpline when actually they were Allah on Earth. But this bit was important. An Ifta is an 'Islamic decree concerning doctrines, religious practices, dealings, good manners and matters that have settled principles in Islamic (sharia) law'. The head of Dar al-Ifta's job was to demonstrate the religious judgment on any given issue. Hind had Egypt's highest religious authority on her side. It was also significant because it seemed to me, with only one witness and not informing their parents, Hind and Ahmed had not performed an urfi marriage as it was meant to be performed. It was these elements of their arrangement that further complicated things. If, despite these slightly imperfect aspects of their ceremony, the Grand Mufti of Egypt was on Hind's side, then this was very significant.

Ahmed tried to match this. He came back from Beirut 'saying that he had visited a sheikh who said that we should pay a *fidya* ('ransom money') equivalent to ten camels or £40,000 Egyptian and fast for 60 days before going for an abortion and maybe then God would forgive me. This was the *fidya* normally exacted for accidental death. But that really made me mad. There was nothing accidental about this.'

They were locked in a bidding war with Allah. If it came to the courts, they'd have to appeal to sharia reasoning. Egypt's constitution calls sharia 'the principal source' of legislation. In reality it is divorce, inheritance and family law issues that are guided by sharia. The rest are mainly secular, derived from English laws and Napoleonic ones.

Hind began to pray more than the five normal times. 'I was worried that people would see the fact I don't cover my hair as evidence that I'm not religious. But I am. I am a believer … I just didn't believe his sheikh. So I said to him, let the sheikh call me – make him say this, write to me, find it in the Qur'an.' It was extraordinary.

'I do not believe this is right,' continued Hind. 'Islam says abortion is *haram* and Egypt says abortion is *haram*.' Ahmed shouted at her before despatching his dad on a mercy mission. Fishawy the elder duly visited Hind. 'He said I could do whatever, have sex with whoever I wanted, but I had to know I couldn't do it in public.'

The etiquette was to have an abortion and then a hymen-repair operation. Extremely commonplace, small hospitals all over Cairo carry out the illegal hymen-repair procedure for ever cheaper amounts: 'Two of my friends recently had one. There are two types you can buy: one that costs 1,500 Egyptian pounds (£150) and the other – just a few stitches before marriage – is 500 Egyptian pounds (£50). But both are getting cheaper. Like mobiles. With different ring-tones.'

It was a gag but there was also truth in it. The video-clips were so unfair because the sex they hinted at was unavailable to viewers who were, aside from dodgy arrangements like urfi marriages, not able to get laid without getting hitched. Girls told me that boys proposed 'making it from behind' – anal sex – before marriage since it was not *haram*. I don't know whether these girls were persuaded or whether they rang TV programmes like *Dial-a-Fatwa* to ask, but if they had they'd have been told that anal sex most definitely is *haram* since it implies domination and no one is allowed to dominate a human. Apart from Allah. Programmes like *Dial-a-Fatwa* had proliferated in the satellite TV era to cater to similar confusions: the market of Muslims unsure of the rights and wrongs of Islam. The concerns viewers rang in with were, according to anecdote, becoming focused on sexual advice and, for instance, the plucking of eyebrows (with the aim of enhancing the allure of the eyes) – was that *haram*?

But Hind's joke about mobile phones getting cheaper being like restoring your virginity had pathos. And, of course, the video-clips were funded by mobile-phone companies. The ticker-tape that ran along the bottom of Khalid's Future TV programme – it wasn't uncommon for some of these to announce that the sender was looking for a boyfriend or girlfriend – secured the phone companies a text-messaging service that paid for the making of video-clips that otherwise had no revenue capacity.

But apart from the geopolitical implications of her story Hind's concerns were also those of a woman who knew her own mind: 'I wasn't prepared to go throughout my life pretending I wasn't experienced. I was bored with the idea of spending the rest of adult life having abortions, then hymen repair operations to fake my virginity, hop into bed with the next man I think I love and lie pretending I don't know what to do. No way. I know what to do.'

It was fair enough and it reminded me of an anecdote (highly choice of course) that her dad had let a newspaper use. When Hind had been naughty at school a teacher had beaten her for discipline. The next day her father marched straight into the classroom and hit the teacher, asking them how much they liked it.

Karma had also felt the hypocrisy in the way the dancers' conduct and profession was pilloried for being seedy, while Hind, barring hell-having-no-fury-like-a-woman-pissed-off, was going further than that. She was saying that, behind the scenes, the new religious classes were much more red-light than the unveiled girls, illegitimate babies or not.

'It was when someone told me that Ahmed had begun hanging out with Amr Khaled that it all made sense. Ahmed's Islamic chat show was very similar to Amr Khaled's. Ahmed had always had real religious moods,' she continued, 'often he would need to be alone in his penthouse and nothing could console him. A lot of Arab stars are becoming similar. I can list many female actors Amr and Ahmed hang around with prone to such religious black moods. In Egypt they're called veiled-again. They're all in Khaled's band.'

Ahmed had even asked Khaled for some verses from the Qur'an to justify his position in the Hind affair. According to one of Hind's contacts – also a Khaled confidante – Ahmed told Khaled that journalists kept ringing him and he needed something religious to tell them.

That evening I went and looked up these actors online. One of them had been acting in a popular soap that ran through Ramadan and then a few months later she had veiled.

'I've been reading religious books and deeply thinking about my life,' she told the religious satellite channel Dream

TV. 'I had this feeling that life is too short. Now I am on the path to either good or bad. I told myself that I want the good and I'll have to work to get it.'

Another actor who starred in the film *Hammam in Amsterdam* also decided to veil after she'd been lying on a beach listening to music: when the music stopped, and she'd heard some Qur'anic recitation. A few weeks later she went to Mecca for Omra and 'finding herself', gave up acting. Another singer whose brother had been nagging her to veil finally did so when her brother was killed in a car crash. Music execs kept chasing her with huge sums of money, trying to persuade her to change her mind but she wouldn't. Now she presents a programme called *Mona wa Ikhwataha* (*Mona and her Sisters*) about the role of Muslim women in society on Iqra'a, the station from which Khaled also broadcasts.

It had happened before when, during the 1970s and 1980s, popular actors and belly-dancers had quit acting, with two of the more popular ones veiling and covering their faces then never making public appearances again. But this twenty-first century lot were different: they seemed willing to continue appearing in public, singing and dancing, spreading the image of a moderate Islam. In 2002, Egyptian actor Abeer Sabry announced she was ending her career to become a more devout Muslim and followed classes by Amr Khaled. But instead of graceful anonymity, she was promptly drafted to present an Islamic talk show on a satellite network and says she is now hoping for a veiled come-back on the silver screen. Sabry, still wearing lipstick, hasn't yet received any offers but insists her modern Islamic look will pay off rather than undermine her career. In an online article in an Egyptian blog about the phenomenon, a director of Dream TV and an entertainment weekly *Al-Kawakeb* also pointed to Khaled's centrality, saying that 'while actors in the 1970s and 1980s were influenced by Sheikh Shaarawi, today's veiled-again actors are doing it because of photogenic sheikhs like Amr Khaled.' The blog also talked directly about Amr's and Ahmed's relationship: 'Khaled, for instance, told young actor Ahmed el-Fishawy, the son of the more famous veteran actor Farouq el-Fishawy, not to quit acting but to be more careful in selecting the kind of work he wants to present.'

Even Haifa, Arabia's Madonna, dipped her toes in the piety trend, saying on one occasion that she intended her next video-clip to have something that made her audience realize that her songs 'are not necessarily without civilized content' and that her presence in a clip 'not only conveys physical arousal and seduction but the communication of a particular message'. But it was another video-clip that signalled how dug in the trend was becoming: Haytham Said's 'Humma Malhum Bina Ya Leel' ('What Have They to Do with Us?'). This was the first one in recent Egyptian pop-music memory to feature a young love interest wearing the veil. The director was Sherif Sabry, who directed all Ruby's video-clips – the bawdiest of them all. But what also caught my eye was that he also directed the videos for Mubarak's governing National Democratic Party (NDP) convention. This man was secular establishment. Things were now changing.

◈

Recently, I'd heard more bitching about Amr Khaled than praise. I was hearing allegation after supposition after gossip, and it felt a bit rotten. Those of his lectures that I'd read revealed a man not without humour. He could sound stern but it was bulked out with sympathetic banter, Qur'anic evidence that the Prophet knew how to have fun, and recognized the importance of having fun. Though he did talk of 'summers without sin' and 'hellfire', he was also very dextrous. Here he was being understanding about sexual attraction: 'But, why did Allah give us this order? Hasn't He created our emotions? So why do things have to be so tight and uneasy? Men and women long for each other by instinct and this is how they were created, so is the issue just to make things difficult?' Could Amr Khaled be held to account for all the woes of young Arabs as Karma and Hind might like him to be? Or might not a lot of it be casual misinterpretation? Maybe the muhajababes had just been plain getting him wrong. Certainly, during his lecture on smoking muhajababe Zina must have been dozing. She might like to believe that smoking and veiling in conjunction were a way of showing she was modern not Ikhwan Islam, but if Khaled saw her smoke he might come rushing towards her with a fire extinguisher. His website showed an award he'd received in 2004 from the World Health Organization for his anti-smoking campaign. After the ceremony he'd surprised well-behaved and reserved WHO delegates by handing out leaflets entitled 'A Message to Smokers', copied 762,000 times. The plan was that as many people as possible would have a few photocopies each. Because of him, he said, the deputy director of the Faculty of Pharmacy in Alexandria University had banned smoking on campus. Zina would have been able to help him with the photocopying, but perhaps would have fallen without the Nicorette.

The day I left Egypt, Hosni Mubarak – having insisted constitutional reform wasn't on the cards – made things a little easier for his opposition. He asked parliament to approve an amendment to the constitution so that the autumn presidential elections could be multi-candidate. Whereas election day in Egypt had been a referendum on Mubarak, this time there would be more than one candidate. One member of Kifaya reported in the press said it was as if the 'dungeon gate' had been opened and now she could 'breathe fresh air', while a spokesperson for the Al-Ghad party said it was probably the most important piece of political reform that Mubarak had introduced. But it was the Muslim Brotherhood, which said it would consider putting up a candidate, that stood to gain most.

If the country's most popular actors, singers and TV presenters were non-smoking, teetotal, veiling and even anti the lewder video-clips – then the Muslim Brotherhood's hands were free. With Islamic rights and wrongs buried by Amr Khaled in chat – in colloquial rather than classical Arabic – of football, homework and racing cars, the Muslim Brotherhood could relax into campaigning about political reform.

15

I Killed the Song
Dubai

So if I left Beirut thinking Prince Alwaleed very important, then I left Cairo thinking Amr Khaled just as big. If Prince Alwaleed's video-clippers were raising the blood pressure of the region then Amr Khaled's calls to be veiled-again seemed to be the rearguard action. For those who bought both – the girls in Beirut Arab University and Zina – it was perhaps not a *bad* worldview. Imbibing media from a Saudi modernizer, Prince Alwaleed, and religion from a Cairene Islamic modernizer was progress, of sorts. Only of sorts because Khaled was ultimately a conservative soul and Prince Alwaleed was unlikely to burn his bra anytime soon (unless it was proposed by one of his producers as a device for a video-clip). For the secular, or the religious, but taking their time, like Karma, the effect was suffocating. The space between the video-clipper and the veiled-again was diminishing. Darah's ambiguous sexuality, Zidan's ambiguous beats, Hind's ambiguously legitimate baby daughter and Karma's belief in dancing as skilled sport were all left with little room.

As if to embody this, news came of the Egyptian Pharaonic rapper, Mahmood, whom I'd been looking for throughout my time in Cairo. One student with whom I'd been in email contact, who was trying to help me track this guy down, told me that perhaps I'd been finding him difficult to trace because he was no longer a rapper. Nor was he based in Cairo. He'd gone to Dubai to begin a contract as a singer not a rapper. They even had the contact details, complete with a Dubai dialling code, to prove it. His line about pre-Islamic rap had been brilliant. Now, the email said, he was just another pop-star video-clipper.

Since I was going to Dubai anyway I arranged to meet him in a creek-side café in the centre of the city. I got there first and waited. In 1990 the proportion of Dubai's GDP that came from oil was 30 per cent. Now, after the visionary policies, nigh *televisionary* policies of Dubai's emir, aware that the oil will not last for ever, this had decreased. Through tax breaks, golden handshakes and fake classic Arabian architecture he had coaxed the world's businesses to Dubai, thereby helping the region to develop other ways of making money. It seemed to have worked: it was now one of the richest 25 countries in the world and, in 2005, Dubai oil accounted for roughly 5 per cent of its GDP. Having become a little themepark version of the Western world, situated in Arabia's eastern nether regions, it had been accused of diverting the Levantine's returning generation.

'Why go back to Beirut or Cairo when Dubai does it so much better?' one Lebanese woman I sat next to on the plane to Dubai had asked. I looked at the skyscrapers lining the creek like mountains and wondered whether the plan was that the region would go from a reliance on oil to a reliance on Rotana.

A car pulled up and two men got out. Mahmood had brought a friend. The taller one, the friend, was more garrulous and quickly ordered us all his favourite *alcoholic* cocktails, the shorter one, Mahmood, sat and watched his friend's flurry of geniality and fluffing. He was much less good looking and charismatic than the taller chivalrous one. I couldn't imagine him as a rapper.

'I have just finished filming a video-clip so you are lucky,' Mahmood declared. 'Two days ago I would have been too busy for you, but now I am free. But not very, so hurry up.' I put to him some of Karma's points. That people like Haifa are bastardizing perceptions of Middle Eastern women. Karim, his tall friend, laughed. Mahmood didn't. 'Be careful, some of those people are my friends. I have performed next to Elissa and am tipped to be the next Amr Diab. Haifa is a close personal friend of mine. I agree, she has no voice, but in that way she is the Marilyn Monroe of the Middle East. You would never have wished for a Western society without Marilyn Monroe, would you? Well, don't wish that on us. Seeing women's bodies on TV will be a very good thing for the Middle East.'

A young Saudi with whom he'd attended university had seen that Mahmood could sing and had poured money into his career, thus enabling Mahmood to buy the shoes, hair, tight pantaloons *and* the record production, he needed to secure the attention of record producers.

'I am descended from a turn-of-the-century sheikh who reformed the Egyptian education system and I am continuing the tradition of participation in revolutionary movements.' He still had the silky words and high-falutin rhetoric of his rapping days, when he'd seen in his rap, pre-Islamic antecedents. 'Through my music, people will acquire a beautiful sensibility and a civilized mentality. They will learn the importance of citizenship that way.' So why did he give up rap? 'Rap was the future once, I'd say about five years ago. But it became clear about a year ago that people don't like this American form of entertainment and prefer a soft sound on their ears.' Did he still stand by the analogy with Pharaonic Egypt? 'Yes, it still sounds good, doesn't it?', and Karim laughed again.

It was this kind of chat – video clips will revolutionize the region by flesh – that meant I was meeting Haitham. He'd signed Rayess Bek for EMI Arabia: the deal that had been the envy of Beirut. If Rotana and associates were driving change from Dubai, where were companies like EMI Arabia? I wanted to know whether they would either function as the chief champion of alternative culture or perpetuate the same old stuff. After all it had been George Martin at EMI in London who had been the only person to sign the Beatles – the band that changed the Western music industry from singleton singers to bands with verve. Would EMI have the same effect in the Middle East?

Haitham was Andre Agassi's *doppelgänger* and had probably looked 35 at 15. His business was trend spotting across Arabia for the next music phenomenon and in this quest he said he never stopped searching for the perfect song, which meant he listened to everything:

'I'd say I'm the only person in the Middle East who listens to Chinese opera.' Because his mission was 'to produce the Buena Vista Social Club of the Arab world'.

'Is it going to be easy or difficult?'

'Up to 50 per cent of those dominating Arab music cannot sing.'

Rayess Bek was causing headaches. Between him and me, he said, being either unusually conspiratorial with someone he barely knew or simply honest, Rayess Bek was pushing it.

'The deal was that he just had to come up with one hit. That's all.' One hit was all Haitham needed to make Rayess Bek break into the mainstream. 'But he does himself no favours. So far it's been eighteen months. At first I thought he was trying. Now I'm not sure. I think he's got this stupid Beirut intellectual hang-up. He doesn't think he should have to write that kind of stuff. And it makes me really, you know,' using his cheeks for stress-balls, he puffed them up and then popped them, 'quite mad. As it stands, there are probably only 500 people in Beirut who will buy Rayess Bek's album. My job is to increase that number.'

On our way to a restaurant Haitham explained he'd recently been in a car crash and the long-lasting effect was that while he hadn't exactly lost his senses of taste and smell, his senses had reversed. Bitter odours and tastes had become sweet, and sweets had become bitter – he wouldn't be eating much that evening. I thought of dolorous Rayess Bek and doleful Haitham flung together across the continent and of each letting the other down. I remembered Rayess Bek shaking his head at the thought of what a bad decision signing to EMI Arabia could potentially have been. How they basically didn't seem to *get* his music. The 'they' over in Dubai that he had talked about as pushing and pulling the

MP3s he emailed over was Haitham. A man who now thought sugar was piquant and salt was saccharine.

But Rayess Bek was one of the luckier ones. Haitham didn't like Zidan's music. Too underground: 'When Western bands do underground so well why would people buy second-class underground music made in Arabia? If you put to one side the samples and snatches of Arabic tunes that are admittedly everywhere.' He was referring to the Chemical Brothers track 'Galvanize' we'd just heard on the radio. They'd sampled a track from a Casablancan Berber singer. 'If you just look at Arabic music on its own, it is in big trouble. It is not innovating.'

Haitham let me stay with him because the hotel he'd picked me up from – Dubai's cheapest – was, he said, an infamous brothel. His one-room studio flat seemed to be the base for a shifting group of boys. Spacious with two people in it, four of ten phone calls he took turned into additional guests in front of his TV, crammed around a coffee table on the floor along with me and another EMI employee, Joseph, over from Beirut for a meeting. In the next few days, Haitham rarely joined us on the floor but instead lay on his bed to one end of the studio flat with his feet up and his laptop on his tummy in a kind of deckchair repose, editing songs. Whatever the song's main riff or melody, Haitham would repeat it over and over under his breath but still audibly, tapping his laptop as he did so.

Everybody else's conversation was almost always about Beirut. Most of his gang of six – apart from Haitham and another Iraqi – were Lebanese as were many of the other tenants on Haitham's floor. Their doors were often left open and Future TV coverage of the Hariri assassination was audible at all times of the day. The boys watched 80 per cent news and 20 per cent video-clips and then the video-clips were only because a change is as good as a rest.

One night, the event all stations were covering was another gathering at the tents and burning pyres in Martyrs' Square. Except this time there was an added *frisson*. The Interior Ministry had put out an order against the gathering. The parliamentary session was meeting for the first time since Hariri's assassination and the political classes were very brittle. Despite Lebanese soldiers circling much of the city centre with barbed wire and barricades, hoping to block the demo, it had been to no avail and the crowds were defiantly big.

Like spotting Walid when I was in Egypt, hours of television-watching turned up a couple of people every half hour whom these expats thought they knew. One girl they particularly approved of had painted the national flag of Lebanon across her cleavage. The loudest hoot of one evening was reserved for the video-clip Future TV broadcast of the personalities and celebrities they'd got to record a fundraiser for Hariri's death. Their song told the Syrian occupiers: 'The Story Is Not Over Yet'.

At another point, Haitham screamed, 'Jeez!' Though Muslims they still took Christ's name in vain. 'Couldn't the shit have warned me?' He'd opened a round-robin email from someone in Beirut and now handed his laptop round like an open cigar case. The email contained photos taken at the scene of the explosion that killed Hariri, one of the dead former prime minister's upper body, on fire, being dragged from the car.

Eventually the boys went out 'cruising for women', and I stayed behind to check my email. There was one from *Superstar* Ahmed. The show's second round had now been cancelled. Of course. The same channel that had just over a month ago been beginning auditions was now busy. It was a cruel change in priorities. Another one from Yusuf ploughed a similar furrow. He wanted contact details for the people I'd met at Future TV. Had I been watching the coverage? The whole thing was rigged, he said.

'Bossy Future TV producers issuing stage directions. They erected TV screens of the demos. They built toilets. They've been painting make-up on the face of some of the demonstrators.' I surfed around. Online there were reports of something the leader of the Druze, Walid Jumblatt, was supposed to have said: that an advertising executive had teamed up with Future TV to create a photogenic revolution, studying hours of footage of the Rose and Orange Revolutions.

At 3 am they came back, turned the light on, and I woke up. I was sleeping on a campbed in the window and Joseph now bedded down on the sofa at right angles to me so his head was near mine. Amiably drunk and nostalgic he asked me for my top five records. I gave them to him and in return he gave me his. I didn't know one of those he listed and he explained that the band was a death-metal band. I thought I knew how to spot a death-metal fan. My brother and his girlfriend would travel Europe for death-metal gigs. Though they didn't scream 'death metal', Joseph looked even less of a goth. His Diesel denim was every inch EMI Arabia employee. Haitham dealt in CDs like they were cards and was always trilling a tune. Why, I wondered, was Joseph in the music business?

In the mid-1990s, Joseph said, he used to do a lot of DJ-ing at beach parties in Byblos – a place I already knew from my time in the Lebanon as both a rave capital and the stomping-ground for Christian and Islamic extremists.

'At one party I was doing a set and everyone was losing it except for one person. He was slightly older than all the rest, looking a bit out of it. Not on drugs.' Joseph eyed him for the hour of his set and then eventually approached him on the pretext of asking for a cigarette. 'At this stage I wondered if he was a paedophile. Why else was he just looking and watching?' He was happy to give Joseph a cigarette and asked about the music not the people, 'I was relieved that he wasn't interested in the crowd. He wasn't a paedophile.' In particular this man wanted to know about one track Joseph had played halfway through his set, which once Joseph had properly identified he was happy to name and even fetched a piece of paper to write the track details on.

'It was a track called "Deicide", by a band of the same name. He wanted me to write down some of the lyrics, which I did.' And they were? He groaned, 'It's a long time ago but I'll try,' and he began to speak-sing, his memory word-perfect as far as I could see, some near religious prose: 'I can strike the light and see through the dark, blind disciples – you will never live again, I killed Jesus just to see him being on his purple throne. I am evil. I am Deicide ... and I killed the song.'

Now Joseph laughed. 'They don't sound so good without music. But they were a great live act and people really got it when I played their tracks in my sets. The lead singer of the band, Glenn Benton, said he'd be dead at 33, the age at which Jesus died. He has a cross burnt into his forehead. But he's still alive. Son of a bitch.'

'Why does that make him a son of a bitch, Joseph?' 'The man asking me questions was secret police and ordered the confiscation of the music and my ID. In Lebanon, without your ID you're in trouble. It's as good as locking you up.' The Joseph who went to pick up his ID had long hair, wore an earring (illegal back then), an eyebrow ring (illegal), a tongue ring (also illegal), had a goatee and – not possessing a pair of smart shoes – wore the slightly oversized shoes of his sister's boyfriend. The Joseph that came out of prison a week later probably looked more like the 2005 Joseph.

'The only thing they'd left was my goatee. Because apparently you're not allowed to humiliate an inmate.' Joseph was now leaning up on one arm. 'Then they told me what I'd done. They were investigating the suicide of a group of people that were thought to be linked to the music, and particularly the one song that I'd played. The lyrics of this song were supposed to have driven them to doing it. Lines like "I want to fuck God" didn't go down well with the judge. My defence was that these lines had been in English not Arabic. People would-n't have understood. But the judge was really pissed. He said, "How can you say this about the Virgin Mary? You abused your responsibility in front of all those people on the beach … you have people from Beirut to Byblos and people who followed you, and the music you played, killed themselves. Your sister goes to these parties – we know – how can you bear the thought of that?" They were alleging that I ran a cult and was responsible for the deaths of these wackos.'

'Weren't you?'

'No.' The first person who had killed themselves because, they thought, of 'Deicide' and Joseph's playing of the track, had lived upstairs from Alessandro, who had sold Joseph the record in the first place.

'The prosecution said that his [the suicide's] dad had been killed in the civil war and he lived alone, coming down to Alessandro's shop every morning to buy a different cassette. One morning he took his father's gun and shot himself in the head in front of everyone at his school. He left a letter saying that he wanted his notebooks and cassettes burying and left it under Alessandro's door for him to get when he opened up the shop. So Alessandro got into trouble too and his shop folded. Now he sells house music from Germany. For a while the government thought I was a ring-leading Christian extremist. But then they realized it wasn't just me. When Kurt Cobain killed himself nine or ten Lebanese copied him. The Lebanese Interior Minister Michel Murr had gone on TV several times and called for tighter controls on imported music.'

A Nirvana 'phase' was a phase in the West, but Christian fundamentalism over here. I supposed the Lebanese government had to think the worst – it was only a handful of years after the end of their civil war and inter-community relations were tense. But still. The long story short was that when Alessandro had sold up, Joseph had bought his death-metal stock.

'With all this music the only job I could get was in the music industry.'

◈

The next day I left Haitham and Joseph snoring and went to meet their boss. EMI Arabia's offices were in a nexus of skyscrapers called things like Knowledge Village, Leisure Village and Media Village. Of course they were loose interpretations of a 'village'. No thatched roofs, daub, cobblestones or hens clucking, but huge gleaming clusters of kitchen-knife towers with their tips cutting the clouds. I didn't know where I was going and got lost at the ankle height of one skyscraper. One door I opened revealed only a brick wall, and another a subterranean crazy golf course, being vacuumed.

When I eventually found EMI Arabia's HQ, in the reception there were familiar records framed: Blue's album *All Rise* had sold 15,000 in the region, and Robbie's *Life Through a Lens* had sold the same. But Arab names weighed in heavier. Artists like Yasser Habeeb had sold 30,000 and a band called Junoon, Sufi hardrockers dubbed 'the U2 of Pakistan', were also on the reception wall.

One of the perks of being in a company fifteen years and graduating from finance director to managing director of EMI Arabia seemed to be that you were able to get your furniture upholstered however you wanted. When Hugh, Haitham's and Joseph's boss, called me into his orange office and invited me to sit down, it was in one of his cow-splodge animal-hair chairs. He was an English man wearing a blue and white striped Oxford shirt, untucked, and his office was a little corner of Richard Curtis's England in Dubai. He immediately gave me EMI Arabia's latest compilation CD and I scanned its playlist. None of Beirut Zidan's acts was on there, even though I hadn't met anyone like him in the region

210

since. Instead a band that I had heard of, Blend, was the sole representative of Beirut's alternative scene.

The Lebanese band Blend had polarized the people I'd met. It was the first Arab act to be signed by an international label; EMI Arabia had got very excited about them. In the singer's own words they were the first Arab band to not sing about love: 'How can we sing about love when so many people are dying in our region?' Instead they sang about 'globalization, corrupt politicians and an apathetic population in the Arab world that lets itself be manipulated.' Their single 'Belong' 'dealt with the search for identity of the post-war generation,' explained the lead singer at the time of its release.

'We young people suffered from a lot of insecurity during the war years and didn't know what the future had in store for us.'

Haitham couldn't stand this band. 'Get him to tell you about Blend,' he had taunted when preparing me for meeting his boss, 'and make sure he admits what a disastrous decision they were.' They had flopped.

Hugh volunteered his scars. 'They are why, I'm afraid, I've had my fingers burnt by counter-culture Arab music. They were the last band I put significant resources into. And it didn't work. They sang in English, not Arabic. This was the first mistake. This was made even worse by their Arabic not being very good … Jad, the lead singer, had grown up abroad during the civil war. Talking to me he was articulate, but that just didn't translate. Sad. It was sad. They wrote their own stuff, unlike most in this region. He would have been good for the genre "Young Lebanese Artist Survives War".

Shakira used her Lebanese origins as a marketing ploy. Blend could have done too.'

His mood was not totally pessimistic. 'Blinkin' Park and Eminem use Arab melodies a lot ... it proves there's an appetite ... I predict in the next ten years there will be a breakthrough and the two will go together to make an Arab star that will sell. Across the world.'

'Across the world' seemed to be their bull's-eye. But what about 'across the region'? Haifa Wehbe, Elissa or Nancy Ajram weren't popular first and foremost because they sold 'across the world'. And Prince Alwaleed probably didn't expect them to. They were region-wide stars. Shouldn't EMI Arabia be looking for region-wide success too? He shook his head and explained why EMI was in Arabia. It made its money by distributing Western hits in Arabia and distributing compilations of Arab hits abroad. EMI's compilations of Algerian artists were selling quite well to France and, at the moment, Malaysia was also buying quite a bit of stuff. The UK less so. The most they had sold in the UK was 10,000 of a compilation album. This orange office with cow-splodge chairs was a caravanserai of music.

I had thought Zidan's music was really good but, even though I had long given up acting as his ambassador, was a bit depressed. Hugh could see this.

'In our defence,' he said, 'there are structural reasons why the rock industry hasn't taken off over here. There's no copyright law. So, if EMI Arabia produces a run of CDs, as soon as they hit the streets – and this is tough since the distribution network isn't the best – they'll be copied a thousand times by pirates and there goes our market. This is why, in ten years, for instance, the Lebanese market had not grown much. All I can fight for is a copyright law. Without that it will continue to be the Saudi princes who want to fund their girlfriend putting a video out – those with funding *already* – who get out there.' He was talking about Prince Alwaleed.

'Rotana has no subscriptions and modest advertising revenues. The Arab advertising market is around $2 billion compared with a UK market of nearly $20 billion. So Rotana is kept afloat as the project of the nephew to the late King Fahd.' This was Beirut Darah's point about the music industry having no market forces because of Alwaleed.

'Your alternative, if you don't have a rich boyfriend, is the Sami Yusuf route. Tap into the growing vogue for trendy new Islam. His latest – 'Supplication' – was released during Ramadan 2004. He sold millions and he was sponsored by Coke. Up against such competition the indie rockers and hip hoppers' – those who don't tap into Sami Yusuf-esque piety or who aren't in the loop of Prince Alwaleed patronage – 'these guys need the Virgins and the Carrefours in the region to survive. Virgin and Carrefour are potentially revolutionary catalysts … If they continue lobbying hard for copyright laws.'

This reminded me why Walid's exhortations for us to shoplift from Virgin were, apart from basic illegality, *so* off the mark. Back at the Virgin Megastore in Beirut in Martyrs' Square – or Liberty Square as it had reportedly been renamed – the spirit of an Arabian Woodstock soared. They'd just got their scalp. That day the Lebanese government of Omar Karami resigned. Haitham's flat became a riot of 'Lebbo' expats with all doors open and chants like 'Karami has fallen, your turn will come, Lahoud, and yours, Bashar' broadcast in stereo. The TV's Breaking News belt hopped around from Karami resigning to Mubarak's announcement of multi-candidate elections in scatty indecision at so much good news. Druze leader Walid Jumblatt went a bit light-headed, saying the Iraq elections were the Arab equivalent of the fall of the Berlin Wall. President Bush had some of the bubbles too: linking the uprising of Gucci-clad revolutionaries with Iraq's January election in some kind of electoral chaos theory. While the principles were similar – people power – you can't cause a government to topple just by *seeing* another country go to the polls. Can you?

16

Gezzing
Kuwait

In Kuwait University there were more parked cars than students. Cars lined the curb outside the library, they filled the ceremonial space in front of the elaborate central building, and this was just overspill from the acres of parking the university provided on its perimeter. Cars indicated that somewhere there were students, I just didn't know where. I saw a Starbucks sign hanging above the door of the law faculty and headed for it, desperate for some coffee and wilting a little in the fossil-fuelled heat. Five steps into the building, an arm hooked mine and swung me round so I was now walking in the opposite direction. He was a young man, dressed in a dazzling white dishdasha with a starched white keffiyeh folded on his head in simple origami. With one hand he had bunched up the lower swathe of his dishdasha to hold it like it was his wedding dress. With the other hand he escorted me away.

'You're not allowed in there. It's men only. That's the sharia law faculty.'

It was about 2 pm and round the corner from what had to be the most un-American of Starbucks franchises, students huddled under scores of little structures that were like kids' Wendy houses. These were modern-day versions of the *diwaniya*, Kuwait's contribution to both architecture and debate. A diwan was once the Emir's office where he met his subjects and now most people have a diwaniya within or outside their house, some kind of large reception room with low seating round the perimeter, which functions as a meeting place for men. Once underneath one of these my escort eventually let go of my arm. Here there was a healthy assortment of dishdashas and denim and nearly all of them had, alongside the normal gym kits and rucksacks, an eye-catching piece of yellow stationery: either a pad, a smaller notepad, a pencil or a sticker. I hadn't found a cult, or a maths class with standard-issue textbooks. I'd found a party of student politicians. If Iraq was in its first flush of democracy, if the Egyptian people were sussing out whether they were pleased or not with Mubarak's announcement, and some of the Lebanese were in shock that they had brought down a government, then I was a bit overwhelmed too. This trip was turning into a Forrest Gump stumble through Important Events. In Kuwait I looked out something a little more humble – Kuwait University's student elections.

The students belonged to something called the Democratic Circle. It had been around since 1974 but was now ailing and the yellow stationery was part of a last push, lest this be their last hustings. Earlier I'd blagged my way into a recruitment fair in the economics faculty and nearly every one of the girls, wearing items I recognized as Topshop's finest, were carrying some bit of this yellow kit. The thick yellow board pads with black-patterned etchings on the front would have got them my vote.

'You're very kind. But of course it's more than about stationery,' said the guy who had prevented me from entering the university's all-male bastion. His name was Mustafa. 'It used to be mixed but it was one of the first victories of the religious parties. People are getting more Islamic … both outside and inside the university.'

He said this as if I might not have noticed myself. Even the mighty capitalists of Dubai and merchants of Coca-Cola had put their fingers in the wind and sensed that, if video-clips were here to stay, the new money was on religious music like Sami Yusuf's. 'The Islamists have been a force to reckon with for most of the past 30 years.' Mustafa now grabbed the yellow pads of his friends and was slapping them down one by one on to the floor. His sudden burst of energy brought my focus back inside the shade of the diwaniya. Each pad became a different university department.

'OK, so the one over there,' he said pointing to a smaller notepad, 'we know we'll never take that: it's the sharia college. That was the building you were trying to get into.' A ripple of polite laughter swirled round the square seating structure. 'And we'll never take that one over there. That's law. Most of the students there are Bedouin.' And now he stepped over to the furthest pad. 'And we'll never take this one, the social sciences, because they are all Bedouin too.' I thought that was odd. Where I'd done a social science degree, it had attracted all the chalet-school girls and gap-year boys earnestly interested in fluffy concepts of identity, gender and other abstract nouns.

'You can go through both degrees never having to be able to speak English, so that's why Bedouins do it. Because they are not the most clever students and this degree never reveals that.' I asked him how he was defining Bedouins. An actual class? Or just a euphemism for thick people who didn't have the intelligence to vote for his party? Again they tittered but Mustafa raised his eyebrows in thought.

'Well, clothing isn't a bad start. Let me see,' and he looked out from under the diwaniya to the few people braving the midday sun. He picked out a likely set of three boys in the middle distance, 'Look at those guys. Even from here we can tell they are Bedouins.' How? They wore dishdashas like his, though they had Gandalf beards. 'Look at their hems. They are quite high, aren't they? They are high so that they don't dirty them with everyday walking about. This proves they are Bedouin. They own very few dishdashas.' It was true that his dishdasha was tennis-white and the boys he'd pointed at looked grungy. I wondered whether they weren't *just* grungy. After all this guy was a teacher's pet and wore a mummy's-boy starched dishdasha. He'd be enough to make anyone dirty their dishdasha.

But I was being obtuse. There was something specific going on with dirty dishdashas. I'd seen them in Walthamstow Tesco as well as the Middle East. Yusuf's cousin had worn a dirtied dishdasha. Yusuf argued that he was lazy and slobby. But hadn't he, and others I'd seen, been doing it to mimic the Prophet's dress? I put this to Mustafa and he grunted.

'Some people say that. Some people say that even if they are rich they scruff themselves up to look pious like Abu Ala al-Maudoodi, one of the founders of Islamic fundamentalism, did. He thought he was the Lenin of Islam. But I prefer my explanation. Most of the Bedouin in this country are poor and they don't think about their clothes like me or you do.

'Our ancestors came from the sea and then started farms in a young Kuwait. In comparison, today's Bedouin have only just come in from the desert. Kuwait didn't even have Bedouin before the 1970s. But the government wanted to control politics in Kuwait, so they bought themselves a voting block by shipping in Bedouin from KSA. MPs in parliament with only a high-school degree? Bedouin. People making most of the important decisions? Bedouin. Go and sit outside the National Assembly and watch the MPs arriving. Count the numbers of high hems.' His keffiyeh had fallen out of shape and he bent his head forward to rearrange it before throwing it all up and flicking flaps of material from around his face back on top. Any re-Islamification at work here didn't seem to have started way before Sami Yusuf or Amr Khaled.

Mustafa now returned to the notepads on the floor. 'But these faculties over here,' and he pointed to the three lined up next to each other nearest him, 'these were our targets. We thought we had a chance with engineering but we knew it wouldn't be by that much so we formed an alliance with some tribes and soft Islamists. And it paid off. We run these now.'

The last time they had taken the Student Union was in 1974. Then they held the union for four years but only by combining with the other centrist party – Mustakela – to take down the Islamists. But this time they was no such strategy. In the words of one of Mustafa's committee members, wearing jeans, the left was split as in the 2000 American elections, with I'm not sure who cast as Ralph Nader.

'Non-Islamists are divided. Our rival centrist party has decided that it would rather win a few individual faculties than unite with us to keep the Islamists out. So if you look

closely you'll find that our rival is fighting on different plat-
forms in the different faculties. Something we would never
do. At any one time they can be found playing Islamist, liberal
or tribal politics. If they're acting as liberal then they are with
women's voting rights, if they're acting tribal like in social
sciences then they're against women's rights. The Bedouin are
against women being allowed to vote. But apart from
anything else, Kuwait lost lots of men during the 1991 war
when Saddam invaded. Women need to be given the vote.'

◈

The next day, four or five hundred, mostly women but some
men, gathered on the patch of grass between the road outside
the parliament and sea. They resembled a crowd of mothers
at a school sports day dressed in smart clothes with sensible
plimsolls. All, or most, had on the blue T-shirts of the
women's-rights movement: the issue was votes for women
and Mustafa and his student politicians had had a hand in
organizing it. The men who came were suited – gleaming
dishdashas – for the TV cameras, snappers and passing cars. I
saw Mustafa and he told me he had been briefed that a group
of tribal politicians were due to arrive and voice their
disquiet, and it was his responsibility to move around
the crowd alerting people. When a group of covered
women arrived half an hour later, heading to the back of the
demonstration, where they sat on the sea wall, most of the
demonstrators fell silent and turned around to look. The
group seemed to have one teacher or leader who was now
addressing her charges, and the girls (or at least they were

supposed to be girls – another rumour was that men would disrupt the demo dressed as women) listened to her obediently. One of the organizers of the demonstration had clambered on to a stepladder and was now addressing the new arrivals with a megaphone.

'Are you here because you are in favour of women being given the right to vote?'

The teacher broke the perimeter of the group and advanced towards the crowd, saying, 'Some of them are not sure – they have come to make up their mind.'

Opinion was divided in this moment of heightened tension. Someone near me told me that one of the Islamist parties – the Ummah Party (obviously, on Mustafa's reckoning, at the clever end of the Bedouin spectrum – if it was Bedouin at all) – had come out, in the last few days, in favour of women getting the vote and that its decision was based on religious edicts by modern clerics citing the female politicians in Muslim nations like Iran and Indonesia as ballast in their argument. But someone a little further away, holding the main banner, asked of no one in particular, 'But the question is, do we want *them* to have the vote?' This reflected the mood among Kuwaitis that women gaining the vote might not be an unalloyed good. I went up to the banner holder when the teacher had returned to her group and the crowd had dispersed.

'Why did you say that?'

'Women are very likely to vote in the kind of Islamists that don't want them to have the vote in the first place. Bedouin women are uneducated and simple, and will like the Islamists' talk of things like the importance of the family.

Islamists have banned men and women being together in classrooms – they've built two campuses, one for each sex, in the new university. Banning working together in the same offices, and banning women driving are on the horizon. What they're lobbying for is that they want all women in hijabs and they are due to ban music. Instead of music classes we're going to get an extension of those lessons teaching the proper intonation of the Qur'an. It is now difficult to have concerts and if people do not pray at high school then they are considered atheists and should be punished. We're going backwards not forwards.'

The girl moved away with the mass of the demonstration, now advancing towards the parliament where a sympathetic MP had just left the building to address them. It didn't seem that muhajababes had arrived here. There seemed to be no middle ground between Islamists cowering under black crinolines and girls dressed in tight T-shirts from Topshop.

There was just one person left behind by the advancing tide.

'She implied segregation means we are backward,' this man said to me. He was wearing a baseball cap, high and large, the blue T-shirt of the women's-rights movement, tight, and had light facial stubble. 'But there is no such thing as normal in Kuwait. No such thing as straight in Kuwait. Everyone is homosexual, including these girls around us.'

Somehow I doubted it. Homosexuality in the Islamic world is still seen as deviant for even some liberal Muslim Arabs. It might be one thing for this man, Elton, to get sympathy. The idea that the Islamists were encouraging him was asking for trouble. But his flamboyant Sardanapalian act was mildly entertaining, so I listened. In segregated high school, where young Kuwaitis are forced into close proximity with the opposite sex, there is a very fine line, he said, between friend and fornication.

'Because there is such hierarchy here lower-class boys who lust after upper-class women get pushed into each other's arms for affection. So we dress up. What do you think of my skin?' – and he jutted out his chin so I could see better – 'I'll tell you the answer. I have light skin. But most Kuwaitis have dark skin. My light skin makes people think I'm weaker and basically a different sex. When I reached 13 I stole my teacher's red marker, drew lipstick on my lips … and it suited me.'

Driving, he said, was where Kuwait really happened. If in Egypt the third space after the home and office had been the mosque or the *ahwa*, then the sports club and now maybe didn't exist at all and people were instead watching Amr Khaled et al. on TV, in Kuwait the third space was, Elton said, the car.

In his large jeep with tinted windows and before he started the engine, he put on some lipstick.

'Imagine: it's Thursday evening and the only thing you are thinking about is where are you going to spend your money and how are you going to meet people. You've probably been to the hairdresser earlier in the day and for four to five KWD [Kuwaiti dinars] got your beard shaven.' This was equivalent to about £10. Not for him the look of a Muhammad. 'Maybe every few weeks you get your hair cut.

Then you need to buy your mobile phone card so you can call people. … In fact, if you have the money you buy yourself a pretty phone number – you know, with pretty numbers: maybe a lot of the same numbers or, if you can get it 1,2,3,4 in it – as well as a pretty phone. But, anyway, my point is that once you've done all of this you have no money. You can't afford to go out. And even if you did, you can't drink. So you get in your car.' With his lipstick on, he started his motor.

'So, OK, it's now about 8 pm on Thursday night. We're in the car. Gezzing. Gezzing means cruising. It's a verb. It can also be used as in, "I'm gezzing".'

'What does that mean?'

'It means cool. So people might say of a restaurant or something, "Is that place gezz?" That's not really a very good answer, is it? Hold on –' He now broke off to call his mum on his hands-free phone and check the derivation of 'gezz'. It was, she said, like 'being *shamra*'. Elton hung up on her with a clap of his hands.

'Yup. *Shamra* means cool too. Like the Eskimos have loads of words for "ice", the Kuwaitis have loads of words for "cool".' In fact, an earlier definition of *shamra* was 'posh': 'Posh has become cool. See, it's all about status.' *Shamra* was from the Arabic word used to describe the actions of Muslims rolling up their shirt-sleeves to wash their hands before praying. 'So it kind of means "to put your nose up". Anyway, where was I?' I wasn't sure whether he was referring to his analysis of the average Kuwaiti adolescent experience or to his route round the city's ring roads.

'Got it,' he said tapping the steering wheel, finding his thread. 'So you've spent all your money for the week and have no choice but to hang out in your car. How do you meet people?' He removed from its cradle the mobile he'd used to call his mum and put it in the glove compartment. He then removed an identical mobile that he put into the cradle and switched on. 'Now, the government wants us to gezz. They encourage us. They've just made it illegal to tint car windows past 30 per cent colouration, so it has to mean they *want* us to see each other.' More wishful thinking.

'How do you know if someone is gezzing, and if someone is driving to the supermarket?' I asked.

'Look at that car. That number indicates where in Kuwait you live. That guy lives in the seventh ring road. We're on the second ring road now. What's he doing here then? Every grocery he could need is provided for on the seventh. He's doing the afternoon gezz. This street is so popular for gezzing that it's got a nickname. Sharia al-Hub.' The Street of Love.

This was bonkers. A crazy game of Scalextric with his teenage libido but nothing more.

'What happens next? Nothing – without Bluetooth,' Elton replied. 'Bluetooth changed my life. Without it, all this would be pointless.' Bluetooth enabled a mobile-phone user to contact another one within a ten-metre radius without needing to know their phone number. In a country where it is rude to be seen to be approaching strangers, and in one so wedded to its cars, it was a very useful tool.

'I see a guy, or a guy sees me and if one of us likes the other they send a Bluetooth. That's why I have a different mobile.' The second phone was his 'gay phone' and it was, he said, registered under his maid's name. Elton was not poor.

But the thing Bluetooth doesn't help you discern is the class of the receiver. 'If a high-class boy makes an advance on someone slightly more lowly than them and the lower-class boy says no then he's in trouble.'

He then showed me some of the messages that had been sent him by Bluetooth. 'She is so sad. She's a he … she dresses up in her car and then sends me pictures.' The video image of his transsexual friend was grainy with unsynchronized pixels, making this baring of their soul to Elton a little more sad than it already was. Elton was incredible. He'd talked himself into spinning segregation as a gay fantasy when actually his culture was clamping down on him. If a moderate Islam was indeed breaking out across the region embracing women's rights, as the Ummah Islamist party declaring its support for women being in politics indicated, then its new red line would be homosexuality. I didn't know whether a liberal Islam would ever be liberal enough to embrace Elton.

17

Fulla Pink

Damascus

On the roads in Damascus, there were posters in fibreglass cabinets like bus-stop adverts. Against a background of the Syrian flag they were unfancy statements of support for President Bashar Assad. Assad was being blamed for Hariri's assassination by the Lebanese, and the Syrian people were rallying round. Cars were bedizened with images of the 39-year-old eye surgeon turned reluctant President of Syria, whose pencil-line lips were too thin for those of a hardman and who, on becoming president, had decreed that there should be none of the portraiture of him plastered around town that there had been of his dad. In this he had largely been ignored. Assad was the man who wouldn't be president. The job was meant to go to his elder brother Basil on the death of their father, Hafez, but the brother had died in a car accident, and because Bashar was a young 34, Syria's Majlis al-Shaa'b voted to lower the minimum age for candidates from 40 to 34. Before becoming president Bashar's only formal political task had been heading up the country's inter-net activity. In 2000 he had the whole country to run.

Flags trailed from the open back windows of cars in the feeble slipstream of those that were moving. It was like Finsbury Park after a football match: there were wails and whistles in support of their man. They might have been on their way home from a demonstration held that day. It had started out as one against Assad and about 100 people turned up but it morphed into another pro-Assad demo when 500 regime rabble-rousers had out-demonstrated the anti-Assad faction.

'We came to tell them that the whole of Syria is behind the president,' said one to a news crew. 'This is democracy. We came and they came and we are the majority.' Despite the support, Assad had within the last few days announced a phased redeployment – first to the Bek'aa Valley in eastern Lebanon and then to the Syrian border. This way, Assad said, he would be fulfilling commitments to the 1989 Taif Accords that had ended the Lebanese civil war and UN Resolution 1559, which called for foreign forces to leave Lebanon. The Americans had already decided such gestures were insufficient.

I was walking north, away from the Old City, when I saw a doll packaged like Barbie in a toyshop. She was sitting quite low in the window and the white jilbab that she was dressed in made her look, from a distance, like a flightless dove. Up close a constellation of watches, bikes, school stationery, umbrellas and CD players – all in the same radioactive pink – were grouped around her.

I went inside, closed the door and cut out the whistling jamboree of the street. Here, there were stacks of these Fulla dolls. Some wore oversized trenchcoats, others jeans and long-sleeved shirts. Those that wore skirts, wore long ones that came down to below the knee and there was not a pair of shoulders on show much less any cleavage. If I could have found any ankles I wanted to see whether they were moulded in the extended form of Barbie's feet – always ready to wear high heels. Most importantly, all heads were covered, in varying degrees.

'Fulla helps girls to practise how to put the headscarf on,' a shopkeeper said, coming out from the back room and obviously finding it odd to see a Westerner in the 'veiled-doll corner' of their shop. The headscarf can be, the shopkeeper continued, a scary thing to put on: 'the end of being, you know, a child.' This doll, therefore, put an end to the nightmares. When a line of Fulla backpacks had been introduced, despite it being the brand's most expensive item at $40, the entire stock had sold out within two weeks of the first TV ad. These ads showed a cartoon of Fulla dancing around her pink house and going through a daily schedule of saying her morning prayers, baking a cake for her friend before donning a black abaya to go outside. When she comes back home at the end of the day she reads a book before bedtime. If Barbie taught a generation of girls the importance of high hems, high heels and the high life, Fulla was pumping the trend for hijabs. And it was the muhajababe Fulla that sold the best – the one that wore jeans, a T-shirt, a colourful headscarf and, according to the publicity blurb, 'a few mascara-ed lashes frame big brown eyes and a hint of fuchsia tints her dainty mouth'. The company's managing director insisted that though they'd been asked, they never had nor would produce a fully veiled Fulla. This seemed confirmation that the brand and the profit margin lay in moderate muhajababe Islam.

But it was a bit odd. Was it wishful thinking that, like my brother had played with his sisters' Barbies when we were all little, a hijab-wearing doll in a pink box sold as a children's toy would be played with by Christian toddlers too?

Diana was someone Eva, the Reuters photojournalist working in the Darfur refugee camps now but whom I had met in Amman, wanted me to meet. Diana, an architect, was also Christian and I had stored this conundrum for her.

I met Diana in a restaurant in the internal courtyard of an old Damascene house, not far from the shop full of Fulla dolls. Despite being technically outside, the restaurant's atmosphere was muffled by an awning in red and white emblazoned with the brand name Syriatel.

'That's Assad's cousin's company,' Diana said, following my gaze upwards as she took her mobile from her handbag and passed it over the table to me. 'Yesterday, everyone on his network got this invite,' she said, referring to the text she was now showing me. 'It was for the pro-Assad demonstration. I couldn't make it. I wanted to. But it's funny. You know someone is in trouble when they get their cousin involved.'

Diana liked Assad a lot but then again, so did a lot of people. That night in a club, a nearly naked man with a flag in his teeth had climbed up to the raised DJ's deck platform and pinned up the Baath party flag – not, significantly, the Syrian flag. The pro-Assad support was more specific than just nationalism. He, or the flag, got a cheer. And though the plan for a Thursday night would, they said, normally be a trip to Beirut now people weren't going 'out of loyalty to Assad'. Diana's loyalty to Bashar Assad – or just Bashar – surprised me: it just wasn't the done thing to be so into your President in *any* country, was it?

'Assad has made it so easy for minority groups like ours to live in comfort, maybe because they are minorities themselves.'

'They' referred to the Assad family. Omitting Bashar's wife whom he met when they were students in London and who is Sunni, the ruling Syrians are Alawites – a sect of Shia Islam that, in Syria, constitutes less than 10 per cent of the population: about the same per cent as Christians. Many Sunni Muslims – some 75 per cent of the population of Syria – do not recognize Alawites as Muslims, but under a secular regime Alawites would, of course, thrive. So it made sense that Diana liked the secularism. 'The Baath party provides for equality between men and women. Any Syrian, from any social, or religious or political background, has the right to join it.'

The next day Diana picked me up from the internet café where I had just checked my email. I'd got a euphoric one from Hind and I told Diana about it.

'The court has ruled that there is enough evidence to force Ahmed el-Fishawy to undergo a DNA test. The first one ever.' This was fantastic news. Without this court agitating on Hind's side, she had no way to prove marriage. Diana asked me why.

'The one witness to their marriage is a friend of Ahmed's and he has since denied everything.' Because of this Hind had to find people who'd admit it was conceivable they'd have fallen into bed with each other. We drove past a whopping great skyscraper going up – soon to be Syria's only five-star hotel, built by the Syrian Saudi Company for Tourism and Investment, 65 per cent of which Prince Alwaleed owned. Diana surveyed it with an architect's eye, as I prattled on how risible it was that a sheikh might advise Ahmed to get Hind to abort the baby and to sacrifice a herd of camels to make amends.

'It doesn't surprise me that some wacko is advising the sacrifice of camels and all will be OK,' Diana responded. 'You've seen the jallaba round Damascus. There's more of them: you know who I'm talking about? The guys who wear their dishdasha short like Muhammad? It means they are salafis. There is a famous bookshop that used to sell Marxist books. Now it sells religious books. Maybe it is very simple, if your mum and dad are Marxists, then you rebel by being religious.'

Some restaurants had stopped serving alcohol and were setting aside separate sections for conservative families. During the Ramadan that had just passed, in the township of Jurmana – which has a Christian community – somebody was jailed because he 'behaved in a way contrary to public morality' by smoking in public while others were fasting. 'But how,' Diana asked me 'can somewhere be secular, if over half the population is veiling?'

Amr Khaled said, in one of his lectures that I'd found online, that he got letters of Christian support by the sackful and, for his religious zeal, I didn't doubt that some Christians would laud him. But Diana had a point. Christians and Amr Khaled Muslims might find each other personable, but what effect would it have on a state so avowedly secular that in 1982 it had crushed a Muslim Brotherhood uprising and killed 20,000?

Perhaps the Syrian government were not much bothered by a tipping of the religious scales by Amr Khaledism right now. The government was, after all, mid-crisis: facing the loss of its vassal state, Lebanon.

Today Hizbollah's leader Nasrallah – the big ursine leader of Hizbollah in Lebanon and President Assad's most effective attack dog there – had hit back at the Walid et al.'s smoking pot and Syria Out! Faction in 'Liberty Square' by organizing his own pro-Syrian demonstration. It was much bigger. The Associated Press put the attendance at half a million, the *New York Times* was a little more subdued with 'hundreds of thousands' and Jazeera went crazy with 1.5 million. Placards at this demo said things like 'No for the American Intervention' and it was all so awesome that I thought to hell with Fulla dolls, Khaled and surreptitious Islam. Hind had got her DNA test. Other questions of personal piety would also sort themselves out in the same way. Instead, the only show in town was macro-politics.

Rami, a Beirut journalist, had given me the name of a Syrian journalist he had never met but who had filed things for his paper in Beirut. She'd stopped sending things to his paper because, he thought, genuine opposition papers had emerged in Syria and she'd been able to file for them. He hadn't much to give me apart from her name, Latifah. So I bought the only opposition newspapers there were in Syria – Assad had encouraged some press freedom – and set about finding the by-line of the young journalist Rami had recommended in Beirut. He'd told me that she used to file pieces to Lebanon from Syria. What would she be up to today?

When I arrived Latifah was out on a story.

'What's the story?' I asked her boss, Naguib.

'She's Arts Correspondent, so it's about art,' he replied, bored by the sound of his commission.

This was a bit odd. Rami (himself a journalist) had said that Latifah 'was alone in filing stuff about young people in Syria. She used to fax and sometimes send by post hand-written pieces. Quite incredible.' But one day, Rami said, they realized they hadn't heard from her in a while. The copy had just dried up. I told Rami that his compassion was very touching but why hadn't he driven the three hours necessary to Syria? 'We don't go to them. Syrians come to us.' The Lebanese could be such arses. But the assumption had been that things had got better for her in Syria and she'd been able to place her hard-hitting pieces in her own country.

Before Latifah arrived, Naguib quizzed me on last night's Nasrallah interview. Nasrallah had said that he would not disarm Hizbollah. The Christians, the Druze, the Sunni Muslims, the Americans and the French wanted Hizbollah to disarm and now Nasrallah was denying them. While we were talking, Latifah crashed into the room and went straight to her desk. She was evidently busy and in one fell swoop removed pens, paper, recorder and headphones from a bag then slouched over some papers – there were no computers in this office – as if she were taking an exam. She then set about transcribing, in long hand, her interviews from her headphones. Naguib rolled his eyes at the drama of it all.

'She's writing up the first of her pieces for next week's edition. She has two pieces to file. Before a TV report she has to put together tonight.' He glanced at his watch, 'I, on the other hand, have the joke page to write.'

When she'd got rid of deadline number one and was getting ready to go back on the road – an assignment I was going to be allowed to attend – I introduced myself and mentioned Rami.

'Oh, yes,' she said, very flattered. 'I remember reading Rami's stuff but I never met him. That's pretty good of him to have recommended me. I thought they'd forgotten about me. They certainly don't like us Syrians that much at the moment.'

Latifah and I and, oddly, her editor, left the office and we hailed a taxi. She now filled me in on that evening's story, if you could call it that. It was National Writer's Day in Syria and her boss wanted a film with three of Syria's most famous writers. That was why Naguib was with us. He was one of the three. It was a very Soviet story – that is, there was no story, and I thought of the most polite way of putting this to her.

'Rami said that you had filed a lot of stories to his paper from Damascus. He talked especially of "investigations".'

'Yes,' she nodded in agreement but also for my next question.

'And now?'

'Yes, I started doing investigations. I sent unsolicited things in from Damascus to Beirut where they'd publish my stuff. I used to write it long hand and fax it. I rarely spoke to anyone… I just kept faxing and faxing until they took notice of what I was writing. And then one day I picked up a copy of the paper and there was my name,' she said, the memory raising a smile. It's a moment that feels like a miracle for any aspirant journalist, I thought, and I couldn't really imagine how fantastic it must have felt. Latifah continued:

'There was one occasion when fax machines didn't work and I had to physically take my copy over the border all the way to Beirut to make sure it got there. Quite easy [though not very] if you live in Damascus … not so easy if you live in Aleppo,' a much smaller town north of Damascus. This was where she'd grown up, in a family in which neither parents had received an education.

'It was an essay I wrote either about Gorky or Gibran Khalil's *Prophet*, I can't remember which, that made my teacher think I had a nice way with words. Mum didn't get it. Neither of them read a newspaper. They'd never *known* a journalist. It's hard to become a journalist in the UK, huh? Well, try it over here. No email, no computer, no training course worth doing, and if the authorities had their way, no stories.'

So what were her stories?

'Unprintable,' Naguib interrupted, and killed our conversation dead.

◈

We were now in a car travelling to the venue for that evening's interview. It was some way out of Damascus and we were passing through countryside with Naguib demanding our full attention. He was a Rabelaisian character and he wanted us all to try and guess which world-famous gangster had a house in the nearby countryside. Unsurprisingly Latifah, the local newshound, guessed right. There were caterwauls of incredulity and I'm afraid we were all sworn to secrecy. Now Naguib got distracted by talking to the driver and left us to talk among ourselves, quietly in the back.

'He said your copy was "unprintable". Was it?'

'Oh, yeeees. My stuff was always being censored. I did a story on oral sex and' – she motioned to cut off her head 'it was edited out. I write a lot about young people ... but I do it from a *secular* point of view. So like, for instance, I recently did a story on hash smoking. Well, that was pulled. Pulled straight out by the proprietor, hours before it went to press. Then there were the students committing suicide in dorms in Damascus – copycat killings. This was pulled too.' The rationale for not running her piece was that they didn't want to increase the number of copycat killings. 'Too many of these stories is why I was made arts correspondent.'

'So you'd rather not be arts correspondent?'

She didn't answer.

I asked her about a Syrian band, Kulnasawa, Diana had told me about. Syria might have been under sanctions by the international community, but those sanctions seemed also to have stymied the free travel of ideas. They weren't very good. Latifah agreed that they were rubbish.

'I am afraid they are as good as the music scene in Syria gets. We do not have the underground music of Lebanon.'

The men in the front seat were now rowing – we had lost our way to our venue, where we probably should have been a long time ago already.

'Did you know that they are about to have a festival at which The Three Esses and Rayess Bek will play?' Latifah asked, talking to the window pane.

That morning I had received an email from Beirut Aisha about a gig organized by Zidan called the Unity Festival. It was scheduled for that weekend: The New Government, Rayess Bek and The Three Esses. I could easily imagine how

Zidan had reacted to the Cedar Revolution with all encompassing pathos and had resigned himself immediately to having to put on a concert for Beirut. It was going to be a gig for 'peace' and, intriguingly, the venue was downtown. Intriguing because the underground scene of Lebanon had rejected downtown when I was there. Perhaps the fact that the gig was being held in downtown Beirut now meant that the area was being redefined as part of the stock of the sacred Hariri legacy? But when I suggested this to Aisha she said I should think of it the other way around: that it represented downtown's embrace of the underground scene.

'What is more interesting is that The Three Esses and Rayess Bek will be on the same stage,' Aisha's email said. The Three Esses had expended a lot of energy dissing Rayess Bek as stuck up, posh, rich, etc. The Three Esses' beats, supposed to be heavier and in the words of one music journalist 'more difficult for the masses to access'. But they, at least, seemed to have buried their differences for the occasion.

Eventually we arrived, and Latifah got ready quickly while the three writers took an age to decide which sample of their writing they wanted to read for the camera. I waited with Latifah, standing next to the fire. We warmed the backs of our legs and drank red wine. She obviously wasn't a devout Muslim.

'Why did you stop sending your writing over the border?' I asked. She swilled the wine around in her mouth then looked me straight in the eye.

'The deal was that I wouldn't carry on doing that when I got this job. It made me look like I thought I was too good for Syria and when proper newspapers emerged I had no reason to need to send my stuff outside. Or so I thought.' She looked back at the posturing writers. 'I don't think any of us realized that it would carry on being stories about writing and ...' She gestured at the three men still umming and ahhing, and she changed tack.

'Recently a writer called Rosa [whose father was a revolutionary and named her after Rosa Luxemburg] wrote a novel that won a prize. So, get this. They say they like the novel and *then* they decide they want it censored. The Ministry of Culture made her cut whole chunks out. There was too much suck and fuck. Her book is now in Syrian bookshops with big black lozenges where words should be.' At the same time as Syria is relaxing about the reporting of politics – this, after all, is why this newspaper could be set up, because before opposition papers were not supported – there has been an increase in fear about reporting social affairs, 'the life of the young especially,' she said. 'Now there is more religion in Syria and I'm not sure where it will take us.'

Naguib came crashing over to where we stood by the fire. Skewering a date with a knife he held it in the flames of the fire and watched it melt.

'We've decided on our writing. We are ready for you,' he announced, looking up at Latifah.

Latifah had or seemed to be having similar problems to Jad and Khalid. She'd had a brief moment of time in the journalistic sun before new different cloud formations appeared. Religion not authoritarianism. It was even a little worse for Latifah. Isolated, she was a one-woman Zen TV. Her write-ups of teenage sex were too much for a nascent civil society to cope with so she got put on arts-reporting duty. When we got back in the car to go home I asked Latifah if she'd like to go to Beirut for the gig.

'Of course I would like. But no Syrians are getting into Lebanon right now. You go, and say hi to Rami.'

The next day when I checked my email I had one from Aisha saying the gig was cancelled. It read: 'Apparently the bands were too underground and posed what people called "a security threat".'

Zidan was mad and, in typically emotive language, told newspapers that he was depressed 'because it was the perfect time for all these bands to perform. We're young, energetic and new. Where is Lebanon's "new spring" if popular, innovative bands like us are told we can't play because we might pose a security threat?' The authorities had allowed concerts in Martyrs' Square, but they were old-school acts, he said: 'The Unity celebrations are positive. But those acts weren't new. Where is the spring ... the new dawn?'

18

The Muslim Fight Club

Damascus

The strength of the Hizbollah demonstration must have cheered Yusuf. He'd mentioned a few of the group's recent devices to recruit and he said that if I got to Damascus I should go to Hizbollah's Central Internet Bureau (HCIB) and find the computer game *Special Force,* Hizbollah's first attempt at attracting to its ranks the likes of Yusuf's video-clip-watching cousin. Taking over two years to make it, the HCIB in Damascus had used maps, films and logs of its commanders to ensure the graphics simulating its some 20-year-old military operations against Israel were true to life. The Bureau was located in an outlier of Damascus half an hour away by taxi in Sayyida Zeinab, a morass of filthy shacks and shops, out of which rose the tall, thin and, given it was as beautiful as an orchid rising out of weeds, orchidaceous minaret of Sayyida Zeinab mosque. It had all Allah's 99 names written on it, in happy technicolour. Compared to this the rest of the town looked like it hadn't been coloured in. I got out of the car and, immediately lost, I ducked into the first internet café I could find.

Here a girl at the next internet terminal was Googling 'Jewry', and seemed to be frustrated, putting in different permutations of the letters plus the letter 'l' as an after-thought without success. I looked at the candy-floss pink hijab, nails and bag and offered to help. She was, she said, trying to find a picture of jewellery for some carrier bags that she was about to have printed. In return for making sure she had bags saying International Jewellery Business instead of International Jewry Business – essentially saving her life – Zeinab asked me if there was anything she could do for me. I asked her to take me to the HCIB. This didn't seem a particularly arduous task but she said she'd have to ask around, she didn't know off the top of her head where it was. The first person she asked, did.

'Ah, I should have known it was there. Did you see a large grand hotel on your way into Sayyida Zeinab?'

I had.

'That's been built by the Iranians who flock here for the Ashura festival every year. The HCIB is next to it. Of course.'

The hotel was the next most expensive thing in the town after the mosque. It had an elegant façade and details were picked out in slim purple lights. We went into the building next to it and up to a second-floor apartment where we took our shoes off before we went inside. An older man, who said he ran the HCIB, was in charge and he ordered a young Hizbollahi to get me my *Special Force*. The shop, or flat, had a funny line of merchandising. There were piles of photos for sale: Nasrallah, Fadlallah, Nasrallah and Fadlallah together and so on. There were also pots of Hizbollah honey 'from the Shebaa Farms'. The boy came back and handed us an edition of the game. 'Fight, Resist, Destroy your enemy in the game of force and victory,' it said on the front in English but there were also Arabic, French and Farsi editions. The director now spoke.

'We created *Special Force* in order to counter the invasion of our region and colonization of our young people by foreign games. The days of fighting the war with just weapons is over, resistance is largely in the mind.' For this reason, the HCIB had produced 15 CDs about Israel's occupation of and then withdrawal from south Lebanon, and now *Special Force*. Selling for just under $7 each, the first 8,000 CD-Roms walked out the door. We asked if he would introduce us to some Hizbollahi and he told us we were in the wrong place for them: they were all fighting in Lebanon.

When we left, Zeinab nearly spat at his denial. We were walking through acres of low garage-like buildings that were, she said, homes, and it had got dark. 'There are a group of boys that I know will play your game.'

This hadn't been the plan. I wasn't sure I wanted to be spreading material that propagated the killing of Israeli soldiers – game or not. It would be interesting to see how well it was made, but I didn't want my research unwittingly to recruit. The posters on the streets now turned from adverts for cereals and new shops like Zeinab's opening soon to posters of the nearly blind, quadriplegic, wheelchair-bound and now dead Sheikh Ahmed Yassin. There were even some where Sheikh Yassin, dead now for just over a year, was freshly pasted *over* one of Nasrallah. Sheikh Yassin had co-founded Hamas in 1987, originally calling it the Palestinian Wing of the Muslim Brotherhood, and was killed by fire from an Israeli helicopter in March 2004. Israel had taken him out because he was the mastermind behind suicide attacks on Israeli citizens. The man who replaced him as head of Hamas – Dr Abdel Aziz al-Rantissi – was also assassinated less than a month later.

'We're now in the Palestinian quarter of Sayyida Zeinab, where they carry on like Sheikh Yassin is still alive.'

There were a pack of boys on the unmade-up road ahead, and Zeinab was acting like she'd seen old friends. When we got nearer to the group, some of whom were kicking pebbles around on the side of the road – the clichéd image of the Middle East – there was clearly one, taller and with bloodshot eyes, who Zeinab knew and cared about more than the rest. She pushed through the knotted group, put one arm around him and, whispering in his ear, sent him off down the lane next to which we were standing. The broken circle watched him zigzag away before disappearing into a house.

'He is a fida'i,' she said. It meant a kind of martyr and now she pointed to a poster of Yassin slapped on the wall, one corner curling like a leaf.

'He is ready to give his life to Yassin if asked.'

'But Yassin is dead,' I said. Zeinab turned to the boys and asked them something about what their names were.

'Of the ten, five are called Yassin after the sheikh. You know – I would do it. I'd blow myself up … if I thought it would make any difference. But I don't think it would.'

We seemed to be waiting quite a long time until, eventually, the young bloke who'd zigzagged away now came jumping back up the alley. As he approached, out of breath, he held out a laminated card like it was an autograph.

'*Ana fida'i, ana fida'i,*' he kept saying.

'Thank you, Yassin,' Zeinab said magisterially as she took his card. 'This is his membership card of Hamas. He says you may touch it. He says that the problem is that he can't get into Palestine to blow himself up. The borders are too tightly sealed.' Young men like Yassin were still wanting to blow themselves up in desperate protest despite the ceasefire signed between Palestinian groups and Israel in 2005.

Now all of their voices broke out into an imperfect choir.

'They are saying that they want you to know that they are not followers of bin Laden. Jihadis don't really know what they want ... and they annoy them because they go around saying they are fida'i too. When they aren't .... He says,' and she was now pointing to the one who had the documentation, 'that if they are fida'i he'd like to see their documents. After all he has shown his. They don't have the documentation like he does.'

For someone with such a subtle understanding of the alliances of Islamists she then made a blunder, asking if any of them were interested in playing *Special Force*, which she showed them. None of them took much interest. They were all asking Yassin to let them have a touch of his membership card.

❖

Up in the northeast area of Damascus, where wide boulevards climb up the hill at its back, is a modern mosque, one of the largest ones in the city, almost Victorian railway-station massive with a vast hood and two minarets. Though the other buildings up there are high, the mosque is in something of a clearing and surrounded by little, low shops: mobile-phone sellers, fruit drink stalls, a laundrette.

I was buying grapefruit juice when I heard the stop-start of non-Arab Arabic. The same not-quite-but-nearly guttural Arab consonants plaited with English that I speak, but mixed with a Brummie accent. Two young men, one in a brown dishdasha, another in what could be called a City-boy, pin-stripe dishdasha – black with fine white stripes – were sitting on a bench. I walked over to them and introduced myself but they picked up their books and jogged off towards and into the mosque. Scooping up my long Dr Who winter scarf that reached my knees on either side and served OK as a headscarf for these moments, I followed them. I went into the white marble entrance hall and didn't stop for a little man sitting in a window who gave chase and prevented me from going any further. Pictures in this atrium showed the central lair of the Abu Nour Foundation into which they had disappeared. Three rooms of wine-red carpet marking out thousands of prayer spots.

It reminded me of all the things I'd told myself I'd be investigating out here and had completely cast aside: the jihadi-riders and paradise-seekers, the British Muslims who dropped everything to become international Muslims in the land of the book. The Palestinians yesterday, with their mummy's boys' denunciation of al-Qaeda, had told me what I wanted to hear. That even among the more disenfranchised of the dirty, outlying towns, fanatics existed; it's just they were quite specific about their team. Though he'd confirmed that he was fanatically, violently and suicidally obsessed by Palestine, Zeinab said Yassin hadn't the brain capacity to think laterally: he was unbothered by events in Iraq, didn't know what or where Afghanistan was and worshipped

Bashar Assad ('Whatever you think of him,' she said, 'he's not bin Laden').

Yusuf in Beirut's Shatila who had grassed on his cousin to me as 'Arab trash' – a jihadi who was into video-clips – had said the region-wide number of those 'freaks' signed up to al-Qaeda was a few hundred, 'OK, a lot. But not much when you think there are 380 million Arabs in the Middle East. The numbers of those who have actually met bin Laden? Even fewer.'

Ahmed, my sometime translator in Cairo, who had been a jihadi five years ago and sought to speak with some authority on the subject, was also dismissive. 'These guys want an international caliphate. Who else wants that? Hardly anyone. Egypt is difficult enough to sort out as it is.'

But this rag-bag of anecdotes didn't amount to a serious consideration of the more violent, pan-Arab pulls on young Arab minds. Instead I'd been gallivanting around the Middle East's recording and painting studios, critiquing pictures and imbibing jamming sessions. The people who interested me most were a privileged Saudi prince (Prince Alwaleed) and a former accountant (Amr Khaled).

Now, up at Abu Nour, hearing these bad bouts of Arabic, I felt pretty stupid. I was getting to the end of my trip and this sighting of lesser-spotted Brummies triggered a crisis of confidence. In this Foundation, the management proclaim that Friday prayers are moderate. Why, there is even one said for President Assad. There is no room for 'political Islam', meaning Iraq, Afghanistan and Israel. Instead it is now Qur'anic exegesis. Pretty obviously the protestations of a place where something really bad had happened.

It used to be that, of the 5,000 who attended classes at this foundation, 1,000 were foreigners who came from all over the world: Americans, Japanese, Norwegians, Turks, Egyptians, Brits, coming both to learn Arabic and about Islam. For those whose Arabic was still embryonic, the Friday sermon was simultaneously translated into several languages including English. It was lauded as a veritable Tower of Babel until the 2004 bombings in Turkey against British and Jewish targets. Syria expelled 22 Turks, three of whom had been studying at the Abu Nour Foundation. Next, it was revealed that the Foundation had taught the first British suicide bomber, Asif Muhammed Hanif. He studied Arabic and Islam at Abu Nour and he blew himself up in an Israeli pub in Tel Aviv. When people started to dig around they found that the mosque's leader, now dead, whom people had professed was a moderate, had, actually, in the early stages of the Iraq war, called for jihad against America. 'I call on Muslims everywhere to use all means possible to thwart the aggression, including martyr operations [that is, suicide attacks] against the belligerent American, British and Zionist invaders.'

It was a low point and Assad decreed there would be no more foreign students. So those foreign voices outside the Foundation, had I been hearing them?

I went to the office of someone called Muhammad Habash. He was the only Islamist MP in the Syrian government, a sometime teacher at the Foundation *and* the son-in-law of the late Abu Nour sheikh. Diana, a secular Christian, had raved about him as the country's great turbaned hope. Of the billboards on the buildings lining the circle of high-density traffic on this roundabout his name was in both Arabic and English, a testament to the number of foreign students of Islam once – and maybe still – in town. Inside an electronically operated side gate and at the end of a path shaded by a plastic pergola was Dr Habash's office, a garden shed without curtains. A group of men gestured for me to sit down and listen to Dr Habash, the small gap-toothed man talking on al-Jazeera about why women should be allowed to lead prayer.

Later, when he was off air and ready to see me, he said that such moderate positions had not been lightly arrived at. They had meant massive arguments with his late father-in-law, who had denounced him during the 2003 elections. But, these were battles Habash needed to be having. Being disowned by mad daddy meant he was loved by people like Diana.

Habash was a social scientist and in his gazebo he ran me through his vision of Syria.

'There are three trends on our streets. Some 50 per cent of Syrians are practising Muslims. These can be sub-divided into conservative, radical and renewal. Then 80 per cent of the people are conservative, 20 per cent are renewal and 1 per cent are radical. The conservatives think that there is only one way to God … that we have to go back to tradition. They believe we have the only reality and that all others are false and our responsibility is to convert others. Radicals are obvious: they believe *you*, Allegra, have no place here and their job is to destroy you. Which you know. And then there is us. Renewers. We believe there is more than one way to

God. God is one. But His ways are many. The Prophet Muhammad came to earth and the Qur'an says 14 times that it asked him to continue and confirm what came before.

'So, for instance, in the Qur'an there are 17 levels of how you treat others. It goes from "Oh, Muhammad, you have to fight", to "Oh, Muhammad, you have to kill others". We in the renewal school say you have to recognize all of the 17 levels. But the radicals? They say you must cancel all the ones before the last one. Which is wrong in all incidences except the following. If Mr Sharon destroys your house you have to fight. It is jihad. Afghanistan is not ripe for jihad but in Palestine – there are rights in that land.'

Someone came in with a cordless phone and handed it to him. He listened, then smiled and put his hand over the receiver to speak to the people in the room: 'They've elected me to the bureau of parliament for the third time: 147 votes out of 250.' When he hung up it had gone slightly to his head. 'Now, why am I so successful?' he asked.

Secularism, it seemed, hadn't brought the Syrians the freedom they had expected and now they were looking to religion for guidance and maybe even governance. This would mean Islamism in healthy measure:

'As Jesus himself said, "Give God his right and give Caesar his right." Even the chief secularist, Hafez, was a believer. Somebody asked Hafez in the days before he died what the Infinity message was. He replied Islam.'

The upsum of this was that Habash, like the Ikhwan in Egypt, was aiming for a secular state, in which a modern kind of Islam is 'a guiding but not sole principle'. The Muslim Brotherhood in Egypt had said while I was in Cairo that imposing sharia law was low on the agenda and that religion is heritage now rather than a blueprint for life.

'If you took the veil, for instance, that government,' he said, describing his model government of the future, 'would acknowledge that it is not an obligation.' Annoyingly he now returned to the veil. I interrupted, 'What about the foreign students?'

'Them? I will get you my Director of Foreign Students. Perhaps I will get her to bring you to my prayers tomorrow.' Foreign students still seemed to arrive in enough numbers to warrant a full-time member of staff.

It was a Friday. Prayer day. Atika, Dr Habash's Director of Foreign Students, was following orders and escorting me a long taxi ride to the mosque outside Damascus, where Habash preaches. She was the waxiest and whitest human being I've ever set eyes on and her outfit of dark navy hijab merging seamlessly into an overdress of a slightly different navy, buttoned from ankles to chin, is the most austere in the room. She looks like a nun.

While the boys downstairs got to look at the pulpit, in this attic room the girls got a peeling white wall and Habash's disembodied voice twice: it is beamed into the room real time through a window joining the two chambers and, with a slight delay, over the loudspeaker. The woman next to Atika was howling with tears – not uncommon during prayers – and clicking the small electronic device stopwatch-like every time Allah's name was mentioned. It was so furious it was like she was sending him a text. Atika winked at me to acknowledge that even she thought this a bit histrionic. Muhajababe she wasn't, but she was not a muhajazombie either. The Q&A session started and the congregation rearranged themselves into more comfy positions. International Women's Day had just passed and someone in the audience asked if it should have been observed. All very civic. We lasted till the end, though dozens didn't, and it was Atika who suggested we leave. I hope it wasn't one of Habash's best because his congregation went home looking bored.

Outside the sun was brilliant, and Atika's skin glowed the unreal white of an English Tudor monarch as we walked to find a cab. I knew I was supposed to be getting down to the serious analysis of how many jihadis are still studying in Syria but old habits die hard. Dr Habash was a *bon viveur* of the Islamic world compared to his Director of Foreign Students. If girls were going to veil, you sensed he'd rather they chose one that complemented the colour of their eyes. So I couldn't resist a question about Atika's headscarf. I was interested to add her reasons to my survey. It was, after all, only small talk to get us to the taxis.

'Why do you veil? It isn't something Dr Habash recommends, or at least *obliges*. So I'm wondering why you do it.'

'I veiled before I found Dr Habash. You're right that he doesn't demand the veil. But I cannot take it off nor do I want to. So it stays.'

'So you veiled young? Did your parents encourage you?'

'No, quite the opposite actually. They were not religious and so I wasn't. But I watched hours of TV and the channels I kept coming back to were the religious ones. It is better to listen to a speech on TV than go to mosque. Often a clerk prepares better.'

'And, let me guess, Amr Khaled?'

'Of course I've heard of Sheikh Amr Khaled. Who hasn't? I'm a Life Maker.'

A Life Maker? Atika explained. Syria had a dialysis-machine shortage, she said. In fact it had an everything-machine shortage – import duty made foreign goods prohibitively expensive with the effect that cars and medical equipment cost a fortune. It all started the day when she'd been watching Khaled's latest weekly programme *Life Makers,* broadcast on the same channel as his previous one, *Words from the Heart.* He was broadcasting one edition every week for around 40 weeks.

'I sent an email to his website and within a month I'd heard back. We'd been given some money. Economic development, through faith,' she said. 'For some of us lucky ones who wrote in and got a reply, he will support us with our projects. Now we just wait for the Syrian authorities to clear the cheques. For others he encourages little things like tending the garden at the top of their apartment block or on their balcony. He encourages them to see the plants as a business. If you can make them live, then you can help yourself. Amr Khaled says that Arabs have lived as para-sites on the rest of the world for too long. Our problem is that we have got used to taking without ever giving. This should change.'

It wasn't 'just another television programme,' he said in an interview I found on Google later, 'but was a project that will revive our countries and save our youth'. There was the same demotic tone but the stakes seemed higher – after amiable introductions he would tell the young Arabs some uncomfortable home truths: 'Thomas Edison is famously known as the inventor of the electric lamp; however he also registered more than 1,093 invention patents over a time span of 15 years. The question we must ask is why haven't we seen a Muslim like him?'

After such questions that any young Muslim would find hard to answer he moved on to demonstrating an accountant's dexterity with numbers: 'The illiteracy index in 1995 saw Arab countries with 45 per cent of their populations illiterate; 30 per cent in other underdeveloped nations; 2 per cent in Europe with Canada having enviably eliminated all illiteracy,' according to Khaled's stats. 'The number of registered patents a year? Egypt 77; Saudi Arabia 171 and Israel 7,652. Number of engineers working in research and development? In Arab countries, 300 for each million citizens while in the US, 4,000 for each million citizen. Number of the sick to each doctor? In Indonesia there are 10,000 sick for each doc. In Spain there are 500. Number of daily newspapers for each 1,000 citizens? Arab countries combined – 53 newspapers; developed countries: 285 newspapers. Number of translated/published books: in 1995, all the Arab countries combined published a total of 1,348 books, whereas Israel alone published about 3,284 books.'

After this battering by statistics he would turn the spotlight on his viewers, asking them to send 'proactive' project ideas into his website with the possibility that theirs would be read out on his programme. Khaled showed his viewers 250 occasions in the Holy Qur'an where Allah used the words that can be translated as 'exert effort', more than 400 occasions on which Muslims were told they 'will succeed and rule earth'; and simply 'to think' more than 50 times. Atika leapt to it.

Khaled's aim was to drum up 'local and international contacts for establishing non-profit organizations that would sponsor and finance small projects'. It was relatively harmless, but it was also appealing to the market to help Arab countries.

In another transcript of an edition that I read Amr Khaled asked why Islam has lasted more than 1,300 years while Communism only a fraction of that. If he had already rubbed up the Egyptian regime something rotten anyway, uttering things like this would, in socialist Syria, take on a new meaning. The Syrian Baath Party is actually called The Baath Socialist Party. Syria hadn't yet got its Gamal Mubarak free marketeer. Would a legion of *Life Makers* like Mubarak change this?

Life Makers was Amr Khaled broadening his constituency from the *rewish* elements of the Middle East (a word first introduced to me by Karma and friends and embodied by someone like Zina) down the social strata. The less than posh Arabs had liked him before: Hassana in the Ikhwan publisher's office had not been a *rewish* rich girl but still she had seen his appeal. But now he was repaying the compliment – with an entire series devoted to nothing short of Islamic and Arab reform. Broadening out from discussions about kissing, swimwear and football into something more like social work. To hear him talk now, it was almost politics.

'Unemployment provides a fertile ground for moral deviation and extremism among youth in Arab countries,' he said.

'Small and medium-sized enterprises create 8 per cent of jobs in developed countries, while all Arab countries together have only 800,000 small enterprises in total.'

A constant refrain in his *Life Makers* series of lectures is this: 'Islam is not only about how to pray or fast. This is not in any way an underestimation of *ibada* (worship). However, many people have stopped at that point and consider Ramadan and the hijab to be the ultimate end. This program aims to correct this.' Bored by the hijab, he'd moved on. The hijab was mission accomplished.

That afternoon Atika and I got back to Habash's headquarters in central Damascus and we sat in her office. She closed the door as she elaborated on her dialysis machine business plan. I decided here that there seemed to be two phases to Amr Khaled's rise. Phase One was pre-eviction from Egypt and Phase Two is post-Egypt. Since these correlate with his two distinct TV programmes, *Words from the Heart* and then the later *Sunna Al Hayat* or *Life Makers*, perhaps they were born in TV commissioning meetings. During the first phase he marked out his turf, the second had seen him put roots down; the first had targeted wealthy Arabs, the second has targeted all of them. The first was about personal piety. The second is much more about politics and economic development, and as such, it is a challenge to the secular regimes. The first was a bit of fun, the second is world domination. He'd performed a gear change from *Cosmopolitan* magazine to *The Economist*.

'Thousands have joined his campaigns to collect clothes for the poor, boycott cigarettes, plant trees in polluted Arab cities and write letters to record companies complaining about the exploitation of women's bodies in music videos,'

Atika listed. How did she know? Because Khaled made a habit, at the top of each project, of giving his viewers an update on how he, and they, had all done.

Atika said the 'positiveness' project had got 15,000 respondents; the 'respecting the woman's body' project, about 100,000 participants; and the 'fighting the five narcotics' scheme had 300,000 participants. If muhajababes were those who lived a contradiction – listening to Nancy Ajram *and* Amr Khaled – then it seemed that Amr Khaled was wise to it. Khaled's campaign at that particular time was 'respecting the woman's body: no to nudity in the mass media'. He meant the video-clips and he was exhorting young Arabs to send letters to whomsoever they found 'exploiting a woman's body in the mass media'. He reported on his programme that the number of people who had sent letters was so far about 10,000. This tested me. On the one hand this was a welcome plea for decorum – no to awful music and no to women dressing like tarts for their manager's financial gain. It's just it wasn't coming from a Germaine Greer figure or a Joan Baez, it was coming from a religious accountant. It probably wouldn't make any difference. He might be able to list hundreds and thousands of examples of people acting on his words, but would it just go the way of his anti-smoking and drinking: whatever way the muhajababe wanted it to go? At one stage, halfway through one of the TV broadcasts, the number of bags of clothes that had been collected was 40,000 with one man's team collecting 6,500. One woman from Saudi Arabia had, Amr Khaled told his audience, collected 120 bags all by herself. His ambition was one million participants. Everything this man touched seemed to become a numerical triumph:

'Six charities contacted me: three from Egypt and three from the Gulf, all ensuring that they will undertake the burden of defending the misuse of women's bodies in the mass media,' was another example of a sentence freighted with numbers. By the end of the update he'd have spent ten minutes filling the viewer in on a dozen examples of his words taking effect.

'It's really big,' Atika said. 'There are *Life Makers* clubs in cities across the region and T-shirts to buy, saying things like "Together we make life" and "We are life makers not life takers".' The movement was widespread. One *Life Maker* in Jordan said in an online chatroom that the person she thought of most when she looked at Amr Khaled was Tyler Durden from *Fight Club*. 'Or at least becoming Amr Khaled is what would have happened to Tyler Durden had he been less anarchist and more religious. Perhaps Khaled is a bizarre version of Durden but with the same goals to change the world into something better than it is now.' In the same manner as *Fight Club*, the Jordanian contended, Amr Khaled's *Life Makers* programme had spread from country to country and young men and women everywhere were setting up little franchises in their own cities. And 'the other difference is that the first rule of *Life Makers* is to talk to everyone about it.'

'So you'd say that you follow Amr Khaled as much as Dr Habash?'

Atika had spent an hour – and seemed happy to spend more time – eulogising about Amr Khaled. I was trying to work out who had the stronger pulls on Atika's affections.

'In return for working for Dr Habash I get to study at the Foundation. Most of the people in my class are foreign so I relax by hearing preachers on the TV. At school people are from so many different countries that we don't converse, because we can't.'

Here in this office, Atika was covered as were, to varying degrees, two of the other girls. One of the daughters of Habash's right-hand man was in the office today – tiny and 12 years old, she'd veiled because she dreamt that Allah asked her. They were all, Atika said, Khaled watchers.

Diana had thought Habash's words of tolerance and liberal Islam were being drowned out by this philanthropic wave of Khaledise. I got one more meeting with Habash before I made my goodbyes and I didn't beat around the bush.

'It seems Amr Khaled is more persuasive than you are.'

He nodded his head slowly and took a deep breath.

'I didn't use to like that brother. He was conservative. But the best thing the Egyptian government did for him was kick him out. He has learnt from living a few years in your country and I think we are now going to start seeing a lot more of him. With his website, his TV channels, his reach. His Islam is unstoppable.'

Epilogue
London

That morning, 7 July 2005, I got on the Tube as usual. The doors opened at King's Cross, people were let on and off, the doors closed but we didn't move on. My temple was resting on a windowpane and one second I was grateful for my seat, the next second feeling and hearing the vibrations of people further down the train banging on doors.

Street level was like one big fire-drill at work: an unusual number of smartly suited people forced to stand idle in the daylight on a pavement. Walking off along the Euston Road, at various points I contemplated hopping on stalled buses but none went near where I worked. I passed the British Medical Association on my left, the Mahatma Gandhi statue in the middle of the square to my right and had just left Tavistock Square when the bomb went off on a bus behind me.

I got into work that day by mid-morning and instead of the usual common-or-garden politicians, BBC Westminster was filled with helmets, medals and dog-collars. Police, military and religious men hauled in to broadcast to a terrified nation.

When I'd returned from the Middle East I'd thought a lot about muhajababes like Zina, muhajaboys like karate-kid Ahmed and muhajaboffins like Atika. All followers, to greater and lesser degrees, of one muhajaboss, Amr Khaled (AK).

My loyalties were torn. AK's web of Life Making, green-fingered, litter-collecting, I'd-like-to-teach-the-world-to-sing Arabs – the saccharine ideals of a beauty contest or Blue Peter initiative – was suffocating those like Karma, Hind, Zidan, Diana, Walid and Mona. Constricting their secular space within a spandex hijab, weighing their sentences down with the it-takes-two-seconds-to-say-it Peace Be Upon Him, and spiriting their moral consciousness back to an earnest man in the seventh century. According to these secularists, the trendy piety was merely a rebranding of religious conservatism. It meant that their mates had gone backwards, not forwards.

In the face of this extremism at home, I started wondering whether AK's religious moderation was an OK consolation prize after all. In his lecture series 'The Youth in the Summer' he creates a ranking system for sin. Sexual desire, though sinful, is 'normal at this age'. But drinking and taking drugs are 'inexcusable'. This seems a short distance from the kind of relativism mixed with diluted faith common among churchgoers in the West.

At 2 pm on 7/7 the police thought things were getting worse rather than better, and they locked us in for a few hours. I put in the first of what would become my regular calls to AK's Birmingham office. When he'd been kicked out of Egypt he'd first relocated to Beirut before eventually moving to the United Kingdom where he enrolled at the University of Wales, Lampeter, to do his PhD, his wife told Islam Online. In fact, she told the website, he'd received a four-year scholarship from the university. He preferred to operate from the UK, 'TV sources close to Khaled' told the website because he'd rather study than be in 'conflict with any authority'. In this article, his wife also said that her husband would not be carrying out any talks in the UK. He was, she said, a full-time student. Mmm, really? AK continued broadcasting on Iqra'a satellite channel and set up a kind of social-work organization in Birmingham.

It wasn't clear which one – Wales or Birmingham – he called home, but the Birmingham office took messages for him, and it was from there that Shaukat eventually rang me back. It's Shaukat, with an accent more Cockney than Arab or Brummie, whom I've dealt with ever since. We had an over-sensitive conversation, in which we established that AK condemned the 7/7 bombers, and eventually I just went for it.

'Shaukat, is he advising the UK government on how to deal with, you know, Islam?'

'Why do you ask?'

'Because he's one of the most famous Arabs in the world hanging out like a student at a university in Wales. It doesn't make sense.' (As he's the sheikh of chic, I couldn't imagine him being the sheikh of student-union shab.)

'Well, if he is, we're not supposed to admit it.'

AK was too busy to speak to me then or that month. Failing an interview with him, I looked for other leads. The *Sunday Times* ran a story about a leaked document that claimed the British government was seeking the advice of four foreign imams, including AK. Islam Online reported an Egyptian reporter as asking AK whether this was true and he obfuscated, saying that like the reporter, he had only heard the rumours. He told the reporter to look at the timing of the report – in the run-up to the UK's general election – and suggested his name was being used for positive association among the Muslim voters the government needed to keep on side.

In August, thinking his schedule would have eased up, I made contact with Shaukat again. AK was still too busy. So I rang both the Home Office and the Foreign Office – the authors of the original documents The *Sunday Times* had seen. They also denied a relationship. In October I found that Baroness Uddin, the first Muslim woman in the House of Lords, had spoken at a conference with AK and so I rang her. Even though they'd been billed as being at the same event, she too denied all knowledge. Again I rang Shaukat and again his boss was busy. In the time I'd been trying, AK had had not a spare 20 minutes. I was even so desperate as to interview David Blunkett's one-time special adviser – Blunkett would have been the minister in charge of the leaked document. Nothing. AK organized and spoke at a large event at Wembley that I couldn't attend because I couldn't get the day off. Officials from Nike, Kim Howells – at the time the government minister in charge of the Middle East – and senior Foreign Office mandarins were at this conference for British Muslims. Of course he was advising the government, at least informally. But then, finally, The *Sunday Times* released the original documents on which their story had been based. There was no mention of AK. The paper had got it wrong. It seemed the merits and problems of AK's fight club extending over here didn't need to be considered after all. I gave Shaukat a break.

Instead AK seemed to have gravitated back to the Middle East. He had visited three times that I knew of when before he hadn't been allowed back on home soil at all, and set up a Cairo office for his Birmingham organization. Egypt, as well as London, had recently suffered terrorist attacks and it seemed to be the Egyptian not the UK government that was making demands on his time. The restriction on AK preaching in public, however, seemed to remain.

Then one day, at the end of an Arabic lesson during Ramadan 2006, Meis, my teacher, started talking about what she'd watched the night before. 'There was something very extraordinary on TV last night,' she said looking out into the black of a Bayswater Tuesday night. Her accent is more Russian than Arabic, and maybe even more Swedish than Russian. Her communist parents left Iraq for Moscow when she was tiny and she and her sister came to London via a decade in Sweden. Both the girls are unveiled Arabs who smoked shisha in both the chichi shisha cafés of the Edgware Road and the grubbier, greasier male-dominated shisha cafés of less salubrious areas. They fast, pray and believe but they also drink vodka Red Bull and smoke. But despite their shishas – AK says that 'society regards the female shisha smoker as an ill-mannered woman' – they are also AK devotees. I hadn't known this about Meis before I went to the Middle East because I hadn't known to ask. Now Meis told me what she had found odd.

'Amr Khaled has been preaching, every day, from the centre of Medina ... something no one else has ever done,' she said that evening. 'It means Amr Khaled has been given serious privileges by the Saudi Arabian government. They own the holy area. Only they can give out permission.' Medina is the second holiest site in Islam after Mecca. The part that he was preaching in was the holiest of holy areas, somewhere lay people never normally access.

I went away and checked this out. In the days leading up to Ramadan he had performed what he called 'The First Reality TV Hajj'. His five-day journey to Mecca (he'd later, I supposed, travelled to Medina) had been recorded in all its 24-hour glory. Broadcast on the same channel as *Words from the Heart* and *Life Makers*, this was the region's first religious reality-TV programme, intended as a challenge to *Superstar*. With a captive audience of millions, AK profiled a series of *Life Makers* projects and then asked viewers to ring in and vote on which they'd like to see funded. The call revenues, about $1.5 million, would also be channelled into the projects. AK also announced that the owner of the satellite channel, Sheikh Saleh Kamel (worth about $12 billion, he controls the majority of the TV station Arab Radio and Television), would fund something called the Life Makers Union. By the end of this Children In Need or Comic Relief type televisual extravaganza there had been a further 12,000 projects proposed. I rang Shaukat.

'If you want to meet him you should think about travelling to Cairo.'

❖

I couldn't afford Cairo. Each time I'd booked travel and days off to be able to get to AK in Birmingham, Wales or London he'd cancelled at the eleventh hour. Now I've followed the AK trail to Copenhagen. I'm not sure if it is going to result in a meeting. Though Shaukat gave me the starter for ten that AK would be here, he hasn't promised an interview.

The air is alcohol fresh. I'm struck by the building I'm now heading towards reminding me of Future TV's white mansion in Beirut. Obviously, it is not Ottoman, but it is large, white and impressive. A state-of-the-art ramp of decking leads into the building over a moat or ditch, steeped in snow. Standing outside the entrance at the end of this drawbridge, there are packs of classic model Danes and Arabs, teams of blonde hair and veils, just as Benetton would have cast them. No one broke the mould on these guys. There is a couple having a smoke, but it turns out they are the organizers. I sneak in to the main hall where there is a starburst of coloured paper stuck to the wall with chunky magnets – work from that morning. I bag a place in a darker corner at the back of this room. It is a Norman Foster hybrid, half-classical architecture, half-glass-house and the walls of window bring the dazzle from the bank of snow outside, inside.

When the cartoons crisis broke, somehow AK got in there first. He recommended that the Danish government should convene a conference and the talk was of him marching on Denmark with 25 Muslims, one from each Muslim country. Another tele-evangelist, Sheikh Qaradawi, al-Jazeera's in-house sage, had opened fire on the event, saying that Muslims shouldn't be engaging with Denmark before they'd had an apology:

'It's like someone telling you, "Damn you", and you tell him "Please, let's talk".'

AK countered that his was the populist's position: he had held a poll on his website asking whether Muslims should 'move from protesting to starting a dialogue' and apparently nearly 97 per cent of 100,000 respondents favoured dialogue. AK said he had received 10,000 letters from Arab youths addressed to their Danish counterparts explaining the meaning of Islam, and of the older age bracket he said he had the support of 170 Muslim religious figures, including muftis of Egypt, Jordan and Syria as well as some Saudi clerics. The debate between AK and Qaradawi was seen to be between a 39-year-old accountant versus an octogenarian holy man; a moustache versus a bird's nest of a beard; a short back and sides versus a turban. But was it right versus wrong?

Now in this house in the city's embassy district are 50 young people, who look the part all right, just no AK. There are twelve Egyptians, four Algerians, four Saudis, and then a lone delegate each from Morocco, Pakistan, Jordan, Yemen and UAE – not quite the one from each Muslim nation paid for by the Danish foreign ministry. The room creaks and splashes with the sound of ice being broken. A girl in a turquoise T-shirt with blonde ringlets cut short about her face is talking with a guy in a navy blazer whose terracotta red scarf is pressed flat underneath his suit-jacket lapels.

'Have you seen *Crash*?' he asks her.

'No.'

'Well, I think it sums up for me what harmony in society is about.'

'Oh yes?'

'Yeah, because they are American-Muslim, American-Irish. American integration is something you Danes should learn something from. You should go see *Crash*.'

'I'm interested that you say that,' blonde ringlets says.

On my right:

'So, if you take the Egyptian Baath party as an example of what I'm talking about –' a lofty Dane begins.

'There is no Egyptian Baath party,' he is corrected. Back with the terracotta scarf:

'Personally, I don't think an Italian living in America should be an Italian in 100 years' time.'

'How can you say that? Are you saying that he can't be an American and eat spaghetti every day?'

'Correct. Have you seen *Malcolm X*?'

This is like expecting them to find the meaning of life in the *It's a Small World After All* ride at Disney Land. They need a task. Someone give them an exercise or a game. If you don't, blandness will kill AK's intercultural initiative.

When the workshops begin I ask a couple of young Arab boys conspiring near me if AK is on his way. They think so. They are waiting for him too but are now told off and given worksheets: My Personal Cultural Profile, on which there are scales.

'Hierarchy: Do you like to live in a low–high hierarchy society or a high one? Situate yourself with an arrow on this scale from 0% to 100%, equality to obedience.

'Relationships: Do you think of yourself as a "we" or an "I"?'

'Rules: Are there many rules in your society or few? Do you take comfort in the grey areas or do you need structures?' and so on.

A Danish TV journalist who looks like a young Willem Dafoe with golden hair, angular features and sapphire eyes but ruddy and pockmarked skin is seated at the table nearest to me and he is being filmed. He now puts up his hand.

'I think it is very difficult to put an X – you can be both an individual and have a group conscience.'

He's just the start of the revolution. Yet another blonde girl puts up her hand.

'I do not like this reference to open societies being "feminine societies" and closed ones being "masculine societies". Can we remove it?'

'See, my Arab friends,' the lecturer says, pointing at the first two dissidents, and making an example of them, the Sartre and de Beauvoir of the room, 'in Denmark, children, unlike in Arab countries, are encouraged to speak their minds. My Muslim friends, please do not be too unhappy. Do not take these interjections as rudeness. Some people might call this outspokenness rudeness … it is not, it is what we call free speech.'

Now an Arab puts his hand up.

'Arabs can also be rude.'

'Yes, but not quite like this. Arabs, you are not so good at –'

'The trouble is,' interrupts a large Arab with his back to me sitting on Willem Dafoe's table, who clearly thinks his fellow Arab is on to something with his last point about rudeness, 'in the Arab world, people think that saying "How are you?" wastes a dollar.'

Muslim heads nod vigorously in agreement. De Beauvoir winces at yet another sweeping generalization even though this time it's not about her culture. It's obvious she's an anthropologist because she's taking every sentence like a bullet. The Arab, with his big back to me, now talks direct to de Beauvoir:

'Hey, I can't help it, I speak my mind. I'm a controversial talk-show host.'

Even though all I've seen of him is the back of his thick rugger-bugger neck, closely shaved head and occasionally a third of his face, I know who this guy is. He is AK's anointed heir; AK is his mentor. The chances of him being chosen at random to participate in this event at random are a quarter of a billion. Moez is who he says he is. He is also an economics graduate from the expensive American University in Cairo. All morning we have to listen to the expensive American accent in the preppy bottle-green Abercrombie & Fitch sweater. He talks whenever he can, likes to use words like dogma, name-check Marx, reference post-Christian societies, and he greatly enjoys delivering, apropos of not very much, two medium-length soliloquies on the French Revolution and Adam Smith. The careless talk of this 27-year-old big mouth, smart aleck, sometime pain in the arse had secured him two English-language Islamic talk shows: *Parables from the Qur'an* and *Stairway to Paradise,* both broadcast from the same channel AK preaches on.

After lunch, Moez is also the afternoon's first speaker. His session will explain Islam. I ask a girl to my left whether the whole point of today wasn't that AK was scheduled to be doing this lecture.

'No, today is Moez's turn.'

AK speaks tomorrow. He has been sent to try me. Will I never meet the man?

Moez starts with not a lecture card in sight. He needs them. He rambles through disassociated, hard-to-follow personal thoughts on the Qur'an and I drift. Moez and his mates got into so many scrapes, so the narrative went, that he knew that unless he changed his life, God could end it. He lost friends to car accidents, overdoses, cancer and in his first year at university he had to have serious surgery. When he came out the other side of all this he made a vow of clean living only to find the lure of 'little tequila bottles and big vodka bottles' too strong. Don't, for a second, get him wrong – he was praying – he was praying five times a day. It's just it was often late at night because that would be when he remembered. Until a blow-out at a New Year's party. He'd have got away with it but for a careless drive home and a near car crash that make him renew his vows to Allah.

But the road to heaven is paved with bad intentions: an exotic foreign student with green eyes whom all his mates wanted to bed tempts him again and he's nearly pulling the apple off the tree when he asks her whether she believes in God. Not only doesn't she believe in his God, she doesn't believe in any God. The attraction disappears like, in his words, the scene in *The Devil's Advocate* when the beautiful woman turns to ashes. His faith won.

His mum 'went mad. "Oh, my God, he's going to be a terrorist. I didn't put him through American schools for this. I could have sent him to some mediocre Islamic school! I can't believe this." She went crazy. And I don't blame her. She's the generation of Nasser who have some serious dogma about religion they'll never be able to let go of.'

She disallowed him from going to a mosque and he'd have to pretend he was going to the sports club instead. During Ramadan 1997, he listened daily to a *juz* (1/30th of the Qur'an), hearing it without understanding a single word. Within two months he knew parts of the Qur'an off by heart and within a year he knew it all. He'd learnt it like he learnt basketball stats. With no help. OK, with a little help from AK's TV programmes.

Moez Masoud: perfect English, excellent Arabic, who mixes the Qur'an with Pearl Jam lyrics and wishes his mother would veil. Sami Yusuf: stripy, preppy jumper with iPod earphones snaking round his neck, passively aggressively shouting, 'I'm hip', lazy student stubble – pioneering pop music as prayer. Moez, Sami, 'veiled-again' actresses and even a doll recruited to jolly up the Middle East's journey back to religion. All of which was proof that the market lay in moderate muhajababe Islam.

Further proof of this was the 360-degree pirouette of a man called Sherif Sabry – director of near-naked popstrel Ruby's video-clip. Sabry is now the proud director of the inaugural muhajababes video-clip: a boy crooning to a veiled girl. It was the first of its kind and it came out towards the end of my visit to the region. Not only was Sabry Ruby's director but he'd also directed the rousing videos at Mubarak's last National Democratic Party (NDP) convention. He was Establishment. He produced work for a government that was so secular it had reportedly kicked AK out of

Egypt for making Islam too popular. Now Ruby's director was directing video-clips AK would approve of and Egypt was welcoming back the sheikh of chic.

If the first muhajababe video-clip were more proof, then the following was absolute proof. I found a newspaper article about Prince Alwaleed. His latest project was a new satellite channel called al-Resalah or The Message, set up with the aim of spreading a moderate view of Islam across the Arab and Muslim world through dramas, game shows and educational programmes, all in an Islamic context. TV execs were excited by this new announcement from Prince Alwaleed and one commented:

'Religious programming is massive. It is like democracy in the Arab world. Every time you open the door for democracy in one Arab country, Islam is likely to come in. Every time you open a religious TV station in the Arab world, audiences will rush in.' This, from Ali Jaber, now head of Dubai TV but once a founder of Zen TV. Zen TV had died a death by video-clip, which in turn seemed to be being swallowed by the trend for religion.

But this was clearly more than just youth culture. It might even be the revolution the baby-booming professors had prophesied. It had taken me a pretty long while to understand the possible significance of all this. All the time that I'd spent looking for the baby-booming revolution in the basement of the underground youth movements of Beirut – seduced by Beirutis – I'd been missing the fact that Prince Alwaleed's soft-focus, soft-porn video-clips had replaced Zen TV's knockabout debate on social and political mores for a reason. They were more popular, more lucrative and, for more and more people as I inched my way along, more fun.

But, having relinquished a youth culture with which I was comfortable for the sexual mores and sounds of a video-clip industry that it took me time to like, I found the real white noise of a young Arab's life much better addressed by a religious man – AK – using the same technology, satellite TV, that had allowed a proliferation of video-clips.

AK had produced an intoxicating brew – interactive websites, Oprah-style confessional values, soft-sofas, colloquial Arabic and matiness – all wrapped in a Californian self-help formula. Liberal commentators in the newspapers at the Egyptian epicentre of Khaledism argue that, for all the revolutionary froth, the phenomenon is ultimately a symptom of the region's passive education system. Khaled's schema that proffers a 'lesson of the week' and gives advice on whether adolescent boys should wear Speedos or trunks is easily digested by young Arabs reared on rote-learning. But you had to hand it to him. He was good. He was so good he'd even persuaded Prince Alwaleed to if not bin his video-clippers altogether then at least set up a new TV channel – al-Resalah – on which the women would be muhajababes not just babes.

Though the democratic advances that had swept the region in the time I'd been there looked unrelated to the phenomenon of veiled girls appearing in video-clips, a suited man appearing on satellite TV to tell youth which swimwear was Islamic and unIslamic, and the appearance in toyshops of a Muslim Barbie doll, the cultural shift that AK embodied – a kind of Islamic reformation because it represented a shift to young people feeling that God understands their lives – had

had a wider effect. It was enabling the region's more moderate Islamists to ready themselves for power. No longer, with AK doing their work, should they feel the need to be bellicose on matters such as whether women should wear the hijab, drink, smoke, or watch video-clips, and whether men should play football on a Friday – there's a section of AK's website for all these issues.

Yusuf in Shatila, Beirut, had been reticent to commit Hizbollah to banning video-clips when once upon a time they'd have leapt at such cheap electioneering; Muhammad Habash in Damascus – the country's only Islamist MP – had talked to me of moderation, and there being no obligation to wear the headscarf. There was obviously a change in policy being worked out by the Muslim Brotherhood in Egypt, as evidenced by the spat between the avuncular Selim and his apprentice, Hassana. The Muslim Brothers demonstrating outside Cairo University had only 'political reform first' to say. Hisham, the Townhouse artist, had been more besieged by government censorship than by Muslim Brotherhood censoriousness.

The newspapers provided more evidence. The Justice & Development Party in Morocco is an Islamist party that since the 2003 Casablanca bombings has toned down the anti-West rhetoric to focus on reform with a view to big gains in the 2007 Moroccan elections. In 2006 its leader told a publication, *Tel Quel*, that 'Islam is a point of reference' for his party.

'Today, nobody contests this point of reference. What's at stake is to have an open and modern reading. I think that the top priority goes to political reform.'

Hamas swept to power in Palestine in 2006 and said that it would not impose sharia law. Instead it would encourage but not issue laws. In Jordan, the Islamic Action Front (IAF) had just had internal elections and moderates won out with the old hardcore withdrawing or standing aside. Some were suspicious, thinking this was a ploy to lull people into thinking the IAF is a new pussycat of a political party. Others took the elections at face value. Whether they would make life easier for nude portrait painter, Daoud, in Amman I wasn't sure. After all, he wasn't very good.

The region's Islamists were trying to make themselves more universally appealing. They were able to do so because AK et al. were doing a lot of their work for them. When AK visited the westernized king and queen of Jordan, a prominent Jordanian Muslim Brother said, 'He enjoys the ability to delve smoothly in his preaching, touch uniquely and emotionally on morals and connect the religious words with happenings on the ground in society.'

But muhajababes will have the last laugh. In the eclectic mix-and-match spirit of youth everywhere, they are still surreptitiously contradicting AK teachings – on smoking, make-up, plucking eyebrows, tight trousers, revealing swimwear, having sex. If they are boys – drinking, driving too fast and not playing enough sport to mask the effects of their lust for a girl in her swimsuit. But by following AK they get to feel like they are good young Muslims, or at least trying to be good. The effect is that the Middle East appears more religious than during its days dominated by the secular governments.

The effect of AK and the perhaps millions of muhajababes and muhajaboys whose attention he has caught has been to free Islamist parties to get on with real politics – political reform – and leave the sermonizing to the man with the mauve TV studio and deeper purple website. Inadvertently, in all their contradictions, the muhajababes have sparked a revolution.

Acknowledgements

I couldn't have written this book without my bosses Jamie Donald and Vicky Flind encouraging me to go on 'holiday' in the first place. If they gave it the green light then it was Sue Lockyer who did all the paperwork. So I'm grateful to all three of them. Then there are my colleagues Penny Davies, Claire Bellis, Mark Himsley and Dave Longstaff who carried me during this period when not having read a single paper before an editorial meeting was not uncommon and not a good idea. Matthew Stadlen, Jessica Atkinson, Natasha Shallice, Kate Ford and Nicola Harrison deserve special mention for all of the above and long emails. And Manisha Vadhia for teaching me more than just how to make a film.

A massive thank you to Meis for Arabic lessons and insights. She's thanked in the book but it was Darah – not her real name – who coined the term muhajababes. A chat with Tanya Habjouqa in a café in Jordan was key. I didn't meet Maysa Ibrahim till the last couple of days but quality not quantity aye. James Howarth, for introducing me to Meis, for hospitality in Amman and advice. To James, Maysa and Tanya – big apologies for any inaccuracies. I should have been listening harder. Going further back in time, thanks to Bruce Wannell for being around. And to Henry Hemming for being a very similar shop selling very similar stuff on the same road as me – except now I hope he sees that I'm cake and he is biscuits. Or I'm biscuits and he's cake.

Then there are the logistics. Had I made it to Jerusalem, Tim Moore was showing every sign of being helpful and thanks to John Harte for putting us in contact; the Arwitzs in Amman for generous hospitality and the Vinters for making this happen; James Lindon and Sasha Morgan for introducing me to Ali Sharaf who was swiftly chivalrous when I found myself stuck in Jordan; Ala'a in Amman; Diana in Damascus; Dergham Owainati in Dubai; Sylvester in Kuwait; Amil Khan in Cairo. Pieces by Jim Quilty, Ramsay Short and Kaelen Goldie-Wilson of the *Daily Star* have been helpful; so has research by Lindsay Wise and Patrick Haenni. I'm also indebted to Rob Andrews and David Carroll for producing the perfect cover image for a song.

Back here, the writing arguably got more difficult. When our flat was infested with bedbugs halfway through the book, the girls of Wilkes Street – Portia, Bekah Phillips, Liz Chong, Kath Randall, Katie McAleese, Kate Phillips, Kathryn McGill and, in absentia, Natasha Phillips (aka Tash) – took me in despite my possibly bringing the pests with me. In addition to letting me sleep on her sofa my sister let me take her laptop to the Middle East. I then destroyed this when I got back to London, which wasn't part of the deal. For never having a tantrum about the sofa, laptop kidnap nor destruction, thank you so much. And thank you, Sasha, for your help on that shitty, depressing, grey, nasty June morning when I poured coffee over my laptop, hadn't backed this book up, had no money to pay for the express service I needed to rescue it nor a cab to get myself across London, and couldn't find my house keys. What a horrible day and thank God you were unemployed at the time. And thank you to Johann for taking us in when we thought the bedbugs banished and then the ceiling collapsed on Rob's head and we had to move out of our flat.

Disaster-management thanks over, my next debt is to Constable & Robinson. Thank you to Nick Robinson for encouraging and supporting me when there wasn't any evidence that I could write a book and to Jan Chamier for championing the eventual book I delivered up, when it was pretty threadbare. They handed it to Becky Hardie who turned my travel burblings into a book. If it weren't for familial etiquette, this book would probably be dedicated to her to make up for nearly driving her mad. Even further along, many thanks to Helen Armitage for performing miracles on it over Easter Weekend. Thanks also to Bruce Connal, Bonnie Lee-Richards, Nithya Rae and Wendy Flay.

Thank you to Liz and Ian Sharples, Pat and John Moore, my brother and sister Alex and Perdy, Lucie and Jane for going without attention for a long time.

But it's to mum, dad and my boyfriend Rob that *Muhajababes* is dedicated. Mum for giving me the arrogance to think about writing a book. Dad, because, though I'm not a daddy's girl, it was dad's priceless outrage at my being black-listed from Israel that lifted my spirits and kept me going when I was very near to wanting to come home. And then to my boyfriend Rob for not dumping me, for being on email at all hours while I was away, and for working on the opposite side of the table when I came back; for injecting cash into my account; lending me a few pitch-perfect phrases, editing some of the stupid stuff out, putting some of the better stuff back in; cooking me breakfast, lunch and dinner, ironing my clothes, putting the cancerous cat down, selling the flat, buying the house, and choosing the book's name while lying in the bath – thank you. The energy mum, dad and Rob have given me detracted from the energy they put into their own projects and so it is to them that *Muhajababes* is dedicated.